Women Leaving Prison

Emerging Perspectives in Pastoral Theology and Care

Series Editor: Kirk Bingaman, Fordham University

The field of pastoral care and counseling, and by extension pastoral theology, is presently at a crossroads, in urgent need of redefining itself for the age of postmodernity or even post-postmodernity. While there is, to be sure, a rich historical foundation upon which the field can build, it remains for contemporary scholars, educators, and practitioners to chart new directions for the present day and age. Emerging Perspectives in Pastoral Theology and Care seeks to meet this pressing need by inviting researchers in the field to address timely issues, such as the findings of contemplative neuroscience, the impact of technology on human development and wellness, mindfulness meditation practice for reducing anxiety, trauma viewed through the lens of positive psychology and resilience theory, clergy health and wellness, postmodern and multicultural pastoral care and counseling, and issues of race and class. The series will therefore serve as an important and foundational resource for years to come, guiding scholars and educators in the field in developing more contemporary models of theory and practice.

Titles in the Series

Women Leaving Prison

Justice-Seeking Spiritual Support for Female Returning Citizens

Jill L. Snodgrass

LEXINGTON BOOKS

Lanham • Boulder • New York • London

Published by Lexington Books
An imprint of The Rowman & Littlefield Publishing Group, Inc.
4501 Forbes Boulevard, Suite 200, Lanham, Maryland 20706
www.rowman.com

6 Tinworth Street, London SE11 5AL, United Kingdom

British Library Cataloguing in Publication Information Available

Library of Congress Cataloging-in-Publication Data

Names: Snodgrass, Jill Lynnae, author.
Title: Women leaving prison : justice-seeking spiritual support for female returning
  citizens / Jill L. Snodgrass.
Description: Lanham : Lexington Books, 2018. | Series: Emerging perspectives in
  pastoral theology and care | Includes bibliographical references and index.
Identifiers: LCCN 2018040858 (print) | LCCN 2018046374 (ebook) |
  ISBN 9781498544030 (Electronic) | ISBN 9781498544023 (cloth : alk. paper)
Subjects: LCSH: Women prisoners—Religious life. | Women ex-convicts—Religious
  life. | Women ex-convicts—Services for.
Classification: LCC BV4595 (ebook) | LCC BV4595 .S63 2018 (print) |
  DDC 259/.5082—dc23
LC record available at https://lccn.loc.gov/2018040858

♾™ The paper used in this publication meets the minimum requirements of American National Standard for Information Sciences—Permanence of Paper for Printed Library Materials, ANSI/NISO Z39.48-1992.

Printed in the United States of America

Contents

Acknowledgments

The passion poured into these pages was first incited by the returning sisters I journeyed with in clinical pastoral counseling practice at the Clinebell Institute in Claremont, California. They were my clients, but more so they were my teachers about life behind bars, the barriers faced during reentry, and what it means to fight against the prison industrial complex. To those sisters, I am grateful.

The stamina needed to persevere in writing this book was fostered by a research grant from the Louisville Institute, a research leave from Loyola University Maryland, and the gracious support of faculty and student colleagues. To those individuals and institutions, I am grateful.

The courage and humility that it takes to try to tell a story that is not your own, especially when it is a story of oppression and injustice, was given to me by the many returning sisters who themselves were courageous enough to share their stories with me in the interviews grounding this book. They emboldened me by their conviction and desire to give voice to the marginalization experienced by women leaving prison. To those sisters, I am grateful.

The wisdom required to know what to retain and what to leave on the chopping block was offered to me through very diligent feedback from a select, and treasured, few: an anonymous reviewer whose expertise was invaluable; the editorial staff, Sarah Craig and Julia Torres at Lexington Books and series editor Kirk Bingaman, who were patient with me in so many ways; and my research assistant, Nancy Stockbridge, who walked with me every step of the way, sharing her knowledge, experience, and passion for abolishing the prison industrial complex and serving both sisters inside and returning sisters. To those individuals, I am grateful.

The grace that I needed as a human, a professor, a friend, a mother, a sister, and so much more was bestowed to me again and again and again by my loving family and friends, and especially my darling son, Sandro. To those dear ones, I am grateful beyond words.

List of Figures and Tables

FIGURES

TABLES

Introduction

Jasmine[1] never thought she would serve over five years in state prison for prescription drug charges. She never imagined that her addiction would cause her to spend more time behind bars than others serve for second-degree murder. And she never dreamed she would miss the first five years of her daughter's life. Yet there she was. Five years gone, awaiting another parole hearing, and wondering what life on the outside would offer her. She dreamed of gaining custody of her eight-year-old son and five-year-old daughter. She imagined getting a job, going to college, and buying a car. She thought about whether or not she could manage to stay sober, especially if forced to live with her mother.

Women like Jasmine are released from state and federal prisons every day after living behind bars for two, ten, even twenty-five years. These women are returning citizens, many of whom are survivors of psychological, physical, and sexual abuse, with histories of substance abuse or mental disorders, and mothers to minor children. And many are women with a profound faith in God or deep spiritual commitments. Religion and spirituality occupy a central role in prison culture and have the capacity to both help and harm women in their reentry journeys.

Jasmine, like many incarcerated women, went to church almost every week as a child and was taught to put her trust in God. But she hesitated to attend worship in prison. The women who went seemed to be a bunch of "holy rollers." Jasmine prayed every day and reflected often on God's role in her life. But she wasn't really working the twelve steps of Narcotics Anonymous and she didn't understand what people meant when they referred to "the God of my understanding." She never entertained the idea of joining a church after her release, because what kind of a church would accept someone with her background?

Every day women like Jasmine are oppressed by the structural injustices of mass incarceration in the United States. The rate of imprisonment in the

United States is higher than that of any other nation (Guerino, Harrison, & Sabol, 2011; Walmsley, 2013), with over 2 million Americans presently behind bars in state and federal prisons and county jails (Kaeble & Glaze, 2016). Each year approximately 650,000–700,000 individuals return to their communities to face numerous barriers to successful reentry (United States Department of Justice, n.d.; Willison, Brazzell, & Kim, 2011). Recidivism rates, the percentage of individuals who relapse into criminal behavior, are hard to track. However, it is estimated that nearly two-thirds of released prisoners are rearrested within three years as too often the structural injustices they face upon returning to community are endemic and too difficult to overcome (National Institute of Justice, 2014).

For many well-intentioned Christians, it is easy to erroneously believe that their day-to-day lives have no impact upon, and are not impacted by, the structural injustices of mass incarceration or the experiences of brothers and sisters enslaved by the prison industrial complex. For many Christians, those affected by the criminal justice system are mistaken as strangers rather than neighbors. Christian leaders and laity alike often fail to engage in prison ministry, believing that some other church, or some other person, is better suited to advocate for, to care for, and to visit the prisoner as Jesus commanded in Matthew 25. *Women Leaving Prison* invites readers to reflect on these and other prejudices and to reconsider what it means to follow Jesus's footsteps by engaging in revised prison ministry praxis.

Women Leaving Prison examines the oft-ignored experiences of female returning citizens. Recognizing that these women face numerous barriers to successful reentry, this book utilizes interpretative phenomenological analysis, a qualitative research method, to explore how women's spiritual and religious beliefs, and their participation in Christian communities are experienced in their transitions. Although "prison ministry" regularly occurs behind bars, spiritual and religious reentry support is a crucial component of a justice-seeking prison ministry program. The book investigates how churches, as well as concerned citizens and people of faith, can welcome and care for these women by investing in reentry ministry as an essential component of prison ministry. The book draws upon interdisciplinary resources to examine the lived experiences of returning citizens toward the cultivation of Project Sister Connect, a model for revised prison ministry praxis that outlines how to facilitate female returning citizens' successful reentry through communal and individual spiritual care and support and how to work toward the eradication of structural injustices.

THE PRISON INDUSTRIAL COMPLEX

Over the past decade, issues related to mass incarceration in the United States have become regular topics in both scholarly and popular discourses.

From *Orange Is the New Black* (Friedman, 2013) to *The New Jim Crow* (Alexander, 2012), from new academic degree programs to bipartisan partnerships, mass incarceration is a common topic of public debate. This is not surprising given that "one out of every 100 Americans is serving time behind bars" (Whitehead, 2012, para. 4). How did we get here? How did the U.S. criminal justice system transform from a system that rehabilitates to a system that restrains and retains millions of citizens? Although it is beyond the scope of *Women Leaving Prison* to detail the birth and development of America's prison industrial complex (the reader is referred instead to Michelle Alexander's (2012) *New York Times* bestseller *The New Jim Crow: Mass Incarceration in the Age of Colorblindness*), acknowledging the structural injustices in today's prison system is essential for understanding the reentry experiences of returning sisters and the goals of Project Sister Connect, this book's vision for revised prison ministry praxis.

More than twenty years ago, Eric Schlosser (1998) published a cover story in *The Atlantic* magazine that detailed the development of the prison industrial complex, "a set of bureaucratic, political, and economic interests that encourage increased spending on imprisonment, regardless of the actual need" (p. 54). Government and private corporations profited by caging people and creating a system of structural injustices to keep people locked up and locked out. The prison industrial complex "produces and reproduces many of our nation's most egregious narratives and practices regarding racial discrimination" (Prison Communication, Activism, Research, and Education, 2007, p. 405), it unequally ensnares individuals and families who are socioeconomically disadvantaged and oppressed, and the impact it has on women is largely ignored. Numerous beliefs and practices perpetuate the prison industrial complex, and the following three merit further attention: the War on Drugs, changed sentencing practices, and the fear undergirding the promotion of an "us" versus "them" society.

In 1971, President Richard Nixon declared a War on Drugs, citing drugs as the number one public enemy, and four decades of presidents followed suit. As a result, "the number of Americans incarcerated for drug offenses has skyrocketed from 41,000 in 1980 to nearly a half million in 2013" (The Sentencing Project, n.d., p. 3). In 1971 when the War on Drugs started, 6,329 women were incarcerated in state or federal prisons (Tripodi & Pettus-Davis, 2013). Today that figure is well over 100,000 (Carson & Sabol, 2012). This is not just a war on drugs. This is a war on women and families (Chesney-Lind, 1998).

The prison industrial complex was also enacted via mandatory sentencing laws. For example, as a part of the War on Drugs, the Anti-Drug Abuse Act of 1986 was employed to leverage a war on crack cocaine. Prior to the Act, the maximum sentence for possession of any drug was just one year; yet by the late 1980s, life imprisonment and the death penalty were permitted for certain drug-related crimes (Alexander, 2012). By 1988, the new Anti-Drug Abuse Act enacted a five-year mandatory sentence for possession of any cocaine-based product, even for individuals with no intent to sell or distribute the drug (Alexander, 2012). Mandatory sentencing laws so markedly impacted the number of individuals serving time, and the length of time served, that while the average time served for a federal drug offense in 1986 was twenty-two months, by 2004 it had skyrocketed to sixty-two months (The Sentencing Project, n.d.). During this same time, many states enacted "three strikes" laws that resulted in life sentences for anyone convicted of a third offense, drug-related or not. Think, for example, of Joyce Demyers, a thirty-six-year-old woman who was convicted in 1994 of a felony cocaine sale in the state of California and sentenced to a term of twenty-five years to life due to two prior robbery convictions. Demyers had "a $5 stake in the $50 drug deal," and the two other individuals convicted in the crime were each sentenced to just four years (Lynch, 1994, para. 7).

A third factor influencing the prison industrial complex is the perpetuation of an "us" versus "them" society. After decades of being "tough on crime," America has created a second-class citizenry that is not only acceptable but desired as it delineates the "good guys" from the "bad." The War on Drugs and mandatory sentencing laws contributed to a new culture of segregation and legal discrimination that many agree is racially motivated (Alexander, 2012; Equal Justice Initiative, n.d.; The Sentencing Project, 2015b). The 1980s offered America a new enemy, the convict or felon, who is literally and/or metaphorically imprisoned for life. Both behind and beyond bars, individuals known to the justice system are veiled in an oppressive shroud woven from unjust laws, policies, and societal stigmas. Americans take comfort in projecting their fear and anxieties onto the drug addict, the murderer, and the pedophile, and although the criminal justice system is intended to rehabilitate, the collateral consequences of incarceration result in felony disenfranchisement that denies returning citizens the right to vote, access to public housing and social services, and many employment and educational opportunities. This has created a revolving door of Americans entering and exiting the criminal justice system. Although 95 percent of all state prisoners are eventually released (Hughes & Wilson, 2015), they reenter a punitive culture largely uneducated on the prison industrial complex and the injustices of the criminal justice system, and dubious about returning citizens' likelihood for change.

According to Schlosser (1998),

> The prison-industrial complex is not a conspiracy, guiding the nation's criminal-justice policy behind closed doors. It is a confluence of special interests that has

given prison construction in the United States a seemingly unstoppable momentum. It is composed of politicians, both liberal and conservative, who have used the fear of crime to gain votes; impoverished rural areas where prisons have become a cornerstone of economic development; private companies that regard the roughly $35 billion spent each year on corrections not as a burden on American taxpayers but as a lucrative market; and government officials whose fiefdoms have expanded along with the inmate population. (p. 53)

The prison industrial complex changed the American mindset around what constitutes a crime, who is labeled a criminal, and how such individuals should be treated both in prison and following their release.

A CLARION CALL FOR SPIRITUAL SUPPORT

The prison industrial complex must be abolished. Christian communities and individuals of faith are called by God to respond to the injustices of mass incarceration and the resulting impact on communities behind and beyond bars. In Matthew 25, Jesus calls Christians to care for our brothers and sisters as we would care for him by feeding the hungry, welcoming the stranger, clothing the naked, and visiting the prisoner. The Epistle to the Hebrews advises Christians to remember those in prison and to empathize with them as though their suffering is one's own (Heb. 13:3). Christians are called to enact care and compassion for the prisoner by following Jesus's example of seeking solidarity with the least and the last.

At present, the majority of ministry to and with women in prison, our sisters inside, focuses on charitable works. Thousands of Christian congregations and people of faith go behind bars to minister to inmates. They offer worship experiences and Bible studies with the aim of evangelism and leading prisoners on the pathway to Christ. These ministries are vital and serve to evidence God's love for all God's children; however, they most often overlook the 650,000–700,000 men and women who are released from incarceration each year (United States Department of Justice, n.d.; Willison, Brazzell, & Kim, 2011). The Christian imperative to care for the prisoner too often stops at the prison gate. Christians' compassionate hearts are hardened by attitudes of "not in my back yard" or "not in my sanctuary." According to Johnson (2011), this is because ministry behind bars is simply easier. It frequently feels safer to Christian volunteers, and inmates tend to express gratitude to outside visitors. The time shared is often experienced as positive by both parties. And, "after completing a quick Bible study or mentoring session, volunteers can be on their way in an hour or two" (Johnson, 2011, p. 198). Women's need for soul care and spiritual support extends far beyond the prison gate. Furthermore, delimiting prison ministry to work behind bars ignores how the structural injustices that contributed to women's incarceration continue to oppress women beyond the bars of prison and upon their release. Prison ministry needs to extend beyond the bars of prison and also beyond the mere provision of charitable works.

Two Feet of Love in Action

Abolishing the prison industrial complex requires dismantling the structural injustices that oppress and entrap women prior to, during, and following incarceration. For Christians, as evidenced by the above sacred texts, this requires following in the footsteps of Christ and walking in what the United States Conference of Catholic Bishops (USCCB, 2012) termed the "Two Feet of Love in Action." Grounded in Pope John Paul II's *Compendium of the Social Doctrine of the Church*, and Pope Benedict XVI's reflections in *Deus Caritas Est* and *Caritas in Veritate*, the Two Feet of Love in Action evidences how the Gospel can be enacted by providing charitable works and striving toward social justice. Figure 0.1 illustrates how justice-seeking spiritual support with returning sisters can draw upon the Two Feet of Love in Action through charitable works that aim to meet the basic needs of individuals and social justice that aims to eradicate the "root causes" of injustice and improve "structures" to be more equitable and just (USCCB, 2012, p. 2).

A movement is underway to help churches to expand their narrow conception of prison ministry to include the provision of spiritual care and support for the friends and families of anyone known to the criminal justice system, the children of the incarcerated, the incarcerated themselves, and the millions of male and female returning citizens transitioning back to their communities. It is relatively easy to provide material support to these populations, to utilize the church van for visits to the prisons, to sponsor summer camp attendance for children of the incarcerated, and to offer bus passes and hot breakfasts to returning citizens; yet material support is a small fraction of justice-seeking spiritual care. Furthermore, although the prison ministries that do seek to assist returning citizens quite often do so in a scripturally and theologically grounded manner, they rarely learn from the wisdom of the experts themselves—the thousands of men and women leaving prison each day. Embarking on a prison ministry aimed at assisting returning citizens requires understanding the spiritual and religious experiences of returning sisters as they undergo the transitional trauma of reentry (McLeod, 2011).

The structural injustices that contribute to incarceration can easily crush the souls, spirits, and psyches of sisters inside. As evidenced above,

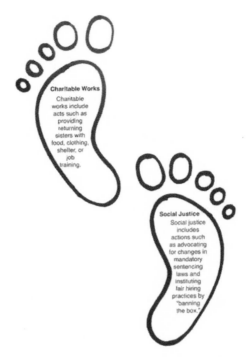

Figure 0.1 "The Two Feet of Love in Action." The Two Feet of Love in Action Evidences How Project Sister Connect Engages in both Charitable Works and Social Justice. Examples of each are provided. *Source:* Copyright 2018 by Author.

Christians are called by Christ to care for and promote the spiritual well-being of women when they are locked up behind bars and locked out as the result of structural injustices beyond bars. Project Sister Connect, the model for revised prison ministry praxis developed in this book, advocates for enacting the Two Feet of Love in Action in a way that provides charitable support and also works toward eradicating high recidivism rates, the barriers that plague female returning citizens, and the structural injustices that contribute to the prison industrial complex. In doing so, Project Sister Connect addresses the multiple environments, often referred to as the ecological systems, in which returning sisters reside (Bronfenbrenner, 1996; Sweat & Denison, 1995). Project Sister Connect aims to engender changes at the micro level, that is, in the lives of individual returning sisters, which often result in changes at the family and environmental level. In addition, Project Sister Connect targets injustices at the structural and super-structural levels, where oppressions related to laws, policies, racism, classism, and sexism are enforced. Figure 0.2 illustrates the ecological levels affected by Project Sister Connect.

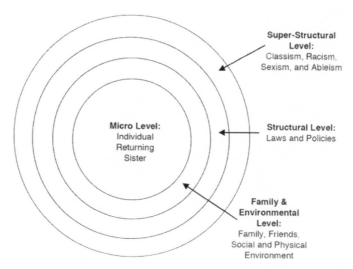

Figure 0.2   "Multiple Environments." The Multiple Environments, or Ecological Systems, in which Returning Sisters Reside that are Addressed by Project Sister Connect. *Source*: Copyright 2018 by Author.

METHODOLOGY

Broadly conceived, this book employs practical theological methods—a critical correlation between theory and practice—utilized toward the construction of a revised ministerial praxis (Browning, 1991). The telos is "toward social and individual transformation" that is grounded in and informed by both interdisciplinary sources and diverse participant experiences (Browning, 1991, p. 36). The book does not adhere to a strict understanding of practical theological methods, however, as it does not engage in in-depth analysis of theological and scriptural insights (Swinton & Mowat, 2006). A significant body of literature is available to the reader that posits theological and scriptural interpretations of prison and prison ministry within the Christian tradition (Hall, 2004; McDargh, 2010; Nolan, 2004; Pounder, 2008). Therefore, this book focuses on filling the gap by addressing how caring people of faith and Christian communities can offer spiritual support to returning sisters, which necessitates an understanding of the literature and wisdom revealed by the social sciences (theory) as well as the voices of female returning citizens and the wisdom revealed by their lived experiences (practice).

Understanding the lived experiences of female returning citizens requires seeking out and elevating the voices of women whose perspectives are too often silenced. To accomplish this goal, this book is grounded in two qualitative research studies that employed interpretative phenomenological analysis (IPA), a research methodology that is "concerned with understanding personal lived experience and thus with exploring persons' relatedness to, or involvement in, a particular event or process (phenomenon)" (Smith, Flowers, & Larkin, 2009, p. 40). In the first study, returning sisters were recruited through residential and nonresidential reentry programs to participate in semi-structured interviews. Women were eligible to participate in the study if they identified as female, were over the age of eighteen, and had served time in either a state or federal prison. The following three research questions guided the study: (1) What are the spiritual and religious experiences of female returning citizens? (2) What role do spiritual and religious communities play in women's reentry? and (3) How do spiritual and religious resources help or hinder women's ability to cope during reentry? More will be revealed throughout the book about participants' backgrounds and demographics, the way their stories are and are not reflected in the literature, and the wisdom they offered regarding the role of spirituality and religion in reentry. The reader is referred to Appendix A for a detailed explanation of the study's methodology.

The stories and experiences of the nineteen returning sisters who were interviewed in the study are woven throughout the book; therefore, a brief glimpse into the participants' backgrounds and demographics is presented in Table 0.1.[2]

In the second study, faith-based mentors were recruited through formally established faith-based mentoring programs to participate in semi-structured interviews. Women were eligible to participate in the study if they were over the age of eighteen, Christian, involved in a formal mentoring program with a female mentee, and an active mentor during the mentee's reentry. The following four research questions guided the study: (1) What were the participants' lived experiences of serving as faith-based mentors to female returning citizens? (2) How did participants' faith communities relate to their service as faith-based mentors? (3) How was participants' spirituality or faith impacted by their service as a faith-based mentor? and (4) What were participants' perspectives on the spiritual and religious experiences of the female returning citizens they mentored? The lived experiences of faith-based mentors are revealed throughout the book, and their experiences were particularly instructive to the development of Project Sister Connect, the model for revised prison ministry praxis, posited in chapter 4. The reader is referred to Appendix B for a detailed explanation of the study's methodology.

A WORD ON LANGUAGE

Sisters inside and returning sisters are, in many ways, the last and the least. Research and engagement with this traditionally marginalized population

Table 0.1   Study Participants' Backgrounds and Demographics

Pseudonym	Age	Race/Ethnicity	Religious Affiliation	# of Prison Terms Served	Years Served during Most Recent Prison Term	Release Date
Tasha	41	Afro-American	Islamism/Moorish Science	1	18	December 2011
Desiree	26	Black	Christian	2	2.5	August 2010
Shanelle	34	African American	N/A	4	2	January 2009
Tammy	52	African American	Christian	1	1.5	July 2005
Latrise	50	African American	Christian	5	2	July 2010
Chelsea	27	White	Baptist	3	2	April 2015
Martha	54	Black	Christian	6	4	November 2007
Lisa	43	Black	Baptist	1	2	October 2014
Danielle	41	Black/Hispanic	Baptist	13	6 months	April 2013
Shawna	50	Black	Holiness	7	7 months	February 2014
Rochelle	46	Black	Seventh Day Adventist	1	13	February 2015
Trina	46	Black	Baptist	3	4	August 2001
Shanice	47	Black	Christian	2	6	2011
Andrea	49	African American	Baptist	1	4 months	January 1998
Deborah	45	African American	Baptist	3	1.5	September 2005
Treva	51	Black	Baptist	1	1	April 2017
Sandra	52	African American	Baptist	1	6	August 2014
Becky	48	White	Methodist	1	2	February 2015
Malea	45	African American	Nondenominational Christian	4	3	March 2011

Source: Copyright 2018 by Author.

requires language care (Bueckert & Schipani, 2006). "One of the simplest methods to keep humanity at the center of discussions about crime and punishment is always to employ humanizing language" (Stern, 2014, p. 10). This book attempts to employ humanizing language in an effort to avoid the use of words and terms that obscure the humanity of people behind bars as well as the people whose jobs it is to administer their imprisonment. Humanizing language or person-first and person-centered language reminds us that inmates, returning citizens, and prison administrators, like all humans, are made in the image of God. Prison ministry is not an "us" versus "them" issue. Prison ministry requires that we acknowledge how our sisters' welfare intimately impacts the welfare of each of us and all of us.

Most women in prison do not want to be called "inmate." Most women leaving prison do not identify as "returning citizens." Most women do not consider leaving prison to be an act of "reintegration," as many never felt "integrated" with mainstream society prior to incarceration (McLeod, 2011). Nevertheless, I am thoughtful in my attempt to employ "language care" based upon my recognition that the language I use can humanize or otherize those I aim to care for and empower, and precise language can enhance my understanding of those whose experiences are like as well as unlike my own (Bueckert & Schipani, 2006). Therefore, throughout the book female inmates are most often referred to as "sisters inside" and female returning citizens as "returning sisters."

I was also careful to employ language care in the book's theological discourse. In my own writing, I employed gender-inclusive language in reference to God. However, because study participants most often referred to God with the gendered pronoun "he," I chose to respect participants' use of gendered language and reported their statements verbatim. When participants used the pronoun he in reference to God, I capitalized it to add clarity.

PREVIEW OF THE BOOK

Women Leaving Prison: Justice-Seeking Spiritual Support for Female Returning Citizens utilizes interpretative phenomenological analysis, a qualitative research methodology, to elevate the essentially silenced voices of female returning citizens in order to explore how their spiritual and religious beliefs and practices, and their relationships with Christian communities, are experienced during their reentry. The book considers how churches, people of faith, and concerned citizens can welcome and care for returning sisters, and how they can facilitate returning sisters' successful reentry through both communal and individual care and support.

Although the majority of scholarly and popular discourse focuses on the incarceration and reentry experiences of men, the prison industrial complex in America impacts men and women alike. Women comprise 7 percent of the total population in state and federal prisons (Carson & Anderson, 2016). Yet failing to recognize the unique experiences of women results in programs and ministries that adopt a one-size-fits-all model. According to Tripodi and Pettus-Davis (2013), increases in women's incarceration rates resulted not only from the War on Drugs and mandatory minimum sentencing, but a "lack of correctional programming designed to meet incarcerated women's needs," thus resulting in increased recidivism (p. 30).

Therefore, part I provides the reader with essential background for understanding women's pathways to prison, their religious and spiritual experiences behind bars, and the barriers common in women's reentry experiences. Chapter 1 introduces the reader to the correlating factors that contribute to female incarceration. By utilizing a feminist pathways perspective (Mallicoat, 2015), chapter 1 evidences first how women are more likely to become involved in crime as the result of attempts to cope with psychological, physical, and sexual abuse, poverty, and substance abuse, and second how women are more likely to be serving time for drug-related offenses than violent crimes. Chapter 1 also explores the cultures of spirituality and religion in women's prisons. Religion has played a role in the American penal system since its inception. Biblical precepts were often used as justification for assigning particular punishments and determining the severity of a sentence (Clear, Hardyman, Stout, Lucken, & Dammer, 2000). The role and significance of religious doctrines in the penal system changed over time when in the twentieth century scientific knowledge replaced religious knowledge as the guiding paradigm for criminal justice (Clear et al., 2000). However, religious life and programming remains central to the prison experience. A higher percentage of inmates participate in religious programs than any other type of programs—surpassing even education (Levitt & Loper, 2009). For example, in a survey of 213 women at a state prison facility, 70.3 percent reported some participation in religious services (Levitt & Loper, 2009). In order to understand returning sisters' spiritual and religious experiences, a cursory examination of their pathways to prison and their experiences behind bars is in order as often this is where their faith was planted, strengthened, or tested.

Chapter 2 then presents the barriers common in women's reentry experiences as evidenced in the existing literature and supported by the experiences of the study participants. The chapter focuses on women's experiences seeking shelter and employment, reintegrating with friends and family, coping with substance abuse and mental illness, satisfying parole conditions, and contending with the oft-internalized stigmas of being a felon and ex-offender. Chapter 2 outlines the factors that facilitate and support successful reentry as well. Finally, despite the dearth of information available, chapter 2 describes what is known about the benefits and outcomes of faith-based reentry services.

Part II of the book presents the findings from the two qualitative investigations into returning sisters' spiritual and religious beliefs and practices during reentry and proposes Project Sister Connect, a model for revised prison ministry praxis that moves beyond bars. Based upon semi-structured interviews with nineteen returning sisters and five faith-based mentors, chapter 3 overviews how women made sense of and understood their spiritual and religious experiences during reentry. It demonstrates how they understood God and God's role in their reentry, the types of spiritual and religious support they did and did not receive from individuals and congregations, the ways their beliefs both helped and hindered their reentry experience, and their experiences with faith-based mentors. Chapter 3 also details faith-based mentors' experiences with female returning citizens and highlights their observations on returning sisters' spiritual and religious experiences.

The book culminates in chapter 4 by presenting Project Sister Connect, a model for revised prison ministry praxis. Rather than reinforcing the abuse and oppression so many returning sisters experienced during childhood, as adults, and as the result of the prison industrial complex, Project Sister Connect is grounded in practices of radical acceptance, connection, and righteous indignation in the face of structural injustices, as exemplified in the ministry of Jesus. Based upon the wisdom shared by returning sisters and reported in chapter 3, as well as the wisdom revealed through the literature in chapters 1 and 2, chapter 4 offers a model for revised prison ministry praxis with female returning citizens that facilitates women's successful reentry by creating partnerships that address returning sisters' holistic needs in an empowering manner that strives toward justice. Spiritual care of returning sisters requires attending not only to the women themselves but to the structural injustices that contributed to their imprisonment and erected barriers to their successful reentry. It requires enacting the Two Feet of Love in Action by working to abolish the prison industrial complex through changes in our micro, structural, and super-structural systems. Project Sister Connect outlines how individual and communal care of returning sisters can be accompanied by Christian advocacy for criminal justice reform. By presenting small, concrete steps for reform, chapter 4 offers a pragmatic approach to changing the laws and structural injustices that impede women's successful reentry.

AN INVITATION

Many readers may believe that mass incarceration does not impact their day-to-day lives. Many readers may assume that they have never met anyone who was incarcerated or who has a friend or loved one living behind bars. Many readers may wonder about the relevance of ministry with female returning citizens if they live in suburban or rural contexts. And many readers may argue that some other church or some other person is better equipped to "do prison ministry."

The reader of this book, however, is invited to identify and to sit with these assumptions and beliefs. The reader is invited to acknowledge how and when these ideas were planted and to reflect upon their resonance with scripture, with the life and ministry of Christ Jesus, and with the witness to God's love documented in chapter 3 of this book. The reader is invited on a journey of examining the power he or she so easily wields each day that is denied to so many by a system with no true clemency or mercy. The reader is invited to recognize the ways that he or she is complicit with the prison industrial complex and the racially and economically unjust policies that create and strengthen it. The reader is invited to consider why any returning sister, after serving her sentence, should be oppressed again and again by facing the barriers of reentry without the spiritual care and support that God commands us to provide. Only in accepting this invitation will the reader recognize that this ministry is not a ministry *for* our sisters, but a partnering *with*, a being in solidarity *with*, returning sisters that enables us as Christians to remember those in prison and to empathize with them as though their suffering is our own (Heb. 13:3).

NOTES

1. Jasmine's story is a composite based upon my qualitative research with female returning citizens and my personal experience serving as a faith-based mentor to female inmates at a state prison.

2. Participants completed a Demographic Form (see Appendix A) that featured numerous write-in responses, and therefore Table A reports participants' responses regarding their race/ethnicity and religious affiliation verbatim or in their own language.

Part I

ESTABLISHING THE CONTEXT: SISTERS ENTERING PRISON, SISTERS INSIDE, AND RETURNING SISTERS

Chapter 1

Sisters Inside

Pathways to Prison and Faith Behind Bars

> Women in prison are among the most vulnerable and marginalized members of society—women who, in other contexts, society would profess an obligation to support and protect.
>
> (Women in Prison Project, 2006, p. 4)

Women in prison are invisible and forgotten. They are "the most neglected, misunderstood and unseen women in our society" (Covington, 1998, p. 1). When rates of female incarceration started to rise in the 1980s and 1990s, scholars began to realize that female and male criminality differ. The crimes committed by women are often "survival crimes" committed in order to "earn money, feed a drug-dependent habit, or escape terrifying intimate relationships and brutal social conditions" (Richie, 2000, p. 7). Feminist criminologists began to view incarcerated women as vulnerable, marginalized, and "compelled to crime" (Richie, 1996) due to "unmet social, educational, health, and economic needs, in addition to a history of victimization" (Richie, 2000, p. 7). Although feminist scholarship often portrays sisters inside as the victims of abuse and structural injustices, these same women are simultaneously judged and relegated to the margins of society by scholars and social service providers alike. Moreover, little has been done on behalf of women with regard to public policy, interventions within the prisons, or reentry programming and services.

Mass culture in America perpetuates its own narrative about this invisible, marginalized population. Popular depictions of sisters inside, such as the hit show *Orange Is the New Black* (Friedman, 2013), perpetuate stereotypes that largely ignore or oversimplify how the complex intersections of race, socioeconomics, family history, violence, and education influence women's

3

pathways to prison. The backgrounds of and crimes committed by women in prison remain under-acknowledged and misconstrued by scholars and popular culture alike.

Given that so many women in the criminal justice system today are simultaneously victims and criminals, survivors and perpetrators, any portrayal of sisters inside and their pathways to prison must evidence how women's involvement in the criminal justice system is influenced by myriad factors, both personal and structural. This chapter draws upon a feminist pathways approach that recognizes the cycle of violence common among sisters inside, a cycle that begins with victimization and leads to offending (Mallicoat, 2015). The aim of this chapter is threefold: first, chapter 1 introduces the factors that contribute to female incarceration by evidencing the backgrounds of sisters inside, illustrating the correlation between involvement in crime and race, childhood and adult experiences of psychological, physical, and sexual abuse, poverty, mental illness, and substance abuse. Second, chapter 1 shows how women are more likely to be serving time for drug-related and property offenses than violent crimes. Utilizing both statistical and narrative evidence enhances the portrayal of these complex dynamics. Third, chapter 1 outlines the historical significance of religion in America's penal system and explores the cultures of spirituality and religion in women's prisons today.

WHO ARE SISTERS INSIDE? UNCOVERING THE BACKGROUNDS OF WOMEN IN PRISON

Although women comprise only 7 percent of the total population in state and federal prisons (Carson & Anderson, 2016), between 1980 and 2011, the number of women in prison in the United States increased by 587 percent (Carson & Sabol, 2012), nearly 1.5 times the growth of men in prison (The Sentencing Project, 2012a). At the end of 2015, there were 111,495 women under the jurisdiction of state or federal correctional authorities in the United States (Carson & Anderson, 2016). Although women comprise a small percentage of total prison inmates (7%), because most women are convicted of nonviolent crimes and therefore serve shorter sentences, women are overrepresented among the population receiving correctional supervision. At year-end 2015, women constituted 25 percent of the adults on probation and 13 percent of adults on parole (Kaeble & Bonczar, 2016). Today, due to shifting policies and practices in criminal justice, many women who previously would have been ordered to supervision in the community are now being put behind bars (Mallicoat, 2015), thus increasing the need for justice-seeking reentry services. Understanding the backgrounds of sisters inside and their pathways to prison necessitates recognizing how women's intersecting social locations, or intersectionality, contribute to myriad, interrelated oppressions that result from structural injustices (Weber, 2010).

Intersectionality

Crenshaw (1991) introduced the term "intersectionality" in her exploration of how racism, patriarchy, and post-colonialism intersect in ways that subjugate and marginalize Black women. Theories of intersectionality are grounded on the premise that every individual occupies social locations in regard to her race, class, gender, sexuality, and other identity markers (i.e., age, ethnicity, and nation; Weber 2010), and that these social locations render some degree of power and privilege or oppression and dependence. The status that one's social locations confer is determined by complex social systems that are historically and socially influenced and determined. For example, being White in America bestows particular privileges that are most often denied to persons of color, and what it means to be White in America today is not only influenced and determined by the current sociopolitical milieu but by the centuries of violence and colonialism perpetrated by Whites in the nation's history. These social systems, which are most often constructed and maintained by those in power, typically result in hierarchies that afford advantages to the few and disadvantages to the many. Such hierarchies are often veiled or ignored by those creating, maintaining, and perpetuating the oppressive systems. "To those who occupy positions of privilege, that is, who benefit from the existing social arrangements, the fact that their privilege is dependent on the unfair exclusion of or direct harm to others is obscured, unimportant, practically invisible" (Weber, 2010, p. 28). Furthermore, because each of us occupies myriad social locations, we may experience privilege as the result of one social location, for example our race, and oppression as the result of another, for example our gender identity or sexual orientation. The way our social locations intersect often obfuscates our ability to understand and explain how these complex social systems operate and perpetrate structural injustice.

Bernard (2013) utilized concepts of intersectionality in her theoretical explanations of female criminality. Traditional sociological theories of criminality posit that individuals engage in crime as a result of feeling strained or thwarted in their attempts to achieve shared cultural goals (Merton, 1968). For example, facing barriers en route to achieving the "American Dream" of material wealth and security may encourage an individual to use alternative, criminal pathways to success. These barriers are not forces that place strain upon individuals but are forces that constrain entire groups, specifically groups of women, who experience oppression as the result of their intersecting social locations. Viewing women's incarceration through the lens of intersectionality "de-emphasizes individual frustrations and pathologies and instead stresses the ways in which power structures and systems of oppression work to circumscribe the life experiences of persons socially located at the intersections of multiple vulnerabilities" (Bernard, 2013, p. 5). If women's intersecting social locations, and their concomitant experiences of oppression, compel or constrain them to crime, it is essential then to understand the backgrounds of sisters inside in order to grasp their pathways to prison and to anticipate their needs at the time of reentry.

Many sisters inside have histories of "multiple marginality" as their intersecting social locations relegate them to the borders of society (Vigil, 1995, p. 125). As marginalized members of society, these women are vulnerable to both abuse and criminal involvement. As noted above, utilizing a feminist pathways perspective helps to evidence how women are more likely to become involved in crime as a result of their racial/ethnic backgrounds, their attempts to cope with psychological, physical, and sexual abuse, and their experiences of substance abuse, mental illness, and poverty.

Racial and Ethnic Backgrounds of Sisters Inside

Racial and ethnic minorities are disproportionately impacted by incarceration. This is true for men and women alike. Although "Blacks and Hispanics make up only 24% of the U.S. population, 63% of women in state prisons and 67% of women in federal prisons are Black or Hispanic, a practice that indicates that women of color are significantly overrepresented behind bars" (Mallicoat, 2015, p. 381). Table 1.1 depicts the racial/ethnic demographics of women in state and federal correctional facilities in 2015.

The racial demographics of sisters inside are changing. Incarceration rates are decreasing for African American women and increasing for both White and Latina women, rendering White women the fastest growing demographic sector in the criminal justice system (Mauer, 2013). For example, between 2000 and 2014, there was a 56 percent increase in the rate of incarceration for White women yet a 47 percent decrease in the rate of incarceration for African American women (The Sentencing Project, 2015a).

Recent changes in incarceration rates along racial and ethnic lines result from numerous interrelated circumstances, and structural injustices,

Table 1.1   Racial/Ethnic Demographics of Female Inmates

White	Black	Hispanic	Other	Total Female[1]
52,700	21,700	17,900	12,700	104,968

Source: Adapted from Carson & Anderson (2016).
[1]Detail may not sum to total due to rounding, inclusion of inmates age seventeen or younger in the total count, and missing race or Hispanic origin data.

relative to (1) women's involvement in crime, (2) the respon
cial system, and (3) differences among state laws. For exam
rates for both property crimes and drug offenses have dec
can Americans and increased for Whites (Mauer, 2013). "Problems with alcohol–the drug most closely linked to arrests, violence and incarceration—are up among white women but down among black women" (Humphreys, 2017, para. 5). White women are disproportionately impacted by the methamphetamine and prescription opioid epidemics (Humphreys, 2017), which increases their likelihood of contact with the criminal justice system. Changes in arrest practices and sentencing laws also mean an increase in arrest rates for use of these drugs among both White and Latina women (Mauer, 2013). In addition to changing trends in drug-related convictions, total arrest rates for violent crimes also influenced racial changes in incarceration rates. Between 2000 and 2009, African American women experienced a 22.2 percent decline in rates of arrest for violent crimes while White women experienced only an 11.1 percent decline (Mauer, 2013).

There is a troubling absence of attention in the literature to Hispanic and Latina incarceration rates as well as those of other racial and ethnic minorities, which erroneously depicts female imprisonment to be a Black/White problem. Statistics and demographics for other races and ethnicities are less frequently presented, and the experiences of these women are largely overlooked in analyses. Therefore, although statistics are available indicating, for example, how Hispanic women represent 14 percent of New York state's female prison population but 44 percent of the state's women sentenced for drug offenses, there is scant analysis regarding what undergirds such unjust racial discrimination (Mauer, Potler, & Wolf, 1999).

Experiences of Psychological, Physical, and Sexual Abuse among Sisters Inside

Desiree was one of the nineteen returning sisters interviewed in the study grounding this book. A twenty-six-year-old African American female, Desiree endured significant abuse during her childhood, which directly impacted her experience behind bars.

> I was broken, as far as coming from a broken home, and you know being abused all my life: sexually, mentally, and physically. I've been kidnapped and raped. . . . Tooken from my mom. Put in the system. Ranned away. Promiscuous. Drugs was here and there. . . . So I had to really look at all that while I was behind bars, laying up on the bed. You know, why me? Why do I need change? It was just, it was awful.

Although confronting the reality of her past abuse was painful, Desiree ultimately found prison to be a healing environment. She noted how sharing her pain, both verbally and in writing, helped her to heal.

> A lot of people [in prison] have been abused mentally and sexually and have never talked about it. A lot of people still hold onto that when incarcerated. But for me, that thing was eating me up so bad, I had to let it out. I had to talk about it. And I would go weeks and weeks and weeks talking about the same thing until I finished with it. Now until this day it's actually gone away.

The majority of sisters inside have experienced psychological, physical, and sexual abuse, a fact that differentiates the typical female from the typical male inmate. Such experiences, during childhood and adulthood, are a common antecedent to women's involvement in the criminal justice system. Abuse and victimization can lead to offending behaviors and, in turn, can result from criminal acts, thus creating a vicious cycle. For example, imagine a fifteen-year-old girl sexually abused by her uncle, who runs away from home to protect herself from further abuse. Unsure about the marketable skills she possesses, she begins prostituting herself to make money to provide shelter, food, and clothing. Her clients further abuse and belittle her and, to cope with and numb the pain, she begins abusing alcohol and drugs. Experiences such as these wherein victimization and crime are mutually reinforcing are all too common. "Abuse is what kicked off alcohol or drug addiction in many of these women; it's what made them . . . get into trouble with the law . . . [and] it's what has kept their self-esteem in low ebb" (Watterson, 1996, p. 36).

The Prevalence of Victimization among Sisters Inside

Childhood victimization. For many sisters inside, their experiences of abuse began in childhood and were perpetrated by immediate or extended family members. These adverse childhood experiences significantly increase the likelihood of both interaction with the criminal justice system and victimization in adulthood. Unfortunately, the U.S. Bureau of Justice Statistics has not collected data on the abuse histories of sisters inside since 1999. At that time, 25 percent of women in state prisons reported sexual abuse prior to age eighteen, and 36.7 percent of women in state prisons and 23 percent of women in federal prisons reported sexual and/or physical abuse before age seventeen (Harlow, 1999). Similar rates of childhood abuse among sisters inside were reported in other studies (Gilfus, 1992; Messina & Grella, 2006; Sargent, Marcos-Mendosa, & Ho Yu, 1993).

Experiences of psychological, physical, and sexual abuse in childhood significantly impact women's entrance into criminal activity and their pathways to prison as juveniles and adults. In an effort to cope with the trauma of abuse, as will be evidenced in greater detail below, they are "more likely to use alcohol and other drugs and turn to criminal and violent behaviors when coping with stressful life events" (Widom, 2000, p. 33). Widom (2000) conducted a longitudinal study that revealed that abused and neglected girls were nearly twice as likely as those who had not been abused to be arrested as juveniles, twice as likely to be arrested as adults, and 2.4 times more likely to be arrested for violent crimes (Widom, 2000, p. 29). Childhood physical and sexual abuse also places girls at higher risk for substance abuse and addiction, thus increasing the likelihood of contact with the criminal justice system and entrapment in the prison industrial complex.

Abuse during adulthood. Childhood abuse also increases the likelihood that a woman will experience abuse as an adult (Brown, Miller, & Maguin, 1999). In a 2014 interview with public radio station WBHM, Dr. Larry Wood, a clinical psychologist at the Tutwiler Prison for Women in Alabama, reported that in over twenty years of service with the Federal Bureau of Prisons, every single woman he counseled reported a history of physical or sexual abuse prior to incarceration (Lovoy, 2014). What are the abuse experiences of sisters inside during adulthood, and who perpetrates such abuse?

Consonant with Dr. Wood's experience (Lovoy, 2014), the prevalence of physical and sexual abuse is much higher among women behind bars than it is in the general population. In a study of 403 randomly selected female inmates at the Metro State Women's Prison in Atlanta, Georgia, Cook, Smith, Tusher, and Raiford (2005) utilized the *Traumatic Life Events Questionnaire* (Kubany et al., 2000) to determine the prevalence among inmates of twenty-one potentially traumatic life events. Within this sample, 78.4 percent experienced physical abuse by a partner; 60.3 percent experienced the threat to kill; 47.1 percent were stalked; 35 percent experienced robbery; 29.8 percent experienced assault by a stranger; and 27.3 percent experienced adult sexual abuse (Cook, Smith, Tusher, & Raiford, 2005, p. 117). Moreover, nearly the entire sample of 403 participants (99%) reported experiencing at least one of the twenty-one traumatic events.

Treva was among the nineteen returning sisters who participated in the study grounding this book. A fifty-one-year-old African American woman, Treva served one year in prison for the mutual, interpersonal violence that occurred between her and her girlfriend. After nineteen years of drug addiction, Treva "stopped cold turkey" in order to try to make her relationship work. But as she was "coming down" off the drugs and working hard to stay sober, she was also navigating an emotionally volatile and controlling relationship. In the heat of an argument, Treva's girlfriend held her up against the wall and

had their forearm up on my neck, my feet up off the ground. I reached around.
I grabbed a screwdriver, and I put it to their back, and I said—I was trying to

push it in 'em . . . I just said, "Get off me" . . . I do like this, made an indenta-
tion in their back.

Her partner then pressed charges, showing the injury on her back, and
Treva served forty-five days in jail. She was told by the judge that if she came
back before the judge she would be sent to prison.

Treva recognized that the relationship was abusive and unhealthy, and she
tried to leave. Without any family or friends in the area, she reached out to
"therapists and counselors, trying to help me get out of that place 'cause I was
letting them know that the relationship had became abusive. I was trying to
get out of there before it turned ugly which it did." But when she tried to pack
her belongings and leave, her partner started throwing her clothes over the
balcony. Treva pulled her partner back from the balcony by her shirt, leaving a mark around her neck, which resulted in the judge sending her to serve
one year in the state prison. But Treva continuously thanked God for sending
her to prison. She shared, "God made that happen. I know that to be true.
The devil tried to tear me down, but God definitely turned that negative into
a positive all the way around." As a middle-aged, African American female
in a same-gender-loving relationship, Treva wanted and sought help to leave
a physically abusive relationship. Yet without friends or family in the area,
and without financial means for counseling or legal representation, she was
dependent upon public assistance. Treva was imprisoned by structural injustices before ever entering prison. In Treva's mind, prison was an emotionally
and physically safe place to be, and she was therefore grateful to God for her
imprisonment.

Sexual abuse in adulthood is also prevalent among sisters inside. According to Cook, Smith, Tusher, and Raiford (2005) in the study cited above,
27.3 percent of the study's 403 participants experienced adult sexual abuse.
In an attempt to provide a richer, more textured understanding of the context
surrounding such sexual abuse, McDaniels-Wilson and Belknap (2008) conducted a quantitative study using a sexual abuse survey with female inmates
at three Ohio state prisons. The study produced 391 usable surveys detailing
the range of sexual abuse behaviors, from less severe abuses like misinter-
preting the level of sexual intimacy to more severe abuses like completed
rape. The study resulted in "data on the victim-offender relationship (VOR),
the offender's gender, and the age of the victim at the time of the violation or
abuse" (p. 1091). The data is rich yet too expansive to present in its entirety;
however, it is illustrative to note that 43.5 percent of the 391 participants in
the study experienced illegally *attempted* penetration (McDaniels-Wilson &
Belknap, 2008). The vast majority of these women said that threat or use of
physical force was used, with the mean number of experiences of violation
being 3.3. Nearly 60 percent of the sample experienced illegally *completed*

penetration, again, the vast majority of which occurred as the result of threat or use of physical force. The mean number of experiences of violation was 3.8. Sadly, only 54.5 percent identified their experiences as rape.

Statistics alone cannot adequately depict the psychological, physical, and sexual abuse experienced by women in prison. Studies utilizing qualitative research methods are essential as they elevate women's voices and lived experiences. For example, Gilfus (1992) conducted qualitative life history interviews with twenty women between the ages of twenty and forty who were incarcerated in a state prison for street crimes, including prostitution, shoplifting, check or credit card fraud, and drug law violations. Of the study's participants, thirteen experienced childhood sexual abuse. One of the many poignant examples was that of Janet, a twenty-eight-year-old African American female, who between the ages of three and fourteen experienced countless acts of sexual abuse at the hands of multiple perpetrators, including a babysitter, her male and female cousins, her grandfather, and her stepfather. Janet left home at age fourteen, began prostituting, and was coerced into a life of street crime as the result of her drug addiction and an abusive relationship.

In addition, fifteen of the twenty participants in Gilfus's study experienced severe physical abuse at the hands of family members. One participant, Marcia, when asked if she'd been abused as a child responded, "No, I just got hit a lot" (p. 72). She explained how both of her parents used to hit her. She stated, "'Cause they both would drink and they wouldn't know the difference. Mmm, picked up, thrown against walls, everything. You name it" (p. 72). This resulted in bruises and welts which, when asked about by teachers, Marcia attributed to having fallen.

Because the majority of the participants in Gilfus's study had experienced abuse at home from a young age, it is not surprising that thirteen of the twenty women ran away from home in childhood. The need to survive the streets then compelled them to engage in criminal behaviors, including stealing, prostitution, and shoplifting, and left them vulnerable to revictimization. Sixteen of the twenty participants experienced rape, assault, and attempted murder. Given the destructive experiences of abuse endured by so many sisters inside, it is no surprise that in a study of sixty-five women in a medium security prison, Bradley and Davino (2002) found that "across the sample as a whole, prison was perceived as a safer environment than was childhood or adulthood" (p. 355).

Finally, not only do women in prison have higher rates of victimization than their male counterparts (Center on Addiction and Substance Abuse, 2010), they also have more enduring and extensive histories of victimization than non-imprisoned women in the United States (Harlow, 1999; Tripodi & Pettus-Davis, 2013). Women in prison suffer from physical abuse at a rate of 6–10 times greater than the general female population (Blount, Kuhns, &

Silverman, 1993, p. 425). Sadly, like childhood physical and sexual abuse, such abuses in adulthood can also compel women to use drugs or alcohol in an effort to cope, and thus places them at higher risk for addiction and increases the likelihood of contact with the criminal justice system and entrapment in the prison industrial complex.

Backgrounds of Substance Use among Sisters Inside

Given her parents', her husband's, and her own addiction, substance use was normative for Shanelle, a thirty-four-year-old African American female participant in the study grounding this book. Shanelle was in and out of prison four times in six years and, although she had nine months sober following her last release, an inability to trust others and a lack of emotional support contributed to Shanelle's relapse. Following her release from prison, Shanelle participated in multiple outpatient drug treatment programs, but she could never stay clean for more than two or three days. She said,

> It was just like nothing was helping me like, I couldn't get past that third day. I was like man I'm tired of this. I'm tired of waking up broke and don't have no food or where are you going to eat at.

Although Shanelle continued to use, her husband got sober; they were living at his mom's house, but Shanelle was running the streets.

> Like I was staying at the house but I was getting high more. So just one day I just, I just got sick and tired like that. And I remember that night just getting on my hands and knees and crying like Lord just help me get into a rehab or something. . . . I need intense inpatient.

Shanelle participated in a one-month inpatient program and, at the time of our interview, had three months clean.

Tammy, a fifty-two-year-old African American female participant in this study, had multiple possession charges and was trapped in the jail's revolving door. She was in and out of jail twenty-four times following a drug court sentence for the possession of a single pill for which she'd been offered a plea of thirty days, but she denied. At the time of our interview, Tammy had had around twenty-five possession charges total. She said,

> There's 25 charges. I might be a little bit over, but not far from it . . . and see it's all possession. Well, I must be an addict. Apparently I have a problem . . . I can't say I'm not a criminal, but rehabilitation would be a better choice for me than keep going to jail.

After running from a warrant for over seven years, Tammy wanted to spend the remainder of her sentence in prison. Prior to her sentencing, Tammy and her prayer partner in the jail spent several days asking God for the judge to see Tammy's potential to benefit from prison substance abuse treatment. And, from Tammy's perspective, her prayers were answered. She was sentenced to eighteen months in prison and only served four before entering a pre-release substance abuse treatment program. Tammy's twenty-four times in and out of jail, her multiple drug court appearances, and ultimately her incarceration in prison, evidence the structural injustices that criminalize individuals struggling to overcome substance use disorders rather than recognizing their struggle as part of a much broader public health crisis.

Prevalence of Substance Use Disorders among Women in Prison

Almost two-thirds of male and female inmates in prisons and jails have a substance use disorder—a rate more than seven times that of non-incarcerated individuals (CASA, 2010). Derivations of Shanelle's and Tammy's stories are common among sisters inside. Although men and women alike experience substance use disorders, women in prison report higher drug use than their male counterparts (CASA, 2010; Greenfeld & Snell, 1999). In a survey of both male and female inmates in state and federal prisons, the Center on Addiction and Substance Abuse (2010) found that 40.3 percent of women versus 36.5 percent of men in federal prisons, and 56.9 percent of women versus 47.2 percent of men in state prisons were dependent upon drugs or alcohol. Women behind bars enter prison dependent upon, and with a history of abusing, myriad addictive substances. Proctor (2012) utilized the Substance Use Disorder Diagnostic Schedule-IV (Hoffmann & Harrison, 1995) with 801 women upon entrance into the Minnesota state prison system. Table 1.2 presents the prevalence of abuse of and dependence upon five addictive substances.

These statistics are supported by the fact that the presence of drugs and/ or alcohol in women's systems at the time of criminal activity is alarmingly high. In 2003, the National Institute of Justice used the Arrestee Drug Abuse Monitoring Program to collect data from 3,664 women arrested at 164 different booking facilities across the United States. Participants completed an interview along with a urine analysis. Across the facilities, 68 percent of women tested positive for cocaine, marijuana, methamphetamine, opiates, or phencyclidine (PCP) and 86.4 percent tested positive for alcohol at the time of arrest.

Substance use relates to criminal activity among women in four significant ways. First is the psychopharmacological manner in which drugs and alcohol can lower inhibitions, change cognitive capabilities, and physiologically

Table 1.2   Prevalence of Substance Use

Diagnostic Category	Prevalence (%)
Alcohol	
Dependence	30.2
Abuse	10.2
Cocaine	
Dependence	30.1
Abuse	5.4
Marijuana	
Dependence	15.6
Abuse	7.5
Stimulant	
Dependence	24.1
Abuse	2.1
Heroin	
Dependence	9.6
Abuse	0.9

Source: Adapted from Proctor (2012).

dispose one to involvement in criminal behaviors that, without the influence of substance, may otherwise not have occurred (Moon, Thompson, & Bennett, 1993). Second, according to Cobbina,

> For a number of women their initiation in crime occurred as the result of their drug addiction. Drug use played a significant role in escalating their involvement in economic crime because women perceived the criminal world as an attractive alternative to obtain money for the purpose of supporting their drug habit. (2009, p. 58)

A third way in which drugs and alcohol relate to women's criminal activity is through the influence of family, peers, and intimates. "Drugs are part of the relationship network of women" (Pollock, 2002, p. 61). Addiction often afflicts the families of many individuals known to the justice system, and a significant portion of female inmates are introduced to drugs and alcohol by family members. In Cobbina's (2009) study, 23 percent of the study's incarcerated participants and 25 percent of formerly incarcerated participants "stated that their initiation into the drug world began as a result of their exposure to illicit substances by their family during adolescence" (p. 38). Finally, many women begin using and abusing substances as a result of their intimate relationships and many maintain unhealthy or abusive intimate relationships due to the role these relationships play in their drug use or dependence. According to Moon, Thompson, and Bennett (1994), sisters inside were frequently introduced to drugs by addicted male partners. This was true for approximately 15 percent of incarcerated women and 8 percent of formerly incarcerated women in Cobbina's (2009) study. These participants reported that their drug use resulted from their relationships with drug-involved males, whether those males pressured them into such behavior and/or made drugs readily available to the women. "As female identity is so often tied to the status of the men in their lives, women often cross many thresholds of acceptable behavior in the name of 'love'" (Moon, Thompson, & Bennett, 1994, p. 48).

Finally, given the preponderance of abuse experienced among sisters inside, it is no surprise that many women turn to drugs and alcohol in order to cope with their experiences of victimization and the concomitant anxiety, depression, and low self-worth that often results. According to the Center on Addiction and Substance Abuse, "Women with a history of abuse are three times likelier than other women to have an alcohol use disorder during their lifetime and four times likelier to have a drug use disorder" (CASA, 2010, p. 47). Drugs and alcohol can aid abused women in their efforts to cope in myriad ways. For example, substance use can mask the relational trauma that accompanies interpersonal violence and abuse. Use or abuse of drugs and alcohol may function as a method of self-medication and facilitate a sense of escape from adverse relationships and situations (Chesney-Lind & Pasko, 2013). Abuse of cocaine and amphetamines can help make women feel more vigilant in order to guard against the threat of further abuse, and both drugs and alcohol can serve as a social lubricant to combat the low self-esteem and social anxiety that can result from victimization (Saxena, Messina, & Grella, 2014).

The war on drugs. Understanding the prevalence of substance abuse among sisters inside is essential as it evidences why so many women are caught, as a result of the War on Drugs, in the prison industrial complex, and why the treatment of substance abuse in prisons is woefully inadequate. As stated in the Introduction, the War on Drugs significantly contributes to the prison industrial complex plaguing America today. In 1971, President Richard Nixon declared a War on Drugs, citing drugs as the number one public enemy, and four decades of presidents followed suit. President Reagan allocated $1.7 billion to fight the War on Drugs in 1986. President Clinton spent $1.3 billion to fight cocaine production in Columbia in 2000. Republican and Democratic administrations alike expended billions of dollars and supported myriad laws that limit the rights of American citizens and increase the control of local law enforcement and the Drug Enforcement Administration. Local police are routinely supported in violating the Fourth Amendment through unwarranted searches and seizures. Provided they have reasonable suspicion, officers can legally stop and frisk individuals and conduct sweeps across small and large groups. Drivers are regularly stopped and searched for drugs under the auspices of enforcing traffic laws; and these behaviors are

...ized among state and local law enforcement through the awarding of cash and military equipment (Alexander, 2012). As a result, "the number of Americans incarcerated for drug offenses has skyrocketed from 41,000 in 1980 to nearly a half million in 2013" (The Sentencing Project, n.d., p. 3). In 2012, individuals convicted of drug-related crimes comprised 51 percent of federal prisoners and 16 percent of state prisoners (Carson, 2014). The vast majority of these individuals are not "kingpins" or high-level dealers; rather, most of them were convicted of drug possession with no intent to sell.

Although the media largely portrays the War on Drugs as a battle waged against men, women are actually more likely than men to be convicted of a drug-related crime (Mauer & King, 2007). In 2012, one-quarter of all sisters inside had been convicted of drug offenses (Carson, 2014) and, as evidenced above, drug use and addiction can lead to other related crimes. In 1971 when the War on Drugs started, 6,329 women were incarcerated in state or federal prisons (Tripodi & Pettus-Davis, 2013). Today that figure is well over 100,000 (Carson & Sabol, 2012). This is not just a war on drugs. This is a war on women and families (Chesney-Lind, 1998). Until this war is eradicated and substance use disorders are viewed as a public health problem and not a moral failing, prisons will be full of addicted sisters. What types of treatments, then, are they afforded inside?

Treatment of Substance Use Disorders in Prisons

A substance use disorder is a brain disease accompanied by cognitive, behavioral, and physiological characteristics. Neuroscientific advances demonstrated how physiological changes in the brain render substance use disorders a disease rather than a spiritual or socioeconomic issue as was erroneously believed for so long. Yet despite the War on Drugs and mandatory sentencing laws that impose extensive sentences to addicted individuals, treatment of substance use disorders in prisons is quite limited and consists predominantly of drug education rather than drug treatment (Chandler, Fletcher, & Volkow, 2009). Incarceration alone does not lead to recovery, and the lack of substance use programs in prisons results in a significant treatment gap. Table 1.3 depicts the percentage of women in state and federal prisons who received particular substance abuse treatments or addiction-related services according to the Center on Addiction and Substance Abuse (2010). It is important to note that women may have received multiple types of treatment or services.

Given that 49.5 percent of women in federal prisons and 67.6 percent of women in state prisons met criteria for substance abuse or substance dependence, the limited number of professional and peer-support services available to sisters inside is egregious (CASA, 2010). Some studies report that as many

Table 1.3 Women Who Received Treatments and Addiction-Related Services

Type of Treatment or Addiction-Related Services	Women in Federal Prisons (%)	Women in State Prisons (%)
Detoxification	0.6	2.1
Any professional treatment	23.7	21.2
Residential facility or unit	16.2	14.6
Counseling by a professional	10.3	9.1
Maintenance drug	0.8	0.8
Other addiction-related services since admission	47.5	38.7
Mutual support/peer counseling	33.7	33.0
Education program	29.4	18.4

Source: Adapted from Center on Addiction and Substance Abuse (2010).

as 80 percent of prison inmates have substance-related problems, with only about 13 percent receiving treatment while incarcerated (Blanchard, 1999; Sheridan, 1996; Staton, Leukefeld, & Webster, 2003). Sisters inside present with greater need for drug treatment in large part due to their co-occurring social and mental health problems, and are more likely than men to participate in and receive help from prison-based treatment programs (Belenko & Houser, 2012; CASA, 2010).

Types of Treatment Offered

As stated above, the majority of substance use treatment offered in prisons consists of drug education (Chandler, Fletcher, & Volkow, 2009). However, beginning in the 1990s, an increasing number of male and female inmates were afforded the opportunity for more intensive treatment through the therapeutic community (TC) model, the most common treatment program utilized throughout prisons in the United States (Taxman, Perdoni, & Harrison, 2007). TC programs vary widely across prisons, but they often involve segregation from the general population. Within the TC model, the individual, not the drug, is considered the problem; therefore care for the whole person is required and entails changing the thoughts, emotions, and behaviors that lead to drug use (Inciardi, Martin, & Surratt, 2001). Unfortunately, TC and many of the substance use treatment programs utilized with sisters inside was developed for men, and many treatment programs use "attack therapy" methods (Pollock, 2002, p. 103). Beginning in the 1990s, researchers began calling for the use of substance use treatment programs that recognize the unique experiences of sisters inside, especially given the prevalence of victimization, abuse, and mental illness that so often accompany substance use disorders among women in prison (Center for Substance Abuse Treatment, 2005; CASA, 2010; Saxena et al., 2014).

Modifying the therapeutic community (TC) model is perhaps the most common method of implementing gender-responsive substance use treatment for sisters inside. In doing so, treatment for substance use disorders is tailored to address the mosaic of factors related to women's substance abuse, such as co-occurring disorders and histories of psychological, physical, and sexual abuse. Gender-responsive treatment consists of services that

> (a) address women's treatment needs; (b) reduce barriers to recovery from drug dependence that are more likely to occur for women; (c) are delivered in a context that is compatible with women's styles and orientations and is safe from exploitation; and (d) take into account women's roles, socialization and relative status within the larger culture. (Reed, 1987, p. 151)

Gender-responsive substance abuse treatment entails integrated mental health and substance abuse treatment (Covington & Bloom, 2006). In these programs women's strengths and assets are utilized in a manner that fosters empowerment and self-reliance within the confines of a supportive, therapeutic community that acknowledges and leverages the unique relational natures of women.

Recognizing the prevalence of substance use disorders among sisters inside, and the inadequacy of prison-based treatment programs, is imperative as returning sisters are at an increased risk for getting trapped "in what has come to be known as 'the revolving door of justice'" (Moon, Thompson, & Bennett, 1994, p. 49). For example, in a longitudinal study of 506 women released from a state prison, one-third of the women who recidivated, meaning they were released and then returned to prison, were dependent upon drugs following release (Huebner, DeJong, & Cobbina, 2010). Women often return to the same people, places, and things that triggered their drug use prior to prison while simultaneously facing the significant stressors associated with reentry. This issue will be addressed more fully in chapter 2, but it is important to note here that substance abuse treatment is more effective if it transcends the walls of the prison and includes a community-based treatment component.

Although there is no silver bullet for treating substance use disorders among sisters inside, it is clear that given the prevalence of victimization and co-occurring disorders (COD) among women in prison, gender-responsive treatment is essential. "Economic analyses highlight the cost-effectiveness of treating drug-involved offenders. On average, incarceration in the United States costs approximately $22,000 per month, and there is little evidence that this strategy reduces drug use or drug-related re-incarceration rates for nonviolent drug offenders" (Chandler, Fletcher, & Volkow, 2009, p. 185). Substance use treatment is far more cost-effective than incarceration and is an important step in the abolition of the prison industrial complex.

Mental Illness

Latrise, a fifty-year-old African American woman, also participated in the study grounding this book. Latrise was first diagnosed with mental illness at age ten. She began having fainting spells, which she attributed to being sexually molested by her sister's baby's father. Latrise shared,

> I guess around the sixth or seventh trip to the emergency room [as a result of the fainting spells], I think, welfare got involved. Child Protective Services. And my mom had to take me to a psychiatrist. But I wasn't allowed to tell the psychiatrist anything about our house.

Latrise did not know what her diagnosis was at age ten, but she remained on psychotropic medication until she was twenty-four at which time she was introduced to heroin. "So the psych meds went, the heroin came, and every now and then when I would get clean, I would go on medication but they would diagnose me and the medicine would be either too strong or not strong enough." Latrise referred to her current condition as "anxiety," and at the time of the interview she was sober and under the care of a psychiatrist.

In addition to battling substance use disorders, the majority of women in prison are plagued by mental illness. The prevalence of mental illness is higher among female inmates than among male, with 73.1 percent of women in state prisons and 61.2 percent of women in federal prisons presenting with mental health problems (James & Glaze, 2006). These statistics are especially striking when compared to the 12 percent of women in society generally who have symptoms of a mental health disorder (Bloom & Covington, 2008). Moreover, according to the Center on Addiction and Substance Abuse (2010), 40.5 percent of sisters inside have both mental health and substance use disorders, and only 19.7 percent of sisters inside have neither a mental health nor substance use disorder.

Much like substance abuse treatment, mental health treatment in the women's prisons is regrettably scarce. Although the exact number of women in prisons receiving mental health treatment is unknown, when combined with men, James and Glaze (2006) reported that only one in three state prisoners received mental health treatment following admission to prison. Moreover, between 1997 and 2004, the percentage of inmates receiving prescription medication for a mental health problem grew, but the provision of mental health therapy remained largely the same (James & Glaze, 2006). "The use of psychotropic drugs is 10 times higher in women's than in men's prisons" (Bloom, Owen, & Covington, 2003, p. 46). Given the prevalence of severe psychiatric disorders among sisters inside, the use of psychotropic medication may not be unwarranted. However, there is no doubt that the efficacy of medication is increased when combined with gender-responsive therapeutic programs.

Poverty/Economic Marginalization

As early as 1900, scholars began to recognize the economically impoverished backgrounds of many sisters inside (Pollock, 2014). Yet as criminologists examined the distinctiveness of male and female pathways to prison, male pathways were thought to entail more structural, macro-level factors and female pathways were thought to entail more micro-level factors, such as biological and psychological conditions (Steffensmeier & Haynie, 2000). Men's crimes were viewed as circumstantial versus women's were pathological. Today, aggregate-level research on the relationship between structural factors and crime evidences that macro-level economic factors, such as poverty, income inequality, joblessness, and being part of a female-headed household, influence both men's and women's pathways to prison (Steffensmeier & Haynie, 2000).

Proponents of the economic marginalization theory posit several factors that worsened women's economic well-being and contributed to the feminization of poverty. For example, along with "women's liberation," the 1970s resulted in the advent of no-fault divorce, an increase in the number of female-headed households, and increased unemployment within those female-headed households (Heimer, 2000; Pollock, 2014). With sex-segregated labor markets, a lack of living wages for workers in the service industries, and women working part-time, low-wage jobs and earning less on average than men, women experience gross economic marginalization vis-à-vis men. As a result, women are driven toward property crimes, such as fraud, larceny, and embezzlement, in order to subsist (Heimer, 2000; Pollock, 2014). "Growing economic adversity increases the pressures to commit consumer-based crimes such as shoplifting, check fraud, theft of services, and welfare fraud, as well as sex hustling and low-level drug dealing" (Cullen, Wilcox, Lux, & Jonson, 2015, p. 250). Not only does poverty contribute to criminal acts, but in the 1970s and 1980s, being poor became viewed as a crime in itself.

At a campaign rally in 1976, Ronald Reagan criticized the welfare state through his portrayal of the "welfare queen"—a woman who collected food stamps, Social Security, and veterans' benefits while driving a Cadillac. Women, with and without children, in need of social assistance were classified as the undeserving poor due to their supposed social and criminal transgressions. "By constructing women in this way, we hold them personally responsible for all of their problems and ignore the role of the government, corporations, or even our role as everyday citizens in perpetuating a cycle that allows low literate, women of color, and living in poverty to cycle in-and-out of our criminal justice system" (Alfred & Chlup, 2009, p. 246).

The feminization of poverty was made all the more apparent by the Personal Responsibility and Work Opportunity Reconciliation Act (PRWORA) of 1996 which "changed the culture of welfare from a system of governmental support to one of personal responsibility and self-sufficiency" (Alfred & Chlup, 2009, p. 244). Through social policies such as this, those in power, particularly White capitalists, perpetuate the myth of self-sufficiency in order to trap women, particularly women of color, in striving toward such mythic self-sufficiency by working low-wage jobs that both directly and indirectly benefit the White elite. Moreover, it is these same White elites who benefit from "tough-on-crime policies that send a non-violent female offender to prison for economic crimes" in a manner that perpetuates the prison industrial complex and keeps for-profit prisons filled beyond capacity (Alfred & Chlup, 2009, p. 242).

Today, over forty years following the introduction of the welfare queen, poverty continues to be criminalized in myriad ways, rendering the feminization of poverty yet another structural injustice plaguing female inmates and returning citizens. For example, some women find themselves caught in the revolving door of incarceration not because they repeatedly commit crimes, but because they cannot pay the fines they were assessed on a crime committed long ago. This manner of criminalizing poverty was brought to light in 2016 when the U.S. Department of Justice investigated the city of Ferguson, Missouri, following the police shooting of Michael Brown, due to the city's jailing of individuals for failure to pay fines for parking tickets or other low-level fines (Perez, 2016). The practices were found to be racially biased and resulted in a debtors' prison from which women and men alike could not afford to escape. Kristof (2016) reported on this phenomenon in the *New York Times* wherein he recounted his visit to a Tulsa county jail where he met, on a single day, twenty-three individuals incarcerated for "failure to pay government fines and fees" (para. 3). He interviewed numerous women, including Rosalind Hall, a fifty-three-year-old woman who had already spent ten days in jail for failing to pay a $1,200 fine for five bad checks she wrote to a grocery store, which totaled just $100. Hall was afflicted by depression and bipolar disorder and, although she earned $50 a month cleaning someone's house, she struggled to pay her $40 a month restitution fee. Hall is not alone. Many returning sisters are ordered to pay restitution in order to assist any victims in recovering from the financial loss caused by the crimes committed. Not only can such fees negate one's ability to provide basic needs like food and shelter, but they may also be greater than one's monthly income.

Given the connection between poverty and crime, it is not surprising that prior to their incarceration sisters inside earned substantially less than their non-incarcerated peers. This was true of Blacks, Whites, and Hispanics. According to Rabuy and Kopf (2015), incarcerated women between the ages of twenty-four and seventy-two earned a median annual income of $13,890 prior to their incarceration as compared to the $23,745 earned by their

non-incarcerated peers. The wage gap between incarcerated and non-incarcerated women was consistent for women of all racial/ethnic backgrounds
(Rabuy & Kopf, 2015). The feminization of poverty, the myth of self-sufficiency, and the wage inequity plaguing women in the United States are all
structurally linked to women's entrapment in the prison industrial complex.

Motherhood

Well over half of all sisters inside are mothers to minor children, making the
impact of the prison industrial complex on children and families abhorrent.
In 2007, an estimated 1.7 million minor children in America had a parent in
prison (Glaze & Maruschak, 2008). Children of color are disproportionately
impacted, as "one in 15 black children and 1 in 42 Latino children has a parent in prison, compared to 1 in 111 white children" (The Sentencing Project,
2009, p. 2). Equally deleterious is the fact that 22 percent of "the children
of state inmates and 16% of the children of federal inmates were age 4 or
younger" (Glaze & Maruschak, 2008, p. 3). And one-third of minor children
with a parent in prison will turn eighteen prior to their parents' release (Glaze
& Maruschak, 2008). The number of minor children with incarcerated parents
is simply unjust.

So too is the number of incarcerated mothers. According to a report published in 2008 by the Bureau of Justice Statistics, "Since 1991, the number
of children with a mother in prison has more than doubled, up 131%" (Glaze
& Maruschak, 2008, p. 2). Nearly 62 percent of sisters in state prisons and
nearly 56 percent of sisters in federal prisons are mothers to minor children,
the largest percentage of whom are between the ages of twenty-five and
thirty-four (Glaze & Maruschak, 2008). Although men in prison are parents
to a larger number of minor children (1,559,200) than women (147,400),
children of incarcerated parents are more likely to be living with their mother
than their father at the time of the parent's incarceration (Glaze & Maruschak,
2008). Over 64 percent of mothers in state prisons lived with their minor
children in the month before their arrest or just prior to their incarceration,
and more than four in ten of these mothers were the heads of single-parent
households (Glaze & Maruschak, 2008).

The alarming number of mothers behind bars begs the question, who is
responsible for raising these minor children? According to Glaze and Mar-
uschuk (2008), 37 percent of the children of incarcerated mothers reside with
their other parent, 44.9 percent with a grandparent, 22.8 percent with another
relative, 10.9 percent in foster homes or agencies, and 7.8 percent with
friends or others. Due to the Adoption and Safe Families Act (ASFA), many
sisters inside face losing all parental rights. Although the goal of the law was
to prevent children from remaining in foster care indefinitely, the ASFA is

federally mandated and requires that a petition for the termination of parental rights be filed if a child has been in out-of-home care (foster care) for fifteen of the last twenty-two months. Depending upon the number of years a woman is sentenced to or serves, and who is caring for her children, she faces the very serious possibility of losing all custody and rights. There are ways around the ASFA ruling, for example, if a child is under the care of a relative (Walsh, 2016) or if a caseworker determines that the relationship with the mother is essential to the child's well-being (Women in Prison Project, 2006). Some states, such as New York and Washington, have even passed bills to make the ASFA more accommodating to mothers behind bars. Yet upon incarceration many mothers must mentally prepare themselves for the possibility that their parental rights may be terminated forever (Walsh, 2016).

In light of the very real threat of losing relationship with their children, how do mothers behind bars continue to parent or be in relationship with their minor children? Foremost, "Women's need to maintain bonds with children during confinement and after incarceration can result in considerable stress, anxiety, and negative adjustment" (Arditti & Few, 2006, p. 104). Beyond the emotional factors, which are examined further below, logistical concerns often exacerbate these stresses. Given the prevalence of children who are cared for by extended family, one might assume that incarcerated mothers are in regular contact with their minor children. However, due to strained familial relationships, geographic distance, lack of transportation, and other factors, in 2000, 54 percent of mothers in state prisons had not seen their minor children since their admission (Mumola, 2000). The majority of parents in state and federal prisons are incarcerated more than 100 miles from their previous residence (Mumola, 2000), a physical distance that mirrors the emotional chasm that can grow between incarcerated mothers and their children of all ages. Sisters inside are typically housed far from home even when sentenced to a state prison in the state where their children reside. In a study of 158 mothers of minor children incarcerated in a maximum security prison in a Northeastern state, Casey-Acevedo and Bakken (2002) found that 61 percent of mothers did not receive any visits from their 285 minor children. The demands of travel, including the expense, are often arduous or insurmountable for both the minor children of sisters inside and their caregivers (Women in Prison Project, 2006).

Moreover, with so many mothers of minor children under the age of four, letters, phone calls, and visits are made all the more difficult simply based upon the child's developmental age. Visitation rules and practices differ among prisons, but very few prisons are equipped to conduct video visitation and some prisons or prisoners are only allowed "non-contact visits" where there is glass separating the inmate from the visitor. As toys are not permitted in the visiting rooms of some prisons (i.e., in the state of New Hampshire), regardless of the distance between the child's home and prison, a sixty-minute visit with no recreation, except making conversation while seated in a chair, is unnatural and boring for most children under four.

According to Kazura (2001), distress regarding the impact of their incarceration on their children's social and emotional development is of significant concern for sisters inside. Many women feel "enormous grief" at being separated from their children and as a result many struggle to cope (Boudin, 1998). "Women who most effectively mothered from prison were those whose children's guardians included them to the largest extent possible in the children's lives and facilitated communication between the mother and child" (Celinska & Siegel, 2010, p. 462). Motherhood behind bars can be both a source of stress and resilience as it often requires arranging for and managing the care of children from behind bars, negotiating one's role as a mother, proving one's fitness to mother, and balancing one's "identity and work as mother, criminal, and possibly substance abuser" (Enos, 2001, p. 35). Yet the way motherhood functions as an identity and a role can facilitate female inmates' resilience. It can also greatly impact women's reentry experiences, a fact that will be addressed in chapter 2.

The backgrounds and demographics of sisters inside, and therefore returning sisters, necessitate services and interventions that are responsive to the ways their intersecting social locations, and the structural injustices that plague them, impact their reentry experiences. Project Sister Connect recognizes that the needs of returning sisters, and the unique challenges they face upon returning to their families and communities, are markedly distinct from their male counterparts' (Galbraith, 2004). Gender-responsive support during reentry requires the provision of wraparound or holistic services, implemented along a continuum of care, by culturally competent providers (Berman, 2005; Covington & Bloom, 2006; Holtfreter & Morash, 2003; Morash, 2010). Returning sisters often need treatment for substance use disorders, co-occurring mental illnesses, and the trauma that can result from victimization and abuse. In addition, returning sisters often benefit from assistance navigating their relationships with partners, extended family, their minor and adult children, and those who cared for their minor children during their incarceration. Project Sister Connect recognizes how female returning citizens' backgrounds, and their intersecting social locations, render them oppressed by the numerous barriers they face upon exiting the prison gate. Returning sisters far too often experience the deleterious effects of racism, classism, sexism, ableism, ageism, and more. Therefore, Project Sister Connect, as evidenced in chapter 4, is grounded in a gender-responsive, justice-seeking approach to spiritual support that engages the Two Feet of Love in Action through both charitable support and the eradication of structural injustices that contribute to the prison industrial complex.

THE PATHWAYS TO CRIME

After examining the backgrounds of sisters inside—their racial/ethnic backgrounds, their histories of abuse and victimization, the prevalence of substance use disorders and mental illness, their experiences of poverty and economic marginalization, and their role as mother—it is evident that women's intersectionality, and the way their intersecting social locations and experiences ensnare them in a web of structural injustices, contribute directly to their pathways to crime. As Richie (1996) argued, experiences of oppression and abuse both directly and indirectly compel women to crime. However, as previously stated, "social and cultural theories [for imprisonment] have been applied to men, while individual and pathological explanations have been applied to women" (Bloom, Owen, & Covington, 2003, p. 51). Early examinations of female criminality were perhaps even more discriminatory, attributing women's criminal behaviors to their stunted evolutionary state (Bloom, Owen, & Covington, 2003).

For more than 100 years, criminologists attempted to explain why people engage in criminal behaviors. Explanations were offered by the Classical School in the 1700s, Positivism in the 1800s, and the Chicago School in the early 1900s, but each of these perspectives took an androcentric approach, assuming that what is normal for men is normal for all people (Pollock, 2014). This book, however, is grounded in the pathways perspective that emerged in the late 1980s and early 1990s (Daly, 1992; Gilfus, 1993) as the result of feminist criminal studies. Life-course and pathways theories drew extensively upon longitudinal and qualitative research, and the narrative experiences of women behind bars, in order to construct a holistic understanding of the interrelated and integrated factors and patterns related to women's incarceration rather than focusing on single causes in absence of the larger context (Brennan, Breitenbach, Dieterich, Salisbury, & Van Voorhis, 2012).

Understanding women's pathways to crime necessitates recognizing both macro- (structural and super-structural) and micro-level explanations for criminal behavior. Macro theories of crime identify large-scale, systemic influences that contribute to the surge in mass incarceration in the United States. In the Introduction, three macro theories of crime were identified including the War on Drugs, changes in mandatory sentencing laws, and a culture of "us" versus "them." Micro theories of crime identify how and why individuals engage in law-abiding versus law-violating behaviors and are found within sociology, criminology, and developmental psychology literature. Many feminist scholars examined macro and micro theories of crime, in concert, and drew upon the lived experiences of women behind bars, to posit distinctive pathways to crime. For example, according to Daly (1992), one pathway to prison is paved by childhood victimization and mental ill-ness/substance abuse; according to Richie (2001), another pathway to prison is paved by extreme marginalization, including homelessness, poverty, and other injustices that result from the intersecting oppressions of race, class, and gender; and according to Covington (1998), a third pathway is paved by relational dysfunction, such as that which can result from interpersonal violence during adulthood and concomitant mental illness and substance abuse. As one of the early theorists to adopt a pathways perspective, Daly (1992) constructed a taxonomy of five prototypical pathways to prison. Table 1.4 depicts Daly's taxonomy of pathways to prison.

Brennan et al. (2012) analyzed scholarship from numerous disciplines that utilized distinct methods and identified significant consensus regarding women's common pathways to prison. In addition, they administered two quantitative measures, the Women's Risk/Needs Assessment (WRNA; Van Voorhis, Wright, Salisbury, & Bauman, 2010) and the COMPAS Reentry Assessment (Brennan & Dieterich, 2007), to 718 soon-to-be-released women at two California women's prisons. Based on their theoretical and empirical research, the authors then constructed a taxonomy of women's pathways to crime. They identified four superordinate pathways to prison that were then further differentiated into eight subordinate pathways, which typified the experiences of all but 16 of the study's 718 participants. Table 1.5 depicts the taxonomy of pathways constructed by Brennan et al.

The taxonomies developed by Daly (1992) and Brennan et al. (2012) evidence how addiction, mental illness, abuse, and other micro- and macro-level

Table 1.4   Daly's Taxonomy of Pathways to Prison

Pathway	Description
Street women	Women who enter street life in order to escape a life of violence and victimization.
Drug-connected women	Women who use drugs, associate with drug-connected friends and intimates, and often end up trafficking drugs.
Harmed-and-harming women	Women who display hostility that resulted from the abuse and neglect they experienced in childhood.
Battered women	Women who engaged in criminal behavior as a direct result of or in retaliation against abusive partners.
Other women	Women who engaged in property and/or economic crimes motivated by greed and economic gain.

Source: Adapted from Daly (1992).

Table 1.5   Brennan et al.'s Taxonomy of Pathways to Prison

Pathway	Prevalence (%)
"Normal functioning" drug-offending women, single parents	20.0
"Normal functioning" drug-offending women, not parenting	14.7
"Battered woman" pathway with depression/stress	12.3
"Battered woman" pathway with higher crime/social influences	11.3
Extremely socially marginalized women with drug trafficking offenses, dependent on or criminally influenced by significant other	16.6
Extremely socially marginalized women with drug trafficking offenses, less dependence on or criminal influence by significant other	11.9
Aggressive, anti-social, nonpsychotic women	9.3
Aggressive, anti-social, psychotic women with history of suicide risk	3.6

Source: Adapted from Brennan et al. (2012).

oppressions directly impact women's pathways to prison. Moreover, they demonstrate the inadequacy of individual and pathological explanations for women's criminality and incarceration.

THE CRIMES COMMITTED BY GENDER

As stated elsewhere, not only do women's pathways to prison differ from men's, but the crimes they commit differ as well. Although the gender gap is shrinking as fewer men and more women are arrested for crimes, the majority of women's offenses fall into only a few categories (Pollock, 2014). Table 1.6 depicts the type and prevalence of offenses committed by women and men in 2015.

As evidenced above, women are more likely than men to be incarcerated for drug-related crimes (Guerino, Harrison, & Sabol, 2011). The Anti-Drug Abuse Act of 1986 that vowed to "get tough on crime" resulted in mandatory

Table 1.6   Offense Type by Gender in 2015

	Men (%)	Women (%)
Violent	54.3	35.8
Property	18.3	27.8
Drug	14.9	25.1
Public order	11.7	10.2
Other	0.8	1.1

Source: Adapted from Carson & Anderson (2016).

sentencing laws requiring that anyone caught in possession of a drug be sentenced. As previously evidenced, the population of women behind bars would not be what it is today if in the 1980s law enforcement had not begun to systematically target drug users and if mandatory sentencing laws had not been enacted (Mauer, 2013).

In addition to drug-related crimes, women are also disproportionately incarcerated for property crimes. Property crimes consist of embezzlement, larceny/theft, fraud, burglary, and forgery/counterfeiting. In 1935, women constituted just 5 percent of all arrests for property crime; by 2010, this figure was 37 percent (Pollock, 2014). For example, in 2012, 7,790 women were arrested on embezzlement charges, 551,074 were arrested for larceny/theft, 62,153 were arrested for fraud, 46,100 women were arrested for burglary, and 24,924 were arrested for forgery/counterfeiting (Snyder & Mulako-Wangota, n.d.). "Much of the rise in female criminality is the result of minor property crimes, which reflects the economic vulnerability that women experience in society" (Mallicoat, 2012, p. 463).

As evidenced above, women are less likely than men to be convicted for violent crimes (Guerino, Harrison, & Sabol, 2011). Violent crimes consist of homicide, robbery, arson, aggravated assault, simple assault, rape, and other sex crimes in which force is used. The majority of violent crimes committed by women are "against family members and in a context of self defense" (Gilfus, 1992, p. 64). Although there is no doubt that women do commit acts of violent assault, and many women who are beaten and abused fight back, as evidenced in the story shared by Treva above, the Bureau of Justice Statistics reported that "women are the victims of intimate partner violence in four out of every five cases" (as cited in Pollock, 2014, p. 10). Moreover, women often become caught in a cycle of violence as childhood victimization is highly correlated to victimization and violence in adulthood. For example, a study conducted by the New York Division of Criminal Justice Services reported that 93 percent of women convicted for murdering a sexual partner, whether a boyfriend, girlfriend, or spouse, were survivors of past physical or sexual abuse (as cited in Women in Prison Project, 2006, p. 6).

As is now evident, women's pathways to prison, and the crimes they commit, differ from men's and are the result of both macro (structural and superstructural) and micro-level injustices. Although there is no stereotypical sister inside, women behind bars share a number of commonalities including experiences of victimization, substance abuse, mental illness, and motherhood that are central to Project Sister Connect, the call for revised prison ministry praxis. Once behind bars, sisters inside are introduced to prison culture wherein opportunities for healing and rehabilitation are both implicitly and explicitly influenced by religion and spirituality.

FAITH BEHIND BARS: THE ROLE OF RELIGION
AND SPIRITUALITY IN PRISON

Since the advent of corrections in the United States, religion has occupied a central position in both prisons and jails. Yet within the disciplines of criminology, sociology, psychology, and theology, there is a dearth of research examining the role of spirituality and religion in prisons and in inmates' lives, which "is particularly odd in light of the historical relationship between religion and corrections" (Meade, 2014, pp. 1–2). As will be evidenced below, both the ideology and practices of the early U.S. penal system were heavily influenced by colonial theological culture. Understanding the spiritual and religious experiences of returning sisters necessitates a basic introduction to the role of religion in prison culture; therefore, this section draws upon a narrow body of literature, written primarily within criminology, to introduce the reader to the historical and contemporary relationships between religion and the penal system, inmates' right to religious freedom, and the religious cultural context in U.S. prisons.[1] In addition, Appendix C depicts the diversity of religious programs found in men's and women's prisons, and Appendix D provides a brief overview of the literature examining if and why, from an empirical perspective, religion "works" as a means of rehabilitating inmates.

The Role of Religion in the Penal System

The word "penitentiary" is derived from the term "penance," meaning "an act of self-abasement, mortification, or devotion performed to show sorrow or repentance for sin" (Merriam-Webster, n.d., para. 1). Historically, Puritan settlers thought crime was a sin that resulted from demonic forces. "The Puritan settlers in the Massachusetts Bay area in the 1600s were Calvinists who placed great emphasis on the concept of obedience to law for it was the external law that helped keep 'sinful' human beings in right relationship with God" (O'Connor, 2002, p. 2). Although corporal punishment was common practice in Europe, early American colonizers considered prisons to be a more "humane" and "Christian" alternative (Sullivan, 2009). The correctional system was meant to morally discipline and rehabilitate individuals who had been convicted for sinful actions. The Pennsylvania Quakers, for example, thought that the divine dwelled within all individuals. They believed that incarceration could pave the path to spiritual conversion, and thus they initiated the earliest prisons in the United States in order to focus on the rehabilitation of criminals as opposed to their physical punishment (Meade, 2014). The hope of both the Calvinists and the Quakers alike was that religion would assist criminals in recognizing their moral failings, turning to God, and desisting from further crime.

In the 20th century, baring the influence of the Enlightenment, social scientific wisdom superseded religious wisdom in its influence upon correctional institutions. Reason and science were thought to provide better guidance for rehabilitating deviant individuals than spiritual conversion. Nevertheless, religion continues to significantly influence prison culture and operations. For example, in 2001, President George W. Bush initiated the Office for Faith-Based and Community Initiatives which endowed faith-based prison and reentry programs with access to federal funding, thus enabling more faith-based organizations to serve both inmates and returning citizens. This act also allowed federal funds to be used in the service of traditionally marginalized and minority religious groups in prisons, including Muslims, Buddhists, and individuals practicing Native American spiritualities (O'Connor, 2002). Today, "nearly every prison has a full-time, paid chaplain who provides spiritual guidance and other religious services to inmates" (Meade, 2014, p. 3). Prisons without paid chaplains may still be served by organizations such as Good News Jail and Prison Ministry, a 501(c) (3) dedicated to building the church of Jesus Christ, that places Christian chaplains in jails and prisons and serves "300,000 incarcerated men, women and youth daily in 22 states and 25 countries worldwide" (Good News Jail & Prison Ministry, 2015, para. 2). Moreover, individuals representing churches and other religious institutions comprise a vast number of the volunteers in prisons.

According to Hallett and Johnson (2014), the United States is now entering an era in which conservatives and liberals alike are in agreement about the importance of faith-based programming in prisons. The prison industrial complex has left those on the political left and right frustrated with the criminal justice system for different reasons. "While the left's concern about mass incarceration has been focused on the racially disproportionate impact of drug sentences and deleterious effects of long prison sentences, prison reformers on the right stress concerns about cost and return on investment" (Hallett & Johnson, 2014, p. 666). Liberals are dismayed by the effects of mandatory sentencing and related injustices and conservatives are distraught by the fact that, due in large part to recidivism, justice spending is leading to higher taxes and big government. As a result, policies and spending that have failed to rehabilitate those it intended to serve frustrate individuals of various political perspectives. Therefore, the role of religion and faith-based programming in prisons is changing with bipartisan support. Hallett and Johnson argued that conservatives are supporting this shift in the American penal system because it is largely funded by congregations and staffed by volunteers, and it decreases the financial burden on taxpayers and lessens government expense and involvement. The movement is receiving the support of liberals because it emphasizes rehabilitative programming that aims to build community and decrease recidivism (Hallett & Johnson, 2014). Bipartisan support is therefore seemingly driven more by economic motivations rather than religious sentiments or convictions.

As previously stated, U.S. prisons were established centuries ago with the goal of facilitating the spiritual conversion and rehabilitation of inmates; yet, according to Erzen (2017), "the purpose of a prison has always been control" (p. 11). Religious programming was and is employed in the service of regulating inmates. Erzen (2017) outlined the danger of the government's overreliance on faith-based programs. She argued that while "'faith,' at first glance, appears to be an innocuous or neutral term," in the context of prisons, more often than not it refers to a narrow tradition of nondenominational Protestant Christianity (p. 4). Therefore, inmates are held as a captive audience that prison officials willingly subject to the proselytization efforts of Christian evangelists. This is especially true, Erzen argued, because these faith-based services represent some of the only efforts at rehabilitation in today's prison context and "perform an essential service in maintaining control and authority" (pp. 11–12). Moreover, in many prison cultures, a judgmental, punitive God image is posited as the ultimate warden who requires compliance and obedience. Therefore, although bipartisan political support of faith-based programming is ideal, the government must not depend solely on faith-based organizations for the provision of rehabilitation services both behind and beyond bars as doing so unjustly inflicts a narrow religious perspective on inmates and returning citizens of all or no faith traditions. Therefore, the perils of the prison industrial complex can only be addressed through collaborative partnership between government and faith-based organizations, a fact that will be addressed in greater depth in chapter 4.

As evidenced above, a narrow religious ideology permeates the U.S. penal system even though the U.S. government refrained from instituting a state religion in 1791. Disestablishment, or the separation of church and state, is a core national value making religious freedom a right for all individuals, incarcerated or otherwise. In 1993, Congress passed the Religious Freedom Restoration Act (RFRA) that prevented the government from burdening or infringing upon any individual's religious beliefs and exercises, if sincere, unless there was a compelling state interest. This guaranteed religious freedom to inmates and "required the government to demonstrate a compelling interest before placing restrictions on the practice of religion by prisoners" (Meade, 2014, p. 69). RFRA remains operant in federal prisons, but in 1997 the Supreme Court struck down its application within state prisons. Therefore, by 2000, Congress again sought to grant inmates religious freedom. At that time, President Clinton signed into law the Religious Land Use and Institutionalized Person Act (RLUIPA). Section 42 U.S.C. §2000cc of the RLUIPA protects the religious exercise of institutionalized persons because, as Senator Ted Kennedy stated, "sincere faith and worship can be an indispensable part of rehabilitation" (as cited in Percival, 2016, p. 103). Despite the separation of church and state, men's and women's prisons alike possess a distinctive religious culture. As Sullivan (2009) stated, "Even when explicitly religious language is absent, the sacred haunts the prison and all who work there" (p. 6).

The implicit and explicit religious ideologies operant behind bars, the preponderance of faith-based programs and Christian volunteers, and the need to protect inmates' religious freedom reveal another structural injustice ensnaring inmates as the result of the prison industrial complex. Well-meaning people of faith, predominantly Christians, are supporting inmates by delivering the majority of the rehabilitative programs in American prisons today, faith-based and otherwise. As evidenced above, many sisters inside need prison to be a place of healing and rehabilitation, and it is encouraging that Christian volunteers and leaders feel called to meet such needs. Unfortunately, the government's reliance on volunteers for the provision of such services can threaten inmates' religious freedom and the separation of church and state if the programs themselves, and/or the leaders of such programs, represent a narrow religious perspective. Simply stated, if inmates desire spiritual, educational, therapeutic, or other rehabilitative programs, the receipt of such services is likely dependent upon inmates' willingness to accept or ignore the religious ideology therein. This is disconcerting given that it is not uncommon for faith-based volunteers to view religious conversion as the key to rehabilitation (Johnson, 2011). Moreover, while spirituality and religion can, as Senator Kennedy argued, be "indispensable" to inmates' rehabilitation (as cited in Percival, 2016, p. 103), this does not mean that all rehabilitative programs need be spiritually integrated or facilitated by religiously motivated volunteers.

THE MEANING AND CULTURE
OF RELIGION IN PRISON

Although there is no monolithic prison culture, prison cultures, and life on the inside, are markedly different from life outside. As previously stated, understanding returning sisters' spiritual and religious experiences necessitates understanding how religion functions inside. Religious culture in women's prisons operates on two levels: the individual level, the way in which each sister inside experiences religion, and the systemic level, the way in which religion is experienced as a group phenomenon (Clear et al., 2000). For example, although Allport's (1950) classic theory of intrinsic and extrinsic religion was highly contested on theoretical and methodological grounds (Kirkpatrick & Hood, 1990), scholars drew upon it to explore inmates' motivations for religious participation. Some sisters inside are sincerely motivated to be religious or to participate in religious programming by intrinsic factors, for example when their religious faith orients their life's direction. Some sisters inside are motivated to be religious or to participate in religious programming by extrinsic factors, for example access to special foods and treats or the opportunity to leave the cell.

Clear et al. (2000) conducted an ethnographic study examining how male inmates' intrinsic and extrinsic religious motivation shapes the religious culture and the meaning of religion in prisons. The study entailed qualitative interviews with seventy male inmates, yet the findings offer some insight into the experiences of sisters inside. First, some inmates develop intrinsic religious motivation because they are confronted with the reality that their choices and behaviors caused their imprisonment. They may view their lack of faith as the cause of their problems and the development of faith as a solution (Clear et al., 2000). Religion presents a set of doctrines and laws that, if followed, can help inmates to amend their transgressive behaviors and make meaning of their time behind bars. According to Clear et al. (2000), this happens in three ways. First, religion, and particularly the evangelical, doctrinal traditions so prevalent in prisons, can help inmates who experience guilt and shame following their imprisonment to heal. Inmates may come to see that their errant, sinful ways of the past are what lured evil into their lives, and that they are, through faith, able to make more holy choices. Christians can seek forgiveness for sins, thus helping to alleviate their guilt and shame.

Second, faith then offers inmates a new life direction (Clear et al., 2000). The doctrines of the Christian faith, and of most faiths, offer a clear way of living that presents an alternative to inmates' previous lifestyles. This belief helps inmates to see how God is active in their lives and to make sense of their imprisonment as something that God orchestrated to help them find a new way of life which, in Christianity, is grounded in following the life and teachings of Jesus. Third, intrinsic religious motivation can help inmates to cultivate greater inner peace. When inmates are denied so many freedoms, religion helps them to cope with such deprivations and losses by offering a sense of peace. The peace is often derived from faith that what truly matters is one's relationship with God (p. 62).

According to Allport's (1950) theory, inmates also experience extrinsic motivations for participating in religious programming. Given the deprivations of prison life, it should come as no surprise that religious programs often capitalize on such deprivations through the provision of treats or privileges (Clear et al., 2000). One extrinsic benefit to participation in religious programming is the furnishing of material comforts such as cookies, doughnuts, extra phone calls, or extra postage stamps. These are minimal by free-world standards, yet can be extremely enticing to male and female inmates alike.

In addition, with minimal visitors, inmates may be motivated to participate in religious programming because of the access it affords to outsiders. Socializing with outsiders can ameliorate the belief that one has been forgotten or left behind by the outside world (Clear et al., 2000). Some inmates desire access to outsiders for manipulative purposes, such as those who convince or coerce volunteers into giving them money or material items, a dynamic that many volunteers are trained to avoid. Yet some religious inmates sincerely desire interaction with outsiders in order to support them in their ongoing transformation or religious conversion.

Finally, participation in religious programming can enable inmates to see friends. Because inmates are often restricted from seeing other inmates on different units, religious programs offer an opportunity to connect. For some, this also means connecting with individuals who are like-minded or who share similar values. This is especially helpful when religious doctrines advocate standards of conduct that depart significantly from the prison norm (Clear et al., 2000). Participating in religious programming can enable inmates to attend chapel services in the evening, meet their friends, and avoid the free time during which trouble often brews.

Extrinsic religious motivations compel nonreligious inmates to participate in religious programming and inmates of particular religious traditions to engage in the rituals and practices of religious traditions other than their own. For example, Lisa, a forty-three-year-old African American returning sister who participated in the study grounding this book, shared how during her incarceration she "practiced Moorish Science, Sunni Muslim, Islam, and I did a little of the Jehovah Witness. But I went to church every Sunday and that was just the regular Baptist, Christian, whatever, one of them services." When asked about the types of religious programs she participated in, Lisa quickly responded that she observed Ramadan in prison. She explained,

> My thing for getting on Ramadan wasn't really for the religion. It was because you get double breakfasts. Early in the morning. And another reason was because my brother was doing it, so I figured somewhere along the line I gotta have some type of self-discipline, and I know I never would have did it out on the street.

Lisa experienced extrinsic religious motivation based upon the "double breakfasts," and she also expressed a desire to have the self-discipline, or intrinsic religious motivation, required for observing Ramadan as a religious discipline. The Religious Land Use and Institutionalized Person Act awards inmates the freedom to participate in religious programming whether their motivation is intrinsic or extrinsic, although the "sincerity" of their religious beliefs can be called into question. In addition, that freedom is restricted by the narrow religious orientation of the majority of programs inside. As previously noted, sisters inside, in some prisons, are held as a captive audience and subjected to proselytization, which they may endure due to extrinsic religious motivation and the rewards, like double breakfasts, that result (Erzen, 2017).

It is important to note that not all spiritually or religiously devout inmates participate in religious programming. I served as a faith-based mentor to a Christian sister inside, and she shared that she would rather pray and read the Bible on her own than participate in church. Although she was interested in singing in the choir, from her perspective the worship service was "ruled by lesbians." Her comment evidenced her homophobia, however many inmates avoid participation in church when they view worship as being ruled by cliques. According to Clear et al. (2000),

> We heard consistent references to the existence of a small number of quietly devout prisoners who stay away from the prison religious programs. This was particularly true in one prison where the religious program was seen as taken over by snitches and sex offenders. (p. 72)

Jailhouse Religion

Jailhouse religion, a desperate attempt to find God behind bars, is a disputable aspect of the religious culture in women's prisons (Johnson, 2011). Skeptics question the veracity and sincerity of inmates' conversions or beliefs because, in part, they seem to occur or emerge when inmates are under duress. Some liken jailhouse religion to the aphorism that there are "no atheists in foxholes." For example, when Charles Colson, the former aide to President Nixon, was imprisoned in 1974 for his role in the Watergate scandal, journalists writing in *Newsweek* and *Time Magazine* questioned the legitimacy of his conversion (Johnson, 2011). They attributed it to a ploy for early release. Maruna, Wilson, and Curran (2006) summarized the views of such critics when they stated,

> Prisoners who "find religion" are thought to be most likely putting on an act to impress parole boards, win plum assignments in the prison (e.g., working with the chaplain), or gain public sympathy. . . . Finding God behind bars seems somehow too convenient to be believable. (p. 162)

Yet in 1976, Colson began doing prison ministry, soon founded the Prison Fellowship Ministries (PFM), and in 1993 received the Templeton Prize for Progress in Religion and donated 100 percent of the $1 million prize to PFM. Whether one deems such conversions to be valid or not, religious conversions are a common occurrence in male and female prisons.

Prison-based Religious Conversions

Given the questioned veracity of inmates' religious conversions, it is no surprise that numerous studies investigate the experience, the outcomes, and the challenges of inmates' religious conversions. Because the majority of prison ministry volunteers are evangelical Christians, volunteers commonly believe that a religious conversion in prison is the key to rehabilitation. According to Johnson (2011),

> In fact, for some faith-based groups or ministries, conversion is not only the first step–it is the only step necessary. In other words, if one accepts Jesus, then one's needs have been met, not only from an eternal, but a temporal perspective. (p. 156)

Churches and faith-based volunteer groups conduct revivals inside men's and women's prisons with the sole intention of saving souls. Many Christians believe that accepting Jesus Christ as Lord and Savior is the radical transformation needed to rehabilitate inmates' lives.

Religious conversions can function as a powerful intervention in the lives of inmates. There is no doubt that more empirical research is needed on this topic, but after interviewing hundreds of inmates in various studies, Johnson (2011) argued that most religious conversions are progressive, occurring over a period of time, rather than dramatic or acute. For this reason, Johnson differentiated religious conversions from spiritual transformations. Religious conversions are the first step in initiating more lasting behavioral and attitudinal changes, that endure over a period of time, which Johnson argued are more aptly called spiritual transformations. In and of themselves, religious conversions are an inadequate means of effecting real and lasting change, according to Johnson. He admitted that this perspective may not be well-received by Christians who identify as born-again and those who feel strongly that salvation, and the lifelong behavioral changes that automatically ensue, result from becoming a new creation in God in a singular moment. Nevertheless, Johnson adamantly argued that conversion can be effective when it "provides a bridge to other faith-motivated individuals and resources that could prove instrumental in having a tipping effect in one person's life" (p. 168).

Johnson's (2011) perspective on religious conversion and spiritual transformation was informed by his six-year study of Prison Fellowship's InnerChange Freedom Initiative (IFI) in which 54 percent of the 125 study participants contended, "I'm not who I used to be" (p. 122). They felt as though they had been given a second chance and new opportunities that were possible only because of God. Second, 69 percent of the study participants felt that participation in the IFI program facilitated spiritual growth, which they viewed as a developmental process. They viewed their life as a journey and a work-in-progress wherein they would continue to strive for greater faith and spiritual maturity. Third, through spiritual transformation participants came to prioritize obedience to and faith in God rather than the prison culture or "inmate code." Fourth, spiritual transformation engendered in participants a positive outlook on life. By viewing events as within God's control, participants were better prepared to receive bad news and to view the future as full of the promise of God. Finally, spiritual transformation compelled participants with a desire to give back. "Now that they have turned their lives around and have a new positive identity, they express an unusual sense of gratitude for this new life and they feel compelled to give back to a society that they have never helped before" (p. 129).

Inmates' Religious Affiliations and Practices

An essential, yet methodologically challenging, question to address is how many sisters inside identify with a particular religious tradition and participate in religious programming. Understanding the religious culture of women's prisons requires statistical, not simply anecdotal, answers to this question. This is problematic for numerous reasons. First, the Federal Bureau of Prisons and the state Departments of Corrections rarely permit outside surveys. Second, much of the data that is available is dated. Third, the studies conducted to-date included methodological flaws. For example, according to Miller, Lindsey, and Kaufman (2014),

> Various studies have indicated that the proportion of inmates who engage in religious activities is 32% (Dammer, 2002), 55% (Bureau of Justice Studies, 1999), or 57% (National Archive of Criminal Justice Data, 2004), depending on the wording [. . .] and timeframe [. . .] of the question. (p. 105)

The deficiencies of the available literature will be ameliorated, in part, by detailing how the nineteen returning sisters whose stories ground this book experienced their faith behind bars. Study participants were asked about their spiritual and religious experiences inside prison as a means of contextualizing their reentry experiences. Therefore, only their spiritual and religious experiences inside will be addressed here in chapter 1, and their spiritual and religious experiences during reentry will be fully detailed in chapter 3.

Inmates' Religious Affiliations

The Bureau of Justice Statistics (BJS) periodically collects demographic information on male and female inmates, such as their age and racial/ethnic background, their history of drug use, and their experiences of physical abuse; unfortunately, BJS does not regularly collect data on inmates' religious

Table 1.7   Religious Affiliations of Male and Female Inmates and the U.S. Population

	Federal Prisons (%)	State Prisons (%)	U.S. Adults, Age Eighteen and Older (%)
Christian	66.2	92.5	78.4
Muslim	9.3	9.0	0.6
Jewish	1.9	4.7	1.7
Native American	3.8	4.1	0.1
Buddhist	1.0	1.78	0.7
Hindu	0.1	0.08	0.4
Pagan	1.4	3.22	0.4
Unitarians			0.3
Afro-Caribbean	2.8	0.92	
Sikh	~0.03	0.1	
Taoist		0.1	
Baha'i	~0.01	0.02	
Other	4.6	0.16	0.5
Atheist or Agnostic	0.1	0.1	4.0
Unaffiliated or unknown	8.8	3.34	12.9

Source: The U.S. Commission on Civil Rights (2008).

beliefs, affiliations, or practices. In 1993, BJS published findings from a survey conducted in 1991 with state prison inmates indicating that 32 percent of inmates participated in "Bible clubs and other religious activities" (Beck et al., 1993, p. 27). This was more than the 20 percent who participated in self-improvement programs and the 17 percent who participated in counseling (Beck et al., 1993). In a nongovernmental study, O'Connor and Duncan (2008) reported that in 2005, in the state of Oregon, 86 percent of sisters inside attended a religious or spiritual service at least once a week. Yet these figures reveal very little about the religious culture of women's prisons.

The U.S. Commission on Civil Rights (2008) solicited data from nine federal prisons and nine state prisons regarding inmates' religious affiliations. Although some data was missing or unusable, Table 1.7 provides an overview of the religious affiliations of male and female inmates in federal and state prisons, in comparison to adults aged eighteen and older in the United States.[2]

The Religious Practices and Experiences of Faith among Sisters Inside

Insights regarding how sisters inside practice their faith can be uncovered by exploring the experiences of the nineteen returning sisters who participated in the study grounding this book. As Danielle opined, "It's prison. It can either break your spirit or build your spirit." The section below presents the following four superordinate themes, the findings derived from the study, regarding participants' experiences of faith behind bars: God's role in their incarceration, the benefits derived from faith behind bars, the corporate and individual faith practices engaged in by participants, and the role of relationship in faith behind bars.

Superordinate theme: God's role in incarceration. Many of the participants felt grateful to God for their incarceration and viewed it as God-ordained. This did not mean, however, that participants all felt positively toward God upon being locked up. Many of the participants felt anger and hatred toward God. According to Shanelle, "I was like mad at God and was like why is He doing this to me?" She questioned why God didn't seem to be helping her out. Desiree had a similar experience. Desiree had been baptized just one month prior to her arrest. She shared, "When I got locked up it was like I hate God . . . I had so much resentment toward Him. Why, if He loved me, why would He put me in this place? And it was just very terrifying." For four months Desiree was so trapped by her anger that she didn't want to hear from God, but her grandmother kept pressing her to stop blaming God and to take responsibility. When she was first locked up, Chelsea, too, was mad at God. But she shared what caused a change in her perspective. She stated,

> I had an issue with God and I was, you know, angry and fighting with God because of it. . . . So I actually lost my faith then. While I was locked up, I was actually locked up with a friend of mine from home, and she more or less drug me into church and beat it back into me, which I'm glad that she did. You know what I mean? But I ended up finding like acceptance with it. I wasn't mad at God any more. I could speak to Him without screaming, you know. I just got more at peace with it.

Chelsea was grateful that her friend "beat [church] back into" her because it was her friend's encouragement that helped her to find peace with God and greater peace with her son's death.

Many participants shared how they felt broken, either prior to or at the time of their incarceration, and explained how they turned to God to ask for help. For Trina, this meant going

> all the way gutter down, before God could reach His hand down . . . for me to be able to reach my hand up and ask for His hand . . . I had to be stripped all the way down to nothing, bare naked, you know. And I think that once I realized that and I could say, "God please. I can't do this no more," He was right there to say, "Come on my path."

Malea had a similar experience. She stated, "One night I was just like, 'Look, Lord, I just can't take this anymore' . . . I cried and I screamed and . . . was like, 'Just do something. I can't keep going down this path.' . . . Every time I got locked up, it was an answered prayer."

Participants' brokenness caused many of them to ask God for help, and even more of them to see their incarceration as God-ordained. Prison was viewed by many participants as God's way of sitting participants down and getting their attention in order to change their lives for the better. Five of the nineteen participants used the phrase "sat me down" or "made me sit" to communicate why God put them in prison. Following the death of her infant son, Chelsea's drug use had her in a very dark place. She said, "I wasn't still. Mentally. Physically. I just wasn't still. And I had lost like all emotion." In order to get her out of that dark place, God put Chelsea in prison. "God just sat me down and just, you know, in His way spoke to me and showed me what really was important in life . . . I needed to sit down and you know just reflect on the past 27 years." Treva also shared how God used prison to sit her down. She said, "Sometimes that is the purpose of you being in jail is to sit down and think about what it is that you've done or what it is that you need to do." Treva went before the parole board after just two months in prison and assumed she would be released, but God had other plans. After being denied parole, she shared how "at first I got mad," but then quickly said to God, "'Well, God, you still want me to sit down for a while. I guess I still needed—still some soul searching I need to do.' I said, 'I'm not gonna be mad. I'm just gonna let you do what you do. I'm trusting your word.'"

Participants shared, however, that the reason God sits you down and locks you up is to change you for the better. God tried to get Shawna's attention by "removing" things from her life. She lost her house. She lost a close friend. But she didn't listen. But when she got locked up, she shared, "I knew that that was the quiet place God took me to get my attention. And I never lost my faith. I knew I had to sit there, but I was okay because I knew I was going to come out and live different." Martha also explained how God locks you up to change you for the better. She saw her incarceration as an "exile," and she said,

> When God puts you alone by yourself and it's just you and Him you're given the chance to talk to Him. And that's what happened to me. . . . When I got arrested, He started shaping me. And on my way out, He started molding me. And then I was just like, as long as He keep me in that mold I'm good to go. And I looked at it like that and He did, He's doing, a marvelous job with me [laughs].

Because many participants viewed their incarceration as God-ordained, it is not surprising that participants also experienced God's protection inside. Rochelle served ten years and never once got into trouble. She attributed this to the fact, "I lean on Him a lot you know for everything. Even before I make decisions, I pray on it. So God has been very good to me." It was Rochelle's "concrete" relationship with God that helped her to manage the prison culture. "I never got into any trouble while I was there and that's very hard to do in that type of situation . . . I'm not going to say it was a miracle, it was God that got me through all that." Danielle also experienced God's protection inside even though she questioned why He didn't protect her from the victimization she experienced prior to her incarceration. She said,

> In the back of my mind I'm saying, "Oh, He ain't protect me out there in them streets and I got raped, or whatever," but I still had faith that nothing is going to happen to me in this prison, nothing that I thought that happens in prisons, and it didn't.

Danielle attributed that to the fact that God was using prison to change her for the better, and therefore would always protect her.

Superordinate theme: The benefits of faith behind bars. The ways participants practiced their faith behind bars, through both corporate and individual faith practices, offered significant benefit. According to participants, spirituality and religion behind bars can function as a protective mechanism, facilitate personal change and growth, and help one to be a "model inmate." First, because so many sisters inside feel broken and tired, particularly early in their incarceration, religion can function as a protective factor. As Desiree stated bluntly, "If you don't have no type of religion while you're incarcerated, you could be so broken, you could be miserable, you could kill yourself. Literally kill yourself."

Second, individual and corporate faith practices helped to facilitate personal change. For Sandra, who served six years in prison, her faith "helped me to deal with a lot of stuff. The negativity. I found comfort reading my Bible, going to the Bible studies, going to the choir rehearsals, singing in the choir. I felt a little bit of relief. Calmness." A number of participants shared how participating in spiritual and religious life inside facilitated happiness and positivity. Shanelle shared how she was initially mad at God and questioned, "why is He doing this to me? But then I would see the other ladies like happy and they would go to church and like something really touched them." So she started participating in Bible study and singing in the choir because she saw the way it made other inmates "happy." She said, "I wanted what they had. It was really nice. Like it helped me to cope with being locked up. Like stressing a lot. And praying. And just letting it go. Talking to somebody." By participating in faith-based programs, Shanelle learned that she could talk with God about why He was "doing this" to her and share with God in order to help her to cope with her experience. Danielle also felt that participating in faith-based programming helped to make her prison experience more positive. She stated, "Having faith and people seeing that your spirit is good, it helped in prison in a lot of ways whereas though you draw a positivity instead of the negative stuff." It helped her to surround herself with happier, positive people and not to get drawn into interpersonal conflict. Although Desiree spent the first four months of her incarceration angry and avoiding God, once she started to participate in a biblical theater program, a "drama ministry," and singing in the choir, she found that her relationship with God was helping her to be happier and to begin loving herself. She stated,

> I started to love myself. The closer I got to Him, He started rebuilding who I was. I found my spiritual gifts. I was just, I started writing about my life story. It was just, I was more happier and [at] peace. I didn't have no worries. It was just moreso of a "thank you," than moreso of a "I hate you."

For Chelsea, the faith she developed inside has fostered in her a sense of humility, empathy, and compassion. She said, "My spirituality allows me to be humble and mindful . . . so it effects me on a daily because of how I respond to certain situations or how I treat people in general." She tries to treat others the way she wants to be treated. She tries to think about the consequences before jumping into an argument. She tries to remind herself that she never knows completely where someone else is coming from, what they've experienced, and why they may have a "nasty attitude." As a result, she also feels that she treats herself better with greater patience, less judgment, and more self-compassion.

Third, as Danielle said, participating in faith-based programs can help inmates to be happier, to gravitate toward positive people, and to avoid "chaos." This then helps one to become a "model inmate." Danielle said,

> You gotta allow your faith to work. You got to. Because you'll actually lose yourself up in there. And get caught up in the chaos because there's a lot of chaos in there. And I'm talking staff and inmates . . . I've seen ladies come in there and they have, they think they spiritually grounded, but they get caught up in it, and they don't be model citizens. I mean model inmates.

Participating in faith-based programs helped some participants to desist from engaging in misconduct, to avoid negative individuals, and to view themselves as "model inmates." As Malea stated,

> I did the church. I did the Bible studies. Every Bible study, it didn't even matter if it was Catholic. I was in it just to stay connected to the fellowship because when you're with the right people . . . I never had a problem with none of my incarcerations because I was with the right people inside the culture.

Superordinate theme: Corporate and individual faith practices. The spiritual and religious experiences of sisters inside are greatly influenced by the way they engage in both corporate and individual practices of faith. Study participants reported engaging in numerous corporate and individual faith practices while inside, but also faced barriers that limited their participation in communal religious experiences. Participants shared how they joined in worship, sang in the choir, went to Bible studies, took Bible-based life skills courses, sought addiction treatment in faith-based programs like Recovery in Christ, and participated in revivals as well as retreats and programs like Kairos. Tasha even shared how she "went to Sunday School every Thursday. That's the day they let us have it on even though it's supposed to be on Sunday. And the ministers would come in from the outside and teach us."

Only about half of the participants went to worship on a regular basis, about a quarter sang in the church choir, and about a quarter participated in Bible study. Danielle was even baptized and married in prison. As evidenced above, "going to church," or participating in worship, was the most common corporate faith practice engaged in by participants; yet they shared a variety of perspectives regarding worship. Chelsea was grateful for the worship opportunities in prison and the friend who, as previously mentioned, forced her into participating. She said,

> I was real grateful that [the prison] had the religious programs they had. Like the church, like they go all out for it. They have performers, dancers, pastors come in. I was just grateful that they had them things in place, and I'm grateful for the friend I had that, you know, pulled me back into it.

Lisa also was grateful for the opportunity to worship inside because of the emotional comfort it offered and the way "God has a sense of talking to your heart." For Lisa, participating in worship in prison "just brings feelings in you. And when you bring out those feelings you find yourself praying about everything that's going on and stuff. And the more the preacher talks it's like he's talking to you. . . . The tears just come naturally." For Chelsea and Lisa, the worship style was energizing and emotionally meaningful. But Andrea, who was raised Baptist, found she couldn't get into the style of worship inside and therefore chose not to participate in corporate faith practices. Andrea said,

> The people that would come in to do church with us, they was the type of people that pray over you, and put they hands on you, people like fall out and stuff. I wasn't raised in no church like that, so it was an experience, really, for me. I was like, "Wow," because I'm like, "Is this real, or isn't it, or is these people faking?" I don't want to judge.

About one-third of participants engaged in faith-based programs such as biblically based life skills courses, Recovery in Christ, and a Purpose-Driven

Life. Sandra spent four years receiving training through the Evangelical Training Association (ETA). According to Sandra,

> They came in and they trained us in church missions. Did that for four years. It was accredited, and I could've transferred it to any Bible college or anything else that came from outside. I was learning about the Bible and stuff. I think I didn't really internalize it. I had the information, but I didn't internalize it.

Sandra went on to share how participating in corporate and individual faith practices inside helped her to desist from crime while incarcerated and to feel "a little bit of relief, calmness. I kept my mind. I focused on all that other stuff that was going on. I didn't smoke cigarettes. I didn't do drugs. Cause there was plenty in there." But even though she participated in the ETA training, had a faith-based mentor, went to Bible study, and engaged in worship, she shared that she did not "internalize" the information. Sandra was the only participant to draw a distinction between spirituality and religion, which evidenced her perspective on how she was able to be religiously devoted without internalizing the teachings. She shared how she wanted to participate in the programming previously mentioned because she "wanted to get more—not religious, but spiritual. It helped me deal with that prison life." When asked about the difference between religion and spirituality, Sandra said,

> Well, spirituality, for me, is something that's within, and how I can look to my God in Jesus for support and relief that I know everything will get better. I try to use that. My faith and stuff to help me get through these trying times. Religion is just something like going to church. Taking communion. Stuff like that. Just doing the ritual. . . . It's good to go to church and commune with everybody. That's just not it. That's just not what it's all about.

For many sisters inside, as noted above, participation in corporate faith practices is motivated by extrinsic rather than intrinsic factors. A number of study participants also shared this experience. For example, when asked what made her periodically participate in Bible study, Latrise said, "Well, and this is sad, boredom." Lisa, who as previously mentioned practiced a variety of religions while inside, observed Ramadan in order to get "double breakfasts." Trina mostly prayed on her own because worship was seen as a "meeting place for people . . . they could meet their significant others and girlfriends from different dorms and stuff like that." In hindsight, Sandra questioned whether a lot of her religious participation inside, her participation in choir, Bible study, worship, and the Evangelical Training Association, was extrinsically motivated and an attempt to "manipulate God." She said, "I don't know if I was trying to manipulate God or doing that, doing all that good stuff, hoping that I could make parole, you know what I'm saying?"

I do not assume that all participants were aware of or willing to share their extrinsic motivations for participating in faith-based programming, yet the participants' experiences do, in ways, reflect the perspectives presented in the study conducted by Clear et al. (2000) and referenced above.

Participation in corporate faith practices inside is not as simple as one might assume. As previously mentioned, Danielle was baptized in prison, she participated in Bible studies, and she went to Recovery in Christ, a once-a-week group that lasted for three months, and was instructed by a male volunteer. But she said,

> The thing is about in prison, when you do have these things you can go to, you have officers that won't even allow you to go whether you have a pass or not. So it's a struggle in prison to actually get to these groups anyway.

When asked why the officers would prevent her from going, Danielle responded,

> Just out of spite. Some of them are really nasty. And there's a lot of things that go on in prison that shouldn't go on with the staff and the inmates. So if you on their wrong side, you ain't gonna get out that cell. I don't care what pass you got. I don't care who says to let you. They gonna make up an excuse to say they never heard the call or whatever. So you gotta really be vigilant and stay on point. And try to practice those spiritual principalities.

Whether study participants engaged in corporate faith practices or not, they all talked about the role individual spiritual disciplines played in their prison experience. For the first ten years of her incarceration, Rochelle did not participate in corporate faith practices because the teachings did not resonate with her own beliefs. Yet during that time she remained close to God. Rochelle said,

> I always had my own personal relationship with God. I talked to God every day all day long. Because He's the one that's got me through everything I've been through, you know, good or bad. You know I lean on Him a lot for everything. Even before I made decisions, I pray on it.

As will be seen below, three years before Rochelle's release she became involved with worship in the Seventh Day Adventist tradition and found that the tradition's approach to scripture greatly strengthened her beliefs.

Prayer and reading the Bible were mentioned by almost all of the study's participants. Almost half of the participants spoke about staying in their cells to pray and read scripture. For example, Andrea stated, "When they [other inmates] rec'd, I really didn't go out and rec with them. I just stayed

in the room, read my Bible, and prayed that when ready for me to go, He'll
be ready for me to go. He'll let me know." Shanice took a similar approach
and engaged in reading scriptures and praying in order to cope with feeling
hopeless, alone, and stuck in a cycle. When Shanice was locked up for the
second time she felt

> scared. For the first time being in, I seen all these big women. I'm like, "Oh my
> God. I don't belong down here." You learn to adapt to it as long as you stay to
> yourself. I read my Bible every day. It was a constant—more and more I had
> faith as I was reading my Bible, like I can do something.

Shanice turned to God and started to realize the impact of her mother's death
during her childhood. She took responsibility for her drug addiction, and she
called on God to help. "I had to call on Him so that [H]e could reassure me
that it would be okay . . . Nothin' ever works out without Him."

Treva's individual faith practices in prison centered around reading and her
morning devotionals. She said, "In the morning I had this ritual. I had different books that I would read before I would leave out for work in the morning.
There would be eight books I would read, and I would read the [scriptural]
passage to it." She noted how she read seven books by Joyce Meyer "within
the first couple of months I was away. I continued on. I kept reading, and
I kept reading, and I kept reading. That's how my faith started getting really
strong. I started reading self help books. It all turned out positive. Jail don't
always gotta be a bad thing."

Participants were not asked if they experienced a religious conversion in
prison, and no one used that language in describing their experiences. Tasha,
however, was raised in the Black church and converted to Moorish Science
very quickly after entering prison. She was the only non-Christian participant
in the study at the time of the interview, yet she spent half her life steeped
in Christianity. Immediately after entering prison, a friend invited Tasha
to a service in the tradition of the Moorish Science Temple of America.
The teachings and the laws resonated with her and "I just proclaimed my
nationality the same day. And I've been studying ever since." I asked Tasha
what resonated with her about the message and she said,

> I felt, I just felt it in my heart, because I knew that I was lost. It was like I was
> overwhelmed with the systemic oppression in society, the society that I was liv-
> ing in at the time. And when I heard that [the teaching] it was just like, it was
> a connection. Like a direct message from God for me. Like this is how you can
> save yourself. With these divine principles.

As previously mentioned, Chelsea also reported "finding" her faith behind
bars as she had "lost it" prior to her incarceration following the death of her

infant son. She realized during her incarceration that if she believes her son is in heaven, she would be contradicting herself not to have faith. She said,

> I came to the realization that obviously my son's in heaven and if I don't have faith then how, it's like I'm contradicting myself saying he's in heaven but I don't have faith. So I want to be at peace with his maker and who has him and who is watching over him now. So I feel like my faith is stronger now than it really ever has been.

Tasha and Chelsea were the only two participants who shared about pivotal transformations in their faith journeys that resulted from their incarceration. Other participants referenced particular spiritual experiences, but they spoke more about the ways prison deepened or strengthened their faith.

Superordinate theme: The role of relationship in faith behind bars. Study participants who regularly engaged in corporate faith practices, as well as those who did not, spoke about the importance of spiritually grounded relationships with the chaplain, faith-based volunteers, and other inmates. As evidenced in Appendix C, one intention of seminaries and formal theological education initiatives in prisons is to create inmate missionaries, inmates who function as spiritual companions and faith-based sources of support for other inmates. Whether formally educated or not, many of the study participants shared about the importance of other sisters inside who bolstered their beliefs. As already noted, it was Chelsea's friend who "dragged" her to church in prison even though she didn't want to go. Chelsea said, "She absolutely gave me my faith back. She would always pray with me and I wouldn't want to hear it, but I didn't want to be disrespectful towards her . . . She just talked me back into it and just got me listening and, you know, I just found peace with it." Tammy spoke about having a prayer partner inside who really taught her how to pray.

> She used to wake me up every morning, before everybody got up, and she would come get me up and we would kneel down. Both of us . . . I've never really had anybody show me how to pray even though I went to Catholic school. . . . And to have somebody right there with you was so powerful.

Rochelle referenced a fellow sister inside who "had a really strong faith in the Lord." Rochelle frequently asked her to pray over her and recounted how her prayers would always be answered. Rochelle told a story about calling home and receiving bad news, after which she began to cry and ran to find this fellow sister inside.

> And she'd be like calm down and she'd hold both my hands. And we'd pray. And she would pray these magnificent prayers, you know. She always had

the right words. And I would feel solitude in her prayers. And they would be answered. And she used to always tell me, she'd say, you know you can pray for yourself. You don't need me to pray for you. Because God will answer your prayers if you believe in Him.

Malea also referenced the importance of spiritually grounded relationships and explained how she served as a "light" to other sisters inside. "I had a spiritual presence about me when I actually got myself together. . . . A lot of those ladies that they put in my unit, I was a light for them." Malea shared about the time a prison administrator came to her and told her that a new woman would be coming to her unit who was incarcerated for charges of molestation.

[The administrator said], "I have this girl coming in, her charges are totally ridiculous." But because they knew me and my character, they knew I wasn't gonna judge her because she did that. You cussing is no different than her doing that . . . Everybody is in sin. I really try not to be judgmental. [The administrator said], "Put her in [Malea's] room," because I sound like a leader and they just gravitated to me.

Participants also spoke at length about the ways their religious and spiritual experiences in prison were influenced by faith-based volunteers. Nine out of nineteen study participants had relationships with faith-based mentors. These mentors' role in the returning sisters' experiences will be addressed in chapter 3. Yet more than the nine study participants referenced the importance of faith-based volunteers who came to lead worship, Bible study, and other faith-based programs. Malea, who herself served as a "light" and "spiritual presence" to other sisters inside, was greatly supported by the leaders of the prison's Kairos program (see Appendix C for more information about the Kairos program). She shared how she's "still connected to a lot of them ladies." But she referenced one volunteer in particular who "was a great mentor. She was a great spiritual leader. . . . She was just always there for you, like open doors, it didn't matter." Like Malea, Sandra also mentioned a relationship she cultivated with a faith-based volunteer that was an important aspect of her faith behind bars. When asked further about what made the relationship so unique, Sandra said,

She talked to me. I would talk to her about what was going on. Then she helped me deal with some stuff the way the Bible would deal with it and stuff. Cause it was Christian. They was Christian and stuff. It was real supportive. . . . Someone I could talk to because I didn't get a lot of visits either.

Rochelle also explained how she felt cared for by the faith-based volunteers who came to lead worship inside. She said,

I liked, you know, the warmth that I felt from that church. How they really cared about the inmates', you know, well-being. And you know, whatever was on our minds if we was going through something they were there as a shoulder to lean on and an ear to listen to. You know, so they really cared.

When asked how she knew that the faith-based volunteers really cared, Rochelle said,

By the way they interacted with us during service. Cause like if it was a person they was used to seeing every Saturday, and they didn't see them no more, they would always ask, "Well where is so and so? Did she get released? Or is she sick? Tell her that we asked about her and hope to see her next service."

Finally, as previously mentioned, although raised Christian, Tasha converted to Moorish Science Temple of America during her incarceration. Because she was sentenced to federal prison and served eighteen years, Tasha did her time in several different state and federal prisons. As a religious minority, Tasha greatly appreciated the care of one particular male leader in the Moorish Science tradition who visited her at three different prisons and "even came to see me when I got released." This relationship meant that upon her release Tasha knew the temple community in her area and had already developed personal connections.

The goal of this section was to present the four superordinate themes that emerged from the analysis of the stories study participants shared about their spiritual and religious experiences in prison. However, it is important to conclude this section by noting that participants' experiences were not universal. For example, Deborah was raised Baptist and her grandmother took her to church every week, but she never had a relationship with God as an adult. She said, "I knew God. There was a God. But I only called on him when I got locked up." Even then, she shared,

I really didn't have a spiritual relationship when I was down there [in prison]. I just did what I had to do. That was it. I went to school down there. I worked, and that was it. Sometimes I went to church. People came in and did church. I didn't get a spiritual relationship until I got on the street, until I got into this process.

Deborah was in and out of prison three times before she had a "spiritual awakening" that was an integral part of her recovery from drug addiction. Lisa's experience was also distinctive as she practiced a diversity of faiths behind bars. "When I was [in prison] they don't really give you no certain religion for you to go to so I practiced a lot of religions. I practiced Moorish Science, Sunni Muslim, Islam, and I did a little of the Jehovah Witness. But I went to church every Sunday and that was just the regular Baptist,

Christian, whatever. One of them services." Deborah and Lisa were outliers in some ways, and other study participants had outlying experiences, yet the distinctive spiritual and religious culture of prison dramatically impacted participants' carceral experiences and how they made meaning of their time behind bars.

The Influence of Faith-Based Volunteers and Prison Chaplains

While sisters inside play an integral role in developing the religious culture of women's prisons, the tremendous influence of faith-based volunteers and prison chaplains cannot be overlooked. Faith-based volunteers and chaplains occupy a markedly distinct role in prison culture from that of the correctional staff (i.e., correctional officers and administrators; Dammer, 2000). They not only aim to meet the spiritual and religious needs of sisters inside, but they often serve as a symbolic representation that God and society cares.

The Role of Faith-Based Volunteers

For millennia, people of faith have responded to the biblical injunction to "remember those who are in prison" (Heb. 13:3 New Revised Standard Version). Given how integral religious ideology has been within U.S. prison culture since its inception, it is not surprising that every day thousands of faith-based volunteers enter prisons across the country (Johnson, 2013). Even in the midst of the prison industrial complex and the overcrowding of prisons in the United States, faith-based volunteers have kept pace and continue to provide the majority of prison-based intervention services.

Today, faith-based volunteers lead worship services, deliver sermons, conduct choral groups and bands, offer religious instruction such as Bible study and confirmation classes, and conduct retreats or religious seminars. Faith-based volunteers frequently aid chaplains by meeting the spiritual and religious needs of sisters inside who affiliate with minority religious traditions, from Hinduism and Odinism to Mormonism and Curanderism, and by educating chaplains, over 84 percent of whom are Christian, on the tenets and nuances of these traditions (The Pew Research Center's Forum on Religion & Public Life, 2012; U.S. Commission on Civil Rights, 2008). Faith-based volunteers are equally involved in religious programming and educational/ rehabilitative programming (Kort-Butler & Malone, 2015). According to Erzen (2017), the prison industrial complex, and the increasing difficulty prisons face in rehabilitating rather than simply penalizing inmates, means that religious volunteers are increasingly meeting the nonreligious needs of sisters inside. The rise of the punitive, in contrast to the rehabilitative, model of incarceration resulted in a growing acceptance of and need for faith-based volunteers to facilitate "job training, GED and college classes, and work-release and other programs. The state saves precious money by outsourcing the labor of running programs in prison to religious volunteers" (p. 164). Faith-based volunteers offer inmates contact with the outside world and show inmates that they are not forgotten.

The Role of Prison Chaplains

Given the religious foundations of America's penal system, it is not surprising that for centuries chaplains have occupied a central role in corrections. Chaplains facilitated worship services, offered spiritual direction and support to sisters inside, and even performed more "secular" tasks such as education and opening the first prison libraries (Sundt, Dammer, & Cullen, 2002). Yet chaplains were not always valued in correctional facilities. As prisons became more heavily influenced by social scientific rather than religious wisdom, in the early 1900s the chaplain was pushed to the periphery (Dammer, 2002).

Given the increasing religious diversity in America and the key role chaplains play in ensuring the religious freedom of inmates behind bars, as well as the unfathomable rates of recidivism in the United States and the impact chaplains can make in facilitating the successful reentry of returning citizens, prison chaplains are arguably more essential than ever. "Prison chaplains represent one of the few potentially humanizing elements in the dehumanizing context of prison" (Kerley, Matthew, & Shoemaker, 2009, p. 88). Chaplains are permitted to interact with sisters inside in the tiers, giving them access to an intimate aspect of their world (Shaw, 1995). Yet the specific duties and responsibilities vary markedly across institutions. Whereas some chaplains are responsible for a significant amount of volunteer management and administration, others spend the majority of their time engaged in one-on-one pastoral counseling. In addition, as the ethos and cultures of prisons differ, the role of chaplains can be focused more or less on containment, rehabilitation, and advocacy. In the introduction to Dammer's (2000) *Religion in Corrections*, published by the American Correctional Association, Sister Helen Prejean stated,

> Some prison institutions give chaplains a lot of leeway. Others keep tight reins on them and restrict their role to strictly "spiritual" ministry. Translated, that means if a chaplain calls an inmate's family, tries to get him an attorney, buys him a pair of socks, brings into the institution a *National Geographic* or any non-religious magazine, he or she can be fired. The rules state "only spiritual ministry, no advocacy." (pp. v–vi)

In general, however, chaplains provide spiritual care and counsel, manage religious programming, and uphold the religious freedom of sisters inside by educating staff and contracting with religious representatives from outside the institution (U.S. Commission on Civil Rights, 2008).

Sundt, Dammer, and Cullen (2002) conducted a study with 264 chaplains, the vast majority of whom were White, Christian men with training in pastoral counseling. Participants were provided with a list of activities typically performed by chaplains and were asked to rank both the frequency and the importance of each activity. Counseling inmates was the most important and the most frequent activity conducted by chaplains, surpassing the facilitation of religious services, the coordinating of religious programs, the provision of religious education, and the supervision of volunteers. Chaplains are frequently responsible for approaching sisters inside with "bad news" like notice of a loved one's death or "a 'Dear John' letter from a spouse or lover" (Dammer, 2000, p. 20). Moreover, chaplains overwhelmingly viewed helping inmates to adjust to prison, and to adjust to life outside prison, as more important than religious conversion (Sundt, Dammer, & Cullen, 2002). Given the increasing number of women behind bars, and the increasing number of women trapped in prison's revolving door, the responsibilities of prison chaplains are diversifying as well as intensifying. As reported by the Pew Research Center's Forum on Religion & Public Life (PRCFRPL, 2012), increased recidivism means that

> chaplains in many prisons are called upon to fight recidivism by counseling inmates and connecting them with religious organizations or other social service providers that can offer job training, substance abuse treatment, education and other assistance before and after their release. (PRCFRPL, 2012, p. 7)

Faith-Based Programming in Prisons

As is now evident, for centuries religious programming has been a central tenet of the American penal system. Although an emphasis on social scientific wisdom pushed faith-based programs to the margins, a shift in the American penal system is now underway following the advent of the Office for Faith-Based and Neighborhood Partnerships in 2001, the recent economic downturn and the inexpensive price point of "moral cures," and the resulting proliferation of bipartisan support for such programs (Hallett & Johnson, 2014; Schaefer, Sams, & Lux, 2016).

The term "faith-based programs" is utilized in diverse ways within the literature, and faith-based programs in prisons vary widely. For example, some faith-based programs offer job and other life skills training, devoid of any explicit religious content, but are taught by faith-based volunteers or organizations. Other faith-based programs promote a particular religious perspective and involve elements of prayer, worship, and religious education. The overall aim of most faith-based programs in prisons is "personal transformation in a comprehensive sense" (Sullivan, 2009, p. 15). Although some faith-based programs are part of an individual congregation's outreach, "mom and pop" prison ministries are far more common (Hallett & Johnson, 2014). These ministries are led by individuals and are rarely affiliated with a denomination or even a local church (Hallett & Johnson, 2014). The primary function of many mom and pop prison ministries is preaching and evangelism, yet the scope of faith-based programming is actually quite wide. Nevertheless, despite protections to safeguard religious freedom, "Christianity dominates in prisons with aggressive and well-organized proselytizing and promoting Christian values in the integrated content of programs" (Thomas & Zaitzow, 2006, p. 250). Ample information about the variety of Christian faith-based programs is available to the reader (Barnwell, 2016; Dawson, 2015; Perry, 2006; Sullivan, 2011). Appendix C offers a summary of the most well-known faith-based programs in U.S. prisons, including Kairos, Prison Fellowship, and Bill Glass Ministries, in an effort to provide concrete examples of the potential role of such ministries in the religious and spiritual lives of sisters inside. In addition, Appendix C includes a glimpse into how 12-step programs, such as Alcoholics Anonymous, and credit and noncredit programs in theological education, function behind bars.

Why Religion Works

Appendix D provides a brief overview of the literature examining if and why, from an empirical perspective, religion "works" as a means of rehabilitating inmates. Unfortunately, studies examining the efficacy of faith-based programs, and the relationship between religion and adjustment to prison, misconduct, and deviance, fail to explain why it is that religion works. The empirical data is simply not compelling, on its own, to vindicate why and how religious beliefs and practices serve to rehabilitate brothers and sisters inside. However, Johnson (2011) posited numerous theoretical reasons, grounded in the empirical data, for why this is true. First, faith functions as a protective factor against criminal activity. When one is involved in a faith community, a local network of social and emotional support is often created, comprised of individuals with common values and standards of conduct. Such communities create connection, cultivate empathy for others, and encourage desistance from acts that harm others. Second, not only does religion function as a protective factor, it also compels individuals to engage in benevolent acts or cultivating "the good" in society. It encourages prosocial behaviors that most often result in beneficial outcomes for the community.

Project Sister Connect aims to provide returning sisters with the social and emotional support of a spiritually grounded community and to foster prosocial ways of being in a way that fosters rehabilitation and growth.

SUMMARY

Providing justice-seeking spiritual support to returning sisters requires understanding the backgrounds and demographics of sisters inside, as detailed in chapter 1, and the way their intersecting social locations contribute to the structural injustices sisters experience as the result of the prison industrial complex. The pathways to prison experienced by women, due to both macro- and micro-level factors, were outlined above, and the different crimes committed by women versus men were defined. Chapter 1 concluded with an overview of the cultures of spirituality and religion in women's prisons as understanding the religious and spiritual experiences of sisters inside offers an important hermeneutic through which to view their spiritual and religious experiences transitioning from prison.

The intersecting social locations of female returning citizens, and the oppressive ways in which the prison industrial complex impacts both women's criminal behavior and their reentry experiences, necessitates a holistic, gender-responsive, justice-seeking approach to reentry ministry as outlined in Project Sister Connect. This approach incorporates the Two Feet of Love in Action by addressing returning sisters' need for charity and justice. First, however, it is important to understand female returning citizens' reentry experiences. Chapter 2 introduces the reader to the reentry experiences of returning sisters by outlining the barriers women face in returning to community, the factors that support women's successful reentry, and the role of religion in reentry.

NOTES

1. The limitations of the available literature necessitate examining both male and female prisons, and men's and women's religious experiences behind bars, even though the cultures and experiences are, in many ways, markedly distinct.

2. The data does not differentiate men's and women's religious affiliations.

Chapter 2

Coming Home

The Reentry Experiences of Returning Sisters

In 2011, there were 111,000 women in state or federal prison (Carson & Sabol, 2012), yet 1.1 million women on probation or parole (Maruschak & Parks, 2012). Although these figures are astounding, they fail to include the number of returning sisters released without parole who are also navigating the barriers of reentry. The numbers of incarcerated women, and women returning to society from prison, are vastly outnumbered by men, yet the needs of female and male returning citizens are, in many ways, quite similar. Men and women alike need housing, employment, and health care in a system of few opportunities and numerous barriers. Men and women alike often need to navigate relationships with family and friends, sometimes with people and communities from which they have been cut off for years. Men and women alike frequently need education, substance abuse treatment, and mental health treatment. And men and women alike have spent months or years behind bars with little power or agency, yet are expected to take command of their lives and make numerous important decisions every day. Male and female returning citizens, in many ways, traverse the same difficult terrain in returning to society.

But the needs and experiences of female and male returning citizens are, in many ways, quite distinct. According to Travis, Solomon, and Waul (2001), "Although female prisoners make up only a small portion of the corrections population, they present risks and challenges in many ways more serious and widespread than do their male counterparts" (p. 13). Project Sister Connect, the revised prison ministry praxis outlined in chapter 4, requires that the reader understand the barriers women face in returning to community, the factors that support women's successful reentry, and the role of religion in reentry.

BARRIERS TO REENTRY

Regardless of the amount of time served, sisters inside experience a range of emotions regarding their impending release. For many, the final days and months in prison are spent navigating excitement, anxiety, and concern as they anticipate the barriers to reentry. Sisters inside often experience stress regarding their reentry well in advance of their actual release. They know that they will likely face multiple, competing demands, and many question if they possess the skills and constitution to cope. Moreover, many sisters do not know the exact date of their release well in advance, which makes planning difficult and can exacerbate their anxiety and fear.

Multiple studies offer insight into the needs of returning sisters. Based on unstructured interviews with forty sisters inside at an Ohio state prison, Severance (2004) identified five areas of concern that burden women as they prepare for release from prison: employment and/or education; relapse and recidivism; children; food, clothing, and shelter; and community acceptance. In a similar study conducted with forty-two women who had recidivated and were trapped in prison's revolving door, Richie (2001) identified the following seven barriers to successful reentry: treatment for substance abuse problems; health care; mental health issues; violence prevention and post-traumatic stress disorder; educational and employment services; safe, secure, affordable housing; and child advocacy and family reunification. Galbraith (2004) asked over 1,000 returning sisters about their specific reentry needs and the list replicated the above findings, but also included the need for "transportation tokens and money for identification" (p. 203). Finally, Bergseth, Jens, Bergeron-Vigesaa, and McDonald (2011) conducted a study aimed at identifying the needs of returning sisters by surveying service providers who work directly with them across both public and private agencies. Service providers identified the following seven needs, which they ranked according to urgency: (1) housing, (2) mental health, (3) and (4) employment and interpersonal functioning (tied), (5) family-related needs, (6) acceptance/support, and (7) substance abuse. This section describes these needs and the barriers they present, along with the unique ways they are experienced by returning sisters.

Barriers to Housing or Shelter

Adequate and affordable housing is essential to reentry, yet returning sisters face numerous barriers in attempting to secure stable housing. First, a history of residential instability is common among sisters inside. According to the Women's Prison Association (2003), 15 percent of sisters inside experienced homelessness in the year prior to entering prison. Residential instability continues for some women following release; however, community supervision (parole or probation) mandates securing a stable place of residence that is free from drugs, criminal activity, and the presence of anyone with a criminal record. As the majority of returning sisters are released on parole, homelessness violates the conditions of their release. For example, Sharon, one of the faith-based mentors who participated in the study grounding this book, recounted the story of a returning sister she mentored who had no other option but to release to her parents' house where her adult son and nephew lived. They were both abusing heroin and prescription drugs, and one day her son, "a total dirt bag," came home with a bracelet with an engraved "M," which he gave her and said it was for "Mom."

> Three days later the cops come kickin' in the door, he done robbed some house. That [bracelet] was stolen property. She turned it over right away, 'cause she said, "I don't know if this is part of it, but he gave this to me." They could have arrested her and she could have went down for that. She was out two weeks when that happened.

Securing housing that meets the stipulations of parole can be challenging for all returning sisters, but especially for those whose families or loved ones are involved in criminal activity.

Second, federal prohibitions also pose barriers to returning sisters in search of stable housing. Public Housing Authorities are required by federal law to deny Section 8, or federally assisted housing, to any individuals who were previously evicted from public housing due to drug-related criminal activity; anyone with a lifetime registration as a sex offender; anyone convicted of methamphetamine production; and anyone abusing alcohol or using drugs in a way that prevents peaceable living. Public Housing Authorities are allowed by federal law to deny Section 8, or federally assisted housing, to any individuals who engaged in a drug-related crime, a violent crime, or any other criminal activity that prevents peaceable living. Public Housing Authorities are allowed to evict tenants if they are associated with drug-related activity, even if they could not have reasonably known or controlled the drug-related activity of other occupants.

Third, landlords also engage in lawful and unlawful discrimination of returning sisters. For example, a landlord can legally deny renting to a returning sister if the landlord thinks she may be a threat to others in the building based upon her past incarceration (Women's Prison Association and Home, 2003). In addition, landlords are simply more likely to rent to tenants with a history of stable housing and employment. Desiree, a twenty-six-year-old African American female who participated in the study grounding this book, had a stable government job for more than two years following her release from prison, but she was unable to rent an apartment. She said,

I thank God that He opened the door for me to be [employed] in the government, [but] it's still certain things I just can't do. Certain places I can't go. I can't apply for an apartment without them saying no. I already tried. It hurts. They look, they go back for 10 years. And then if your credit jacked up you still can't get one.

Despite her positive employment history in a government position for the past two years, and the fact that she had the funds for an apartment in the District of Columbia, Desiree's credit history prevented her from the stable housing she desired and reminded her of past mistakes and regrets.

Finally, as a result of these and other barriers, most returning sisters end up residing with their families in the same communities in which they were convicted. This makes it difficult for returning sisters who are attempting to change "people, places and things" to maintain new ways of being. Given the prevalence of physical and drug abuse among returning sisters, residing with family or friends often means returning to an abusive environment or an environment not conducive to their rehabilitation. Research indicates that most returning sisters return to disenfranchised communities and did not receive adequate services in prison to facilitate their success (Richie, 2001). For example, Chelsea, a twenty-seven-year-old White female and participant in the study grounding this book, was lucky enough to secure a spot in a program for women in transition; however, she had one week between her release and her entry into the program, during which she stayed at her mom's house. She said,

It was scary because, you know, it's a horrible neighborhood. My family is still in the acts of addiction. It was scary because I know how quick I could have been sucked back into that life. . . . It's, you know, the same stuff that's been going on for the past, since you know, before I got locked up.

Chelsea attributed her ability to stay clean during that week, and to avoid recidivating, to God. "That's my God. I'm telling you. 'Cause I don't know how, but He made sure I found a way."

Barriers to Employment

As evidenced in chapter 1, women typically enter prison with limited work experience. Somewhere between one-quarter to one-half of sisters inside have never held a job (Bloom, Chesney-Lind, & Owen, 1994; Cho & LaLonde, 2005). Lack of employment history, combined with the way a criminal record can impact employment, makes finding a job upon release a significant challenge. According to the Sentencing Project (2007), "Only 4 in 10 women are able to find employment in the regular labor market within one year of release" (p. 9).

As previously noted, the conditions of community supervision often require returning citizens to return to the communities from which they came. For many returning sisters, this means a lack of public transportation, limited job prospects, and little access to industries suited to their skill sets. Moreover, they often do not possess the social capital in these communities that can be essential to obtaining employment in today's economic and employment landscape. Education is another significant barrier in obtaining employment as 42 percent of women in state prisons have not completed high school or passed the General Educational Development test (GED; Harlow, 2003).

Based on unstructured interviews with forty women incarcerated at an Ohio state prison, Severance (2004) found that 35 percent of the study's participants expressed concerns regarding their ability to secure employment or educational opportunities. For participants with felony convictions, which is the vast majority of sisters inside, there are numerous positions which they legally cannot occupy, including various trades and licensed health care professions. In addition, although significant progress has been made to "ban the box" and prevent the inclusion of questions about conviction histories on job applications, such legislation has not been enacted in all fifty states, and numerous returning sisters will be denied employment regardless of their qualifications or expertise. Moreover, given public access to criminal history records, it is quite easy to search the Internet for a job applicant's record and to identify previous arrests and convictions. Another barrier to employment is technology, as it changes at a rapid speed, and gave participants with previous reentry experiences in Severance's (2004) study concerns about their ability to keep pace. A lack of employment history was another significant area of concern. Yet participants had also developed strategies for addressing these barriers (Severance, 2004). Participants who lacked previous employment experience expressed desire to do something they enjoyed, such as cleaning. Participants shared that they wanted to participate in work-related reentry programs, knowing that such programs might help them to break down certain employment-related barriers, and to get a foot in the door through personal relationships.

Unfortunately, for many returning sisters, the longer they are unemployed following release, the stronger the lure toward engagement in criminal activity, as financial support from family, community, and government is often quite limited. According to a study of 134 female returning citizens conducted by Holtfreter, Reisig, and Morash (2004), logistic regression analyses indicated that poverty increased women's odds of rearrest by 4.6 and their odds of violating supervision by 12.7. Unemployment and financial instability and poverty, therefore, directly contribute to recidivism. Given the economic marginalization experienced by so many returning sisters, both prior to and following incarceration, employment training programs need to prepare women not only for jobs that they are eligible for, given the barriers they face, but that pay a living wage. This is especially important given the correlation between financial overdependence or reliance on others and criminal behavior (Berman & Gibel, 2007). This topic will be addressed again in chapter 4 as it is an important component of Project Sister Connect, the model for revised prison ministry praxis.

Danielle, a forty-one-year-old Black-Hispanic female who participated in the study grounding this book, was in the midst of a job search at the time of our interview. She saw her limited employment history, and her limited, prison-based job training, as significant barriers to her employment prospects. Danielle stated,

> I don't know how to actually get a job besides McDonald's, because that's all I ever had. And I only worked there four months one time and four months again. . . . But that's it. So I don't even have a work history. I have skills, and I have certificates in this and that. But never used nothing. Because I got them all in prison. And when you get out, like I said, you don't have the resources to go for none of that stuff because everything is for men.

Danielle is just one of the thousands of returning sisters whose risk of recidivism are greatly increased if she cannot access the necessary resources to help her to secure stable employment.

Relational Barriers to Reentry

As women return to community, they are faced with reestablishing relationships with friends, family, and children and, for some, choosing to end relationships that do not support their rehabilitation. Women who are successful in reconnecting with family reduce their likelihood of recidivism (Petersilia, 2003), are less dependent on social welfare programs (Arditti & Few, 2006), and can prevent intergenerational cycles of poverty (Arditti & Few, 2006). However, not all pre-prison relationships are toward returning sisters' health and well-being. Addressing the relationship reintegration issues of returning sisters impacts both micro and structural levels.

Barriers to Reintegrating with Family

As evidenced in chapter 1, many returning sisters had strained or abusive relationships with their families of origin and/or families of choice prior to their incarceration. Some experienced psychological, physical, or sexual abuse at the hands of a family member. Some experienced their families as enablers of or triggers to their addiction. And some family members are addicts themselves. Nevertheless, reintegrating with family is considered to be an important objective by many returning sisters. Why is this so? First, women tend to maintain and work toward relationship goals more than their male counterparts (Covington, 1985). As a result, they are more likely to feel or experience the impact of both positive and negative relationships. Women are socialized to function as caregivers, and therefore are more apt to adopt an identity as a caregiver for family members, even when those members may be abusive (Leverentz, 2011).

> Many women define themselves in terms of their ability to provide care to their parents, siblings, and other adult relatives. These relationships are an important aspect to the women's sense of self, which has direct implications for their attempts to desist from further offending. (Leverentz, 2011, pp. 240–241)

Sandra, a fifty-two-year-old African American female participant in the study grounding this book, shared about the familial stress she experienced during reentry. Sandra's mom died during her incarceration, leaving Sandra's two minor children in the custody of her stepfather. Upon her release, Sandra went to live with her stepfather and children, and "thought I could just come home and pick up where I left off, and help with stuff." But Sandra did not return to the world she had left. "Just everything had changed. My mother was gone. The house looked different. Everything was different." What hurt Sandra the most, however, was that she felt as though her stepfather did not want her there.

> They wasn't receive me as I wanted them to receive—as I thought they should receive me. . . . The first thing he said to me [following release] is, "If I didn't let you come here," he said, "I woulda been the worst person in the world." That's what he said to me when I walked through the door. I felt I wasn't welcome then.

This dynamic did not just impact and relate to Sandra's relationship with her stepfather, but her relationship with her two minor children as well. In the face of the interpersonal stress, Sandra turned to the coping mechanism she knew best: drugs. She started using just three days after leaving prison and "then my stepfather put me out."

Reentry and Motherhood

Nearly 62 percent of sisters inside state prisons are mothers to minor children, and over 64 percent of these mothers of minor children lived with their children in the month before their arrest (Glaze & Maruschak, 2008). In addition, nearly 56 percent of sisters inside federal prisons are mothers to minor children (Glaze & Marushak, 2008). As mentioned in chapter 1, sisters inside are more likely than brothers inside to be their child's or children's primary caregivers and the heads of single-parent households. Given the prevalence of motherhood among sisters inside, relationships with children are a significant issue facing the majority of returning sisters.

As previously noted, incarcerated mothers face numerous stressors such as maintaining contact with their children, relating to their children's custodians or caregivers, fretting over the impact of their incarceration on their children, and fearing the possibility of losing parental rights all together. Yet as they prepare for release, these stressors are often compounded as they anticipate what life as a mother beyond bars will be. Most mothers plan to resume their parental role following their release (Hagan & Dinovitzer, 1999), which for many means residing in the home of a mother, grandmother, aunt, husband, boyfriend, or other relative who assumed care for the child during the mother's incarceration. In a study on motherhood conducted with returning sisters in Hawaii, Brown and Bloom (2009) reported that 188 of the study's 202 participants were mothers of minor children and 14 were mothers of adult children. Of the 188 mothers of minor children, only 3 possessed the resources needed to establish their own independent households following incarceration. The vast majority lived with adult relatives (46.3%), in a program or clean living house (25%), with a spouse or partner (17%), or with an adult friend (10.1%). Only 47.3 percent of the 202 women reunited with their children immediately upon release, and for some that meant living with an adult child.

During their incarceration, many mothers feel a strong bond with their children, which may not be reciprocal, and many believe that reintegration will be easier than it is. Unfortunately, the children of mothers behind bars experience emotional, social, material, and financial consequences that research shows can render the relationship irreparable (Travis, Solomon, & Waul, 2001). Reintegrating into the lives of their children is difficult for returning sisters as younger children may no longer view them as "mom" and older children often harbor resentment in response to their mother's absence (Severance, 2004). Moreover, many mothers lose the parental capital that they likely once possessed as an authority and a moral leader, and they find themselves pushed to the periphery of their children's lives (Brown & Bloom, 2009).

In the previously referenced study conducted by Severance (2004), children were identified as one of five significant concerns faced by returning sisters. One-quarter of participants reported significant concerns regarding reintegrating with their children post-release. Participants reported experiencing "fear and uncertainty" about resuming their maternal duties, and they questioned their ability to manage motherhood in the midst of competing demands (p. 80). According to Severance (2004), as a result "some women desire to delay reunification with their children until they have both achieved stability and successfully avoided the temptation to fall back into old patterns of drug use and crime" (p. 81). Unfortunately, Tasha, a forty-one-year-old African American female and participant in the study grounding this book, experienced both the illusions regarding the mother-child bond and the subsequent desire to delay reunification.

> When I went to prison my son was 10 months, my daughter was three [years old] . . . I think I was under the illusion that I was going to come home and we were going to rebuild our relationship and live happily ever after. But there was nothing to rebuild because we didn't have a relationship in the first place. There was just a bigger disconnect than I realized.

Tasha's son has a disability and, although he's a young adult, he cannot live unassisted. Her cousin, who raised her son for the eighteen years of Tasha's incarceration, wanted her to "get him like ASAP." But with all of the stressors and demands Tasha faced during reentry, she didn't feel equipped to be the primary caregiver for her son. This put strain on her relationships with both her cousin and her son, and it caused her to feel ashamed. She shared,

> Like one time I came home and I was fresh out. And she told me she said, "Even a dog know how to be a mother to their child." And I was so hurt. I was devastated. I stopped dealing with her after that. If she needed me to do something, let me know and I'll take care of it. But far as like talking to her and allowing her to really be in my inner circle and have a front seat in my life I just couldn't do it. Because I can't let people talk to me like that and belittle me. I'm already going through enough.

Tasha felt overwhelmed and, from her perspective, she was doing the best she could to reintegrate with family and community after eighteen years behind bars. Her cousin's comments resulted in feelings of shame and the need for self-preservation.

Although returning sisters face numerous barriers upon release in adapting to their changing roles and responsibilities as mothers, for some women, their time behind bars created a shift in their family system toward a more supportive, functional way of being. Arditti and Few (2006) conducted a study with twenty-eight participants in which many participants indicated that "incarceration actually helped strengthen their family ties because the family had to pull together for the well-being of the children and to help her get back on her feet" (Arditti & Few, 2006, p. 111). In addition, the study results indicated that social support, particularly from family, was a key component in helping returning sisters to reintegrate into their maternal role.

Although the majority of mothers hope to regain custody of their minor children following their release from prison, in some situations this is simply not wanted or not possible. Nevertheless, parenting, whether custodial or not, can actually help women as they navigate reentry (Richie, 2001). If returning sisters are supported in their parenting, then "having even a noncustodial relationship with one's children can be an important stabilizing force in women's lives as they make difficult transitions" (Richie, 2001, p. 379).

Reentry and Intimate Relationships

For men, research suggests that marriage aids in desistance from crime (Laub & Sampson, 1993). However, for women, relationships, particularly abusive relationships, often serve as a pathway to prison. Chapter 1 provided an overview of the eight pathways to prison posited by Brennan, Breitenbach, Dieterich, Salisbury, and Van Voorhis (2012). Three of the eight pathways included relational abuse or dependence, and of the study's 888 participants on which these pathways were based, over 23 percent were involved in an abusive relationship that contributed to their incarceration and over 16 percent were dependent on or criminally influenced by a significant other. Gilfus (1992) evidenced how the dynamics of an abusive relationship between drug-dependent individuals can often result in incarceration. In such situations, both partners are drug-dependent and engage in a division of labor to secure drugs. The women are often responsible for getting money, frequently by shoplifting or prostitution, and the men, if responsible for anything, frequently work as pimps, engage in robberies, or fence the goods stolen by the women. The women in these relationships are almost always directly engaged in criminal behavior, while the men may or may not be. For some women, these relationships entail psychological, physical, or sexual abuse, but not for all. But the relationship, whether functional or not, is central to the women's identity. In Gilfus's (1992) qualitative study with twenty incarcerated women, fourteen of the study participants defined themselves and their identities in relation to a significant other. These significant relationships then required "caretaking" that necessitated illegal activity. Whether the abuse occurred during childhood or adulthood, women commonly enter prison with a history of dysfunctional familial and intimate relationships.

Therefore, upon release, women struggle to break the cycle of abuse, especially because for many it is the norm, and prison does not always function to rehabilitate or change this perspective. In Gilfus's (1992) study, sixteen of the twenty participants had been in abusive intimate relationships, with some participants recounting as many as five abusive partners. Reentry invites returning sisters to decide which familial and intimate relationships are toward their health and which are not, yet such decisions are not always easy or even apparent. Guidance in navigating relationships during reentry important component of Project Sister Connect, as will be shown in chapter 4.

Sandra, a fifty-two-year-old African American participant in the study grounding this book, experienced both the help and hindrance that can come from reliance on an abusive romantic partner. Just two days after her release from prison, Sandra became overwhelmed. "I couldn't figure out where to, how to start the process, getting a job and all that stuff." She felt "scared, alone," and she coped by using drugs. She was honest with her parole officer and he helped her to get into a recovery house. It was then that she met a man and got into an abusive relationship.

> Well, at first, he was all nice and good. Then we started living together, he was controlling, and he got abusive. He thought he could talk to me any kind of way. When I said something back, he slapped the shit out of me.

But for nine months, despite the abuse she endured, Sandra remained sober. She got a job working at McDonald's and paid her share of the lease on their apartment. But she grew weary. When asked how these factors contributed to her relapse, Sandra stated,

> For one thing, I was living with him. I felt as though I was working, both of us was, my name was on the lease and his name was on the lease. He couldn't be controlling me like that because I'm paying my part, he paying his part. Who does he think he can run me like that? That's why I would mouth back. The way he dealt with it was hitting. I got tired of working hard and going to outpatient [drug treatment] to deal with that shit. I got tired of working at McDonald's at a bullshit job, dealing with them customers, then have to come home and deal with his ass and still pay the bills. I said fuck it. So I started using.

As previously mentioned, women face difficult decisions as they navigate romantic relationships during reentry and often feel constrained by material and emotional needs along with previous patterns and ways of being. These dynamics become even more complicated when one's romantic partner is also a co-parent.

Reentry Barriers Related to Medical Problems, Mental Illness, and Substance Abuse

Due to the prevalence of long-term substance abuse among sisters inside, as well as the poor medical care received by so many women prior to incarceration, inmates' medical needs are often quite significant. Although prison-based health care is mandated, a significant portion of the medical attention inmates receive is acute or emergency care, leaving ongoing needs unaddressed or inadequately treated. Yet the medical needs of sisters inside are most often chronic, as numerous chronic conditions, including asthma, diabetes, and HIV/AIDS, are prevalent in prisons. Moreover, communicable diseases, including HIV/AIDS, hepatitis, and TB, are problematic in many prisons (Women's Prison Association and Home, 2003).

When women release to the community, they often do so with significant health concerns. In a study of 262 female returning citizens, with an average age of thirty-six, 77 percent had a chronic physical and/or a mental health condition (Mallik-Kane & Visher, 2008). According to a study conducted by the Urban Institute, nine out of ten female returning citizens have chronic health conditions that necessitate ongoing treatment and/or management, and six out of ten possess some combination of physical, mental, and substance use disorders (Mallik-Kane & Visher, 2008). Regrettably, "treatment is inaccessible until a complex public assistance application process, which is dependent on a permanent address, is completed" (Women's Prison Association and Home, 2003, p. 3). As a result, eight to ten months following release, 58 percent of female returning citizens had no health insurance (Mallik-Kane & Visher, 2008).

Returning sisters oftentimes release back into community not only with medical concerns but with undiagnosed and/or untreated mental health conditions. As noted in chapter 1, mental health needs are grossly undertreated in state and federal prisons. In a study of forty-two female returning citizens, Richie (2001) found that the majority of participants reported receiving inadequate mental health treatment in prison, both for major psychological problems as well as more moderate depressive, behavioral, and learning disabilities. Over half of the participants described severe emotional problems that went untreated inside. When mental health needs go untreated, women are released back into the community at a distinct disadvantage and often struggle to navigate relational, occupational, and physical demands. Returning citizens with mental health problems face greater employment- and housing-related challenges than mentally well or stable returning citizens (Mallik-Kane & Visher, 2008).

As noted in chapter 1, a significant percentage of sisters inside have substance abuse problems, but the growing treatment gap means only a small percentage receive treatment services in prison. Therefore, "advocates and service providers agree that substance abuse treatment is one of the most significant needs for women returning to their communities from jails and prisons" (Richie, 2001, p. 372). According to a study conducted by the Urban Institute, four in ten women received substance abuse treatment in prison, whether through a formal treatment program or self-help programs such as Narcotics Anonymous (NA) or Alcoholics Anonymous (AA). However, eight to ten months following their release, only one-quarter of the study's participants continued in substance abuse treatment. Moreover, the s. term, prison-based alcohol and drug treatment conducted in a setting where drugs are less prevalent than the streets, does not "adequately prepare them [returning sisters] to abstain from substance abuse or manage their addiction once they are released into the community" (Richie, 2001, p. 372). Not only is there a treatment gap, but the efficacy of prison-based programs is debated. Reentry entails stressors, such as old neighborhoods and relationships, which can trigger most returning sisters, but are especially challenging to those who did not receive adequate substance abuse treatment in prison. Therefore, relapse is often a direct contributor to recidivism.

In a study of thirty-eight returning sisters with co-occurring substance use and major depressive disorders who received treatment in prison, Johnson et al. (2013) found that women often relapsed in the first few days following release, a period so short that they were unable to access post-release services that were previously set in place. Based on qualitative interviews with the study's thirty-eight returning sisters, the following five relapse triggers were identified: experiencing difficulty in romantic relationships; experiencing emotions that were uncomfortable and with which they could not cope; experiencing mental health problems, including depression, anxiety, anger, and mood swings; finding oneself in the midst of people, places, and things that trigger relapse; and facing a lack of housing and employment (Johnson et al., 2013, pp. 174–175). Moreover, many of the women in the sample "experienced serious problems (e.g. unsafe living conditions, violence) within days of being released," which required the use of coping mechanisms they may not yet possess given the nascent stage of their recovery (Johnson et al., 2013, p. 173).

Latrise, a fifty-year-old African American participant in the study grounding this book, had been in residential addiction treatment prior to her incarceration, so she knew something of the process. Latrise was in active addiction when she returned home from prison, and after a few months of living on the streets, she knew she needed treatment. Latrise said,

> When I came home from prison and it had got real bad for me, when I say real bad, real bad. I was addicted to heroin and alcohol and crack. And I started calling to see if I could come up with some kind of program, but in the process I had let my insurance run out. So no place was willing to accept me without the insurance. And the places that was willing to accept me without the insurance I had to get on psych meds, and I just couldn't take no more.

Latrise found a Christian recovery center where she could live for eighteen months and learn a new way of life for $135. Although she did not have the money, the program accepted her anyway and, after she got high, her cousin took her there. "My hair hadn't been combed in about two weeks. I hadn't had a shower in Lord knows how long. I had something like a Walmart bag with a brush in it and pair of shorts or a skirt or something." But Latrise stayed in the program. She detoxed without any medical assistance. And she remained clean for nearly three years.

Barriers to Satisfying Parole Conditions

Many returning sisters are released to the community on parole, a form of community supervision that permits conditional release from prison. Parole places stipulations or conditions on women and requires them to adhere to particular rules of conduct. For some women, satisfying parole conditions can function as a barrier to successful reentry. For example, female parolees are expected to secure and maintain employment. Although state and federal conditions differ, it is not atypical for returning citizens to be required to secure employment within fifteen to thirty days of release. This task would be challenging for any citizen, but is especially challenging for returning citizens given the employment barriers they face as noted above. Unfortunately, the pressure of satisfying this condition of release often results in significant stress. For example, in a study of sixty female returning citizens, Wilma, a forty-eight-year-old African American shared how the stress of employment and finances, combined with her low self-worth, made satisfying parole conditions too much to handle (Johnson, 2014). She was repeatedly reminded by her parole officer of the requirement to secure employment and the consequence if she did not. Wilma continued to look for a job, but she felt "unworthy." Wilma stated,

> All of that just weighed on me and I went back out trying to hustle to make money to pay my bills and ended back up on drugs again. After thinking about it, I realized my parole officer, who I saw as nagging me, was just trying to help me. (Johnson, 2014, p. 375)

Like many returning sisters, Wilma turned to drugs when her daily stressors became too much to manage. She commented that in hindsight she saw that her parole officer wanted to help her, but the pressure of producing a paycheck clouded her perspective (Johnson, 2014).

Returning sisters on parole may also struggle to pay their monthly parole supervision fees (Johnson, 2014). The participants in Johnson's study often relied upon their families to assist them in meeting the $30 monthly fee, yet their families were also financially strapped. Thirty-three percent of participants were one, two, or three months behind in their payments, and for 28 percent of participants this created both personal and familial stress.

Although parolees can apply for an exemption if their other expenses, such as child support, medical fees, and restitution fees, surpass their employment income, most do everything in their power to make that bill. This was described by Harriet, a sixty-four-year-old White woman, who stated that she would pay her supervision fee even if it meant having no money for food (Johnson, 2014).

Contending with the Ex-convict Stigma

Following a criminal conviction, many women adopt, and have thrust upon them, identity labels such as offender, criminal, convict, or felon. These labels are accompanied by deeply engrained prejudices and stigmas. According to famed sociologist Erving Goffman (1963), a stigma is "an attribute that is deeply discrediting" (p. 3). Goffman surmised, "By definition [. . .] we believe the person with a stigma is not quite human. On this assumption we exercise varieties of discrimination, through which we effectively, if often unthinkingly, reduce his [*sic*] life chances" (p. 5). Women face myriad stigmas when reentering society following incarceration. I invite the reader into a moment of free association. What words enter your mind when you read the terms female ex-offender? Female ex-convict? Female ex-felon? Far too many of the adjectives associated with these nouns focus on returning sisters' deficits rather than their strengths.

Moreover, most returning sisters suffer from multiple stigmatized identities due not only to their history of incarceration but to their race, substance abuse, and mental illness (LeBel, 2012). They are thought to have abandoned their children, be drug-addicted and/or sex workers, and be violent, illiterate, and a liability upon society. As a result of internalizing society's stigmas, women degrade themselves, adopt the deviant label, and are shamed into low self-esteem and powerlessness. This is particularly problematic because many sisters inside who want to change have fluid or fragile identities, which are negatively impacted by stigmas, when they are seeking to redefine who they are and where they are going.

In much the same way that racism and sexism can become internalized and function not only as systemic and interpersonal oppression, but as intrapersonal oppression as well, stigmas that are projected onto sisters inside by society-at-large are often internalized and then serve to further imprison women in feelings of low self-esteem and self-worth. According to O'Brien (2001),

> Offenders in the criminal justice system find their very selfhood is defined by the crimes they have committed. The related stigma often follows them out to the "streets" where statistics attest, they often fall back into former patterns of behaviors and associations, that then lead them back to prison as recidivists. (p. 287)

Therefore, the stigmas women face in prison, and when transitioning from prison, can negatively influence the formation of a healthy identity and contribute to the erosion of their self-concept. The double, triple, and quadruple stigmas faced by returning sisters often challenge successful reentry. According to Dodge and Pogrebin (2001), when women reenter society and find themselves with few social bonds it can serve to confirm "their deviant master status. [. . .] The difficulty, if not impossibility, of attempting to disavow one's deviant label is a formidable task for many women offenders" (p. 42). In addition, research shows that the "ex-inmate stigma" impedes the process of securing a job (Harris & Kelly, 2005) and, when combined with the lack of social bonds and economic marginalization (Lund, Hyde, Kempson, & Clark, 2002), can present an insurmountable barrier for some returning sisters (Johnson, 2014).

LeBel (2012) conducted a study with 204 formerly incarcerated persons, 171 men and 33 women, who were receiving reentry services. Utilizing the Rosenberg Self-Esteem Scale, LeBel concluded that respondents who felt stigmatized and discriminated for between five and ten individual reasons, such as their status as a former inmate, their race, their economic status, and their past drug or alcohol use, reported significantly lower self-esteem in comparison to those who reported less discrimination. Therefore, incarceration leads to beliefs that one is stigmatized by society, which leads to feelings of discrimination, and results in lower self-esteem. Sadly, "a criminal conviction–no matter how trivial or how long ago it occurred–scars one for life" (Petersilia, 2003, p. 19). As will be shown in chapter 4, churches and people of faith can play an important role in helping women to avoid internalizing the "felon" or "convict" stigma and aid them in embracing how they are beloved children of God. "Congregations can let women know that, though society stigmatizes and judges them, God loves them—and so do the people of God" (Robinson-Dawkins, 2011, p. 89).

Going "Home": Where Returning Sisters Go upon Release

When women are released from prison, they most often say they are "going home." Yet a significant number of women, even if they had a permanent home prior to prison, will not return to that same pre-prison bed, apartment, or home. Due to differences between state and federal prisons, and the distinctiveness of reentry services across the nation, prior to exiting prison, some women are presented with a choice to participate in reentry services. Some are not. Some women are presented with a choice to return to the community on parole. Some are not. Some women are presented with a choice to go to a halfway house. Some are not. Even without the stipulations of parole, few women are given a plethora of attractive choices regarding where "home" will be when they exit that prison gate. But, for those who are able to utilize them, reentry services can be an important factor in facilitating women's successful integration in the community.

Just as the pathways to prison are distinct, so too are the pathways to "home." Utilizing the inmate case files of the returning sisters released in a period of just under two years in a Midwestern state, Vigesaa, Bergseth, and Jens (2016) conducted a non-experimental study comparing the characteristics of female inmates who are released from prison via the following three pathways: (1) to the community on parole, (2) to a reentry program that included "prison-based treatment and services followed by stepped-down gender responsive residential services" (p. 314) in a halfway house, and (3) to a halfway house on parole. The authors found that the women on the halfway house and the reentry pathways had fewer risk factors, particularly related to substance use and mental health, and had participated in more rehabilitative work in prison than the women who paroled directly to the community. The results "suggest an apparent mismatch between treatment need and treatment participation" (p. 322). The reentry programs were serving those "outside" who had already been served "inside" and whose risk for recidivism was less than their community-based peers. The authors posited numerous explanations for this, including the fact that those on the reentry pathway had served more time and therefore had greater opportunity to participate in treatment. In addition, correctional administrators may refer lower risk inmates to programs as they are presumably more "successful." Individuals and churches seeking to provide faith-based reentry services and spiritual care to women "coming home" need to think about who programs aim to serve—those who have already started a rehabilitative journey or those who, for whatever reason, have not?

Desiree, a participant in the study grounding this book, decided to leave the city where she had familial support in order to get the type of assistance she needed. She needed help breaking her "addiction to the streets." She needed to change people, places, and things. "It was a hard transition because I could have slipped back into the old me," Desiree stated.

> And a lot of people do. . . . When you go home, right back in, because the system is designed to break you in some way, form, or fashion. But it's also designed to help you, if that makes sense. It helps you with benefits, but it don't help you with what you need help with.

For Desiree, the system helped her with reentry services, it helped her to find a transitional program that met her material needs, but it didn't help her to break her addiction to the streets and change her lifestyle.

Philosophically and in regard to terminology, there is little consistency about whether "reentry services" begin pre-release or strictly following an exit from prison. Wilkinson (2004), Director of the Ohio Department of Rehabilitation and Corrections, argued that "reentry is a philosophy, not a program" (as cited in Petersilia, 2004, p. 5). Therefore, Wilkinson, Petersilia, and others argue that reentry services should begin at the time of sentencing or once one is admitted to prison, not upon an inmate's release. Yet reentry ministries and services most often do start at the gate and not behind bars. "A variety of different interventions may be categorized as reentry programs and services, including programs or services provided during incarceration and within the community, community corrections centers/halfway houses, mentoring programs, and reentry courts" (Vigesaa et al., 2016, p. 309). Project Sister Connect posits recommendations for individuals and churches who seek to offer spiritual care and reentry services to women following their release from prison. However, as will be seen in chapter 4, it is recommended that the ministry and relationship-building efforts begin pre-release when sisters are still inside.

STUDY PARTICIPANTS' LIVED EXPERIENCES
OF THE BARRIERS TO REENTRY

Brief insights into the reentry experiences of study participants were integrated within the above presentation of the literature. Although the aim of the study grounding this book was to uncover participants' spiritual and religious experiences during reentry, and participants were not asked explicitly about the barriers they faced, they all referenced difficulties and hardships that reflect the literature presented above. Therefore, it is worth sharing a bit more insight into the lived experiences of study participants and the barriers they faced related to addiction and "the streets," housing, and interpersonal relationships. First, the lived experiences of returning sisters and the barriers they faced are recounted. Second, the perspectives of faith-based mentors regarding the reentry experiences of the returning sisters they mentored are presented.

Returning Sisters Explain the Barriers to Reentry

Sixteen of the nineteen participants had a history of addiction, which often entailed a familiarity with "the streets." In addition, many participants lacked a healthy social or familial support system. Therefore, one of the major barriers to reentry that study participants faced was avoiding the lure of the streets and the people who got you high, especially when an alternate support system was not available. According to Tammy, "A lot of people come out, they don't have anywhere to go. They've burnt bridges. So where are you going? Back to the streets." Danielle also spoke about this dynamic when she said,

> So who embraces you [when you leave prison]? The people who you was trying so hard to run away from, to get away from. It's the corner people. The drug dealers. The people that mean you no good. And they have open arms for you just to suck you back in when it's though it should be the church, or the community.

As previously mentioned, following Chelsea's release from prison she had one week to wait before she could enter a residential program for women in transition. During that week, she returned to her mom's house and the threat of street life and addiction. She said, "It was scary because, you know, it's a horrible neighborhood. My family is still in the acts of addiction. It was scary because I know how quick I could have been sucked back into that life." Tammy also found herself trying to avoid the lure of the streets during her participation in a prison pre-release program. She intentionally went to Narcotics Anonymous (NA) to remind her that the streets had nothing to offer her. She stated,

> I'd always go [to NA] to hear the stories. Because while I'm there [in the pre-release program] it lets me know it's still going on out there. Everything is still the same. The streets is still the same. They don't change. And you have to be reminded sometimes of that. You gotta remember where you come from or you'll go back. . . . And they [NA members] just showing you the evidence. This is your choice.

As Tammy said, returning sisters exercise the choice to go back to street life or not. Yet for some, the choice is between life on the streets or an equally destructive situation. Danielle was in and out of jail and prison thirteen times. She shared, "I've been broken. I've been built up. I've been broken. I've been built up." Within that process, the revolving door of incarceration, Danielle tried to avoid the streets, but the alternatives were just as damaging. "You don't want to live on the streets. So you go back to that abusive man. Or you go back to the people that got you high because that's all you know and you don't have nowhere else to go."

With the streets and the friends and family that got you high waiting for you, participants explained how devastating a lack of secure housing can be during reentry. According to Rochelle,

> One of the biggest things that women need help with transitioning from prison is housing. Housing and mental health help, you know because a lot of people that

are mentally ill need medication. And it's a lot of people that have addictions to things and they need help. But the biggest thing that most of us need is housing. Because nobody wants to be homeless.

A lack of secure housing was uniquely stressful for Rochelle because she received subsidized housing prior to her incarceration, a benefit that due to her time in prison she could no longer secure. She shared,

> Before I got incarcerated I had a voucher. I was living on a Section 8 voucher. And when I got locked up all that was terminated. So I was really worried and scared. I said oh God, how am I supposed to . . . you know . . . if they do get my disability back, how am I supposed to survive off of that when rent be so high? What am I going to do? And I didn't want to go stay with my grandmother. I didn't want to go live with any of my family members because I'm used to being on my own. I left home when I was 16.

Becky also faced significant concerns related to housing as her parents initially did not want to welcome her into their home and she had nowhere else to go.

> To even have nowhere to go and have to go back to their home to be released was hard. At first they weren't going to let me come there and then I just prayed. When God made it open, I said that's where I'm meant to go.

Becky was forty-six years old when she was released from prison on house arrest and went to live with her parents. She spoke about how difficult it was to be dependent on them.

> I went back to my mother's. It was so hard. It was hard, for one, because they had to support me again because the jail still collects the funds for you. I couldn't get food stamps. I couldn't get transportation. They had to provide everything. They were on a fixed income. My father's heart only had 25 percent working so they weren't—he wasn't able to work. It was like I was going home to help them and I couldn't even help them.

Becky's experience in many ways echoed the concerns noted above by Rochelle; even when family is able to shelter you following release, the dependence faced during reentry can be overwhelming. Moreover, Becky was dependent on her parents for housing, but she was not provided with a home that functioned to support her parole or her recovery from drugs. Her parents were also sheltering her drug-addicted son and nephew, and her parents' bedroom door had a deadbolt and the windows were locked in order to secure her father's prescription pain pills. Moreover, due to her son's and nephew's use of heroin in the home, Becky's husband refused to allow her minor children to visit, thus preventing Becky from reestablishing a relationship with her kids during her house arrest.

Trina also spoke about the importance of housing that "lets [returning sisters] know they don't have to come back home to the same stuff they left." Although Trina had been released from prison for the third time years prior, at the time of the interview Trina was part of a residential program for women in transition. Based upon her three reentry experiences, Trina felt strongly that women need more residential reentry opportunities. Shanice also shared about the importance of reentry programs. She recalled her release from prison and said,

> It was the most horrible experience that I've ever had. We really don't get nothin' out of this. We don't have no programs to go to after we get out. . . . We had to rely on what parole told us to do, so that's what we did. . . . Knowin' that, I knew I was gonna use [drugs] again, because there was nothin' put in place there for me to grab onto. . . . They just put us out and, "You're released."

Treva also noted the benefit of residential reentry programs. She'd been released from prison two months prior to our interview and found the process of gaining entry to a transitional program challenging. Treva stated, "This place is hard to get into. You can't just get into [this transitional program] like you think you can. I had three interviews in order to get in here." Shawna actually asked the parole board for a "delayed parole sentence," which extended her time in prison, as she waited for an interview to get into a residential reentry program. Shawna knew she needed the wraparound services of a reentry program in order to succeed. She said, "I wanted to change my life and I knew that if I didn't start things rolling in that format to change, you know, when it's your time it's your time. And that was my time."

Yet halfway houses and residential reentry programs do not ameliorate all barriers to successful reentry. Shanelle, after serving four incarcerations in the state prison, was lucky enough to secure a place in a halfway house that allowed her to regain custody of her eleven-year-old son. Unfortunately the program was far from where she had lived in the past and she had no interpersonal support system. After being around other women in prison around the clock, Shanelle felt isolated during reentry. She said,

> So I was all alone. Not really all alone because there was like my counselor at the halfway house, there was other ladies, but I guess like they was going their separate ways and I was going my separate way. So it was like, well I'm from [another town] so I don't know my way around. It was just like me and my son.

Despite the barriers and adversity faced during reentry, many participants felt they needed prison. As evidenced in chapter 1, many of the participants felt grateful to God for their incarceration and viewed it as God-ordained. As Chelsea stated, "I would not change [my incarceration] for anything in the world. People are like, 'You're not mad about all the time you got?' I was like absolutely not. I needed it . . . it was a good opportunity to wean the bad people out of my life . . . it was an eye-opener." Trina had been asking God for help. She had already been to prison twice, was in the throes of active addiction, and knew "I didn't want to live like I was . . . and I knew when I got locked up this time I was saved. I didn't look at it like here I go again." Trina knew that her incarceration was God's answer to her prayers.

Faith-Based Mentors Explain the Barriers to Reentry

In walking alongside returning sisters, faith-based mentors watched as their mentees faced a significant amount of adversity. Karen was in a mentoring relationship with a returning sister whose husband divorced her two months before her release and whose oldest child was killed just months following her release. In recounting her mentee's experience, Karen said,

> She's overwhelmed. In the beginning it was wonderful. It was so nice. Especially because her ex-husband was still there. He was home with her kids. It was good until her son was killed. Then she started having a really rough time.

Furthermore, Karen's mentee struggled with mental illness, "some kind of schizophrenia," which required consistent psychiatric care and medication and significantly contributed to the crime that resulted in her incarceration.

Faith-based mentors also accompanied returning sisters as they worked to reestablish familial relationships. Eunice's mentee had inherited some money, and it concerned Eunice that the mentee's family might be "using her." She was very protective of her mentee and was concerned when the mentee told her that she and her ex-husband were trying to get back together. Eunice reflected,

> She missed the birth of some of her grandkids and just some of the things that she's missed. It makes you do more than what you would normally do just trying to make up, but you can't make up . . . I guess I'm overprotective . . . because, see, my thought is your family use you, that hurts worse than anybody else and can bring you down. And we don't want that.

Eunice was concerned that the mentee's family might be trying to reestablish relationship for financial gain, and that her mentee, due to the guilt and shame she had in missing so many years of their lives, might not realize it.

Melanie also noted the difficulty female returning citizens face in tr_ _ to reestablish relationships with family. As a faith-based mentor, Melanie mentored women who successfully integrated with family and others whose recidivism was encouraged by unhealthy and difficult familial relationships. According to Melanie, oftentimes

> [the family] reluctantly accept them, but [the returning sister is] thinking that everything is fine. I'm coming back home, but the family is still a little reserved. Then they come home, and the relationships are rocky. There was some things that were unresolved that haven't been dealt with, or there are people in the home that they didn't know were in the home now. It creates a whole dynamic. I've seen one young lady within a month there was a huge altercation at her home. She was arrested because of that. You know what I mean? It was unmet expectations and she was just thinking of coming home to live with her sister, and everything's gonna be fine. She didn't know what was going on in her sister's home, because she and her sister never really talked.

Melanie's story illustrated the stress experienced by both returning sisters and their families in the attempt to reestablish relationship following a sister's release.

As noted above, Karen attempted to support her mentee as she renegotiated her relationship with her ex-husband. Karen's mentee also tried to reestablish relationship with her minor children, who were in her ex-husband's custody during her incarceration, but she realized that they'd grown. Karen shared,

> [My mentee] came out. She started looking for a job right away. She talked about the transition with her kids. You know, how she used to do things with them before she became incarcerated. She had to come to a realization that hey, this is four or five years later. I can't do the same thing with them I used to do. This is how they've been doing it. Because they pretty much had been taking care of themselves.

Karen continued to communicate via text messaging with her mentee as she navigated a new way of relating to her children, and Karen offered her scriptural passages to comfort her and give her strength.

Faith-based mentors walked alongside their mentees as they navigated barriers of reentry related to family, money, mental illness, housing, and more. Eunice, however, was concerned that her mentee's attitude was a barrier to reentry. As noted above, Eunice described herself as "overprotective," and she expressed a great deal of motivation for her mentee to pursue getting a driver's license because, from her perspective, one of the barriers her mentee faced was complacency. She explained, "So that was my thing. Trying to help her get the [driver's] license because she was suffering from watching television." She was "complacent." And Eunice worried that, "when the money runs out, then she—nothing—I want her to have something fall back on once her money runs out."

FACTORS THAT SUPPORT SUCCESSFUL REENTRY

When tasked with overcoming the barriers to reentry detailed above, research reveals numerous factors and sources of support that can aid returning sisters in a successful transition from prison. Parsons and Warner-Robbins (2002) interviewed twenty-seven returning sisters who participated in Welcome Home Ministries, a faith-based reentry program, in order to determine the factors that contributed to successful reentry. The authors identified twelve factors, which they ranked in order of the frequency they were reported, that helped participants to "make it." The factor cited the most was a belief in God or a higher power. The Welcome Home Ministries is a faith-based reentry program, so in many ways this finding is not surprising. However, participants were not asked any direct questions about spirituality and religion, and 96 percent of the women spoke about the role of God in their lives. For example, one participant stated, "I gave my life to God. He is the only one who has kept me from going back out and using drugs. If I didn't have Him and my sisters from Welcome Home and support from my family" (p. 12). The second most commonly cited factor that aided in reentry was freedom from drug addiction. Because twenty-four of the twenty-seven participants were previously addicted to drugs, their sobriety and recovery was a major contributing factor in their ability to integrate in society. Third, participants spoke at length about the support that they received from the other participants in the program as they navigated the vicissitudes of reentry. Fourth, participants noted the importance of visits by the nurse-chaplain prior to their release and the healing that resulted from those pre-release relationships that continued during reentry. The final eight out of twelve factors that aided participants in "making it" included: "supportive friends (not former drug using friends)," "supportive family," "role models (other women who have made a successful transition to the community following incarceration)," "the personal strength of determination," "children as a driving force to change," employment, helping others, and "learning to deal with feelings and issues from the past" (p. 11).

Cobbina (2009) compared a matched sample (based on race, age, marital status, offense type, and incarceration history) of fifty women who were released from prison around the same time, twenty-four who desisted from crime for the first two-to-three year period of parole and twenty-six who recidivated. Cobbina's study posed numerous research questions, including an examination of the factors that supported the successful reentry and desistance from crime of the twenty-four successful female returning citizens. By conducting qualitative interviews, Cobbina found that "many women identified the importance of receiving support from family and children; others discussed the role of finding employment; and most reported that having access to external programs and support systems facilitated their reintegration efforts" (pp. 99–100).

In Cobbina's study, 40 percent of participants commented on the positive impact that familial support played in their reentry, a finding overwhelmingly noted by African American participants. Familial support was provided in the form of finances, transportation, childcare, clothing, food, and general care and emotional support. Participants in Cobbina's (2009) study spoke about how employment facilitated their reentry by helping them to cultivate stability and build social capital. The paradox, however, is that social capital is often needed in order to secure a job, and a significant portion of the study's participants secured a job through networking. "Specifically, 42% of women landed a job by turning to friends, family, and former employers for help" (p. 102). Others were able to secure a job simply by word of mouth, which was more common among those who participated in transitional or halfway house programs. "For ex-offenders who manage to secure a job, they may feel as if they have accomplished half the battle as it relates to their transition into the free world" (p. 105). This is especially true given the positive way that employment influences identity and status, economic stability, social relationships, and status in the community.

Finally, 88 percent of the returning sisters who desisted from crime in the study conducted by Cobbina (2009) participated in community-based organizations that provided material resources and services. Participants shared the importance of concrete assistance like clothing, food, and transportation passes, and yet also commented on the importance of self-empowerment and doing for oneself. They noted the significant difference that could be made by a kind, supportive parole officer—someone who was also a "friend." This finding is particularly striking given that the twenty-six women who recidivated cited their parole officer as a barrier to their successful integration.

Returning sisters are truly the experts on the factors that support their reentry and it is most beneficial to hear their voices and to learn from them directly. Yet the thousands of administrators and staff working with women in reentry also maintain their own perspectives on the factors that facilitate successful reentry. In a study of 134 prison administrators at the state, institution, and programmatic level, participants reported that it is not only the programmatic offerings, for example, the particular skills taught and services rendered, that facilitate successful reentry, but also by the supportive relationships that are forged with staff and others (Koons, Burrow, Morash, &

Bynum, 1997). The care and support received by officers, staff, and administrators can make a significant positive impact on women's reentry experience.

STUDY PARTICIPANTS' LIVED EXPERIENCES
OF THE FACTORS THAT SUPPORT REENTRY

The returning sisters who participated in the study grounding this book were
not asked about the barriers they faced during reentry, and they also were
not asked explicitly about the factors that supported their reentry, except as
those factors related to their spiritual and religious experiences. However,
participants' stories revealed numerous insights regarding "what works" in
reentry. A brief glimpse into the insights they shared, grounded in their lived
experiences, is warranted.

First, participants noted the importance of having someone to meet you at
the gate. When Andrea was released, there was no one to meet her or to give
her a ride. In recounting her experience, she shared, "Matter of fact, one of
the COs [correctional officers] carried me from [the prison] to the light rail,
which was nice, because down there if you ain't got a ride, it's like how you
gonna get where you got to go?" Andrea took the light rail into the city and
went back to her old neighborhood. Sandra also spoke about the importance
of someone meeting you at the gate. She shared about the prison ministry she
envisioned starting and the ways that it would help returning sisters. In this
ministry, volunteers would

> go to the prisons and let them know that you're available for when they come
> home . . . [volunteers] can meet you inside and bring you home. . . . They can
> bring you home or take you to the place–take them to a safe place as soon as
> they get out.

Having someone to meet you at the gate is part of a larger support system,
which many participants referenced the importance of. After serving eighteen
years in prison, Tasha now works in a government-sponsored reentry services
program and dedicates her life to helping other women avoid facing the barriers she did during her reentry. Tasha shared,

> I think women need positive support systems. . . . I think women need other
> women in their lives who are willing to support them unconditionally, whole-
> heartedly, and consistently. And meeting them where they're at on their terms.
> I think that's the most important thing that women need. . . . Because I think
> that we thrive in relationships and I think that's the best way for a woman to be
> successful and really, really grow is when they have other women in their lives
> who are successful and who want the same thing for them.

Tasha attributed the success she's experienced following her release from prison to the strong women in her life and their ability to connect her with "the right resources at the right time." These women gave her "some behavior to model [and to] know what's possible."

Tasha highlighted the importance of strong female relationships, but for Shanelle, it was the love and support of her husband that aided her reentry. After serving four sentences in the state prison, Shanelle reflected on how it was that her husband helped her to free herself from the revolving door and establish a life outside.

> I stayed out because of my husband. I have a husband and he's been, he's been on me. Like he's been helping me stay out. I guess cause, I don't know. I guess cause I wasn't running the streets no more. As soon as I met him, I met him almost nine years ago, so he's just been keeping me humble, and stable, and make sure I don't gotta run the streets or nothing. So that's how I stayed out.

Unlike Tasha and Shanelle, Sandra did not have the support system that would have helped her in reentry. Yet she spoke at length about how one individual, much like her sponsor in a twelve-step program, could help to aid women in reentry. Sandra said,

> If I was coming home today, what would make a difference is maybe having somebody for the first 30 days . . . take them new places and stuff like that. Have somebody that would be with you for the first 30 days. Like my sponsor. She being with me every day until she gonna let me go. She been with me every day for the first 90 days [following her relapse]. . . . Or just someone to come and talk to and ask them how they doing. What can we help you? What is your challenges, and like that, with coming home?

Sandra and her twelve-step sponsor speak every day on the phone and see one another at meetings on a regular basis. The support she receives from this relationship modeled for her the type of support that she thinks would have been helpful during her reentry, although with an added provision of material resources and logistical/transportation support.

According to Tammy, supportive relationships entail acceptance and guidance without judgment. She spoke about the women's transitional program she was a part of and noted,

> This place here, when you come in this door, they don't treat you like a criminal. They don't treat you like an addict. And they don't take advantage of the fact that you've been abused. In abusive situations. Any of that. They don't even look at you that way. So when you come in the door they already going to give you a chance. This is what you're going to do. This is the steps.

Tammy was encouraged and strengthened by being welcomed into a non-judgmental, supportive transitional program that believed in her and gave her a chance. She noted the importance of support as well as structure in helping a woman to succeed in reentry.

Participants also spoke at length about the need to have somewhere to go, whether that means living with others, like friends or family, or participating in a residential program. Shawna explained how she was released at the same time as other inmates and how grateful she was to have somewhere to go that would support the change she wanted for her life. Shawna stated,

> When you're locked up you hear some of the women talk. Because the day that I got out, other women got out too. And, like, "I'm not going where I'm supposed to go." "I'm just going here or there." I said, "Well I'm going where I need to go. I'm going where I need to go, because this is the start of a brand new life for me." "Girl, you put yourself in that program," He [God] always in your ear. [I thought], "You put yourself in the program. You don't have to go there." [God reminded her], "Yes, I do. If I want to live different, if I'm making a change in my life, I need to go there, and I'm going." So once I was released, my sister met me downtown, I came straight to the [program].

Shawna's experience evidences the ambivalence she felt upon release. She felt the lure toward the streets, yet she knew that with that choice the change she desired would not come. God was in her ear telling her where to go.

Trina went to prison three times. The last time she was released, she went "straight to a program in shackles." With experience in reentry, Trina knew what kind of support she needed in order to improve her chance at a successful reentry. So she participated in a six-month residential program. She stated,

> I told myself that I would do everything that I didn't do the first time. And then some. And I did. I started from the door with my feet on the ground. Paying the payment, not just the help they afforded me, but outside help that I need. Grievance counseling. One-on-one therapy. To really work on what was inside of me. I went there with nothing. The clothes on my back from the sister in the jail, the jail shoes and everything. And I can honestly say I didn't want for nothing. The whole time there. I wanted to make me well.

As Trina's experience illustrates, returning sisters not only need programs and structure, they need material provisions as well. Many participants spoke about leaving prison with only the clothes on their back or with nothing more than a grocery sack of belongings. More will be said in chapter 3 about how participants experienced church-sponsored material support; but here, it is important to recount the laundry list of needs that, according to participants, can help to support reentry. According to Andrea, female returning citizens need "clothes. They need all types of stuff. They need help getting their IDs." Desiree added that they need

> housing. Clothes. Learn how to use transportation again because a lot of them lose their way. . . . I had to learn how to work a phone. . . . When I first got a touch screen like this I was, what am I supposed to do with this? I don't know how to work it?

And, of course, participants spoke at length about the need for employment and help with addiction and mental health issues.

BEST PRACTICES IN REENTRY PROGRAMMING

Given the numerous barriers to reentry, as well as the factors that support returning citizens, in April 2008 Congress passed the Second Chance Act (SCA; Public Law 110–199) with bipartisan support in order to reduce recidivism and improve the lives of returning citizens. This marked a turning point in criminal justice as significant federal resources were made available to support the hundreds of thousands of returning citizens leaving prisons each year. In addition, SCA provides federal funding in the form of grants for faith-based mentoring and other faith-based reentry services.

The National Reentry Resource Center (NRRC) was established by the SCA, and has invested more than $540 million, to date, in tackling reentry and recidivism (The Council of State Governments Justice Center, n.d.). Given the significant funding invested in the provision of reentry services, and the importance of using tax-payer money judiciously, there is an emphasis on utilizing evidence-based practices that have empirically demonstrated efficacy. Therefore, NRRC, in partnership with the Urban Institute, created the What Works in Reentry Clearinghouse, "a 'one-stop shop' for research on the effectiveness of a wide variety of reentry programs and practices" (The Council of State Governments Justice Center, n.d., para. 1). The clearinghouse contains studies that examine the outcomes and efficacy of numerous reentry programs, thus providing a sense of "best practices" in reentry services. To be included in the clearinghouse, studies must be quantitative and include both a treatment and a control group. The clearinghouse features the results of evaluation studies on eleven different programs for female returning citizens, all of which were designed to impact recidivism, employment, and/or substance abuse.

Reentry outcome research is problematic, however, as recidivism is most often used to evidence the efficacy of a program, and recidivism is measured and defined in numerous ways. Furthermore, if prison is intended to be

rehabilitative and not simply a means to safeguard society from female criminals, then recidivism alone cannot be the only measure of reentry success.
Scholars recommend including measures related to societal reintegration,
supportive relationships, substance abuse, and employment in an effort to
evaluate programs based upon the holistic impact they have on the lives and
likely success of returning citizens (Petersilia, 2004; Vigesaa et al., 2016).

If we broaden the scope and consider that "best practices" in reentry must
impact more than just recidivism, it requires an examination of how reentry
programs meet the needs and address the reentry barriers of returning citizens as noted above. Scroggins and Malley (2010) attempted to do just that.
They utilized the Internet to analyze 155 women's reentry programs in the
ten largest urban/metropolitan areas in the U.S. in order to determine if the
services offered address the needs most common and pressing among returning sisters. Although the study's methods lack rigor as websites frequently do
not offer a complete or accurate portrayal of an organization's services, practices, or culture, the findings are interesting and worth noting. For example,
regaining custody of minor children is often a pressing goal, as noted above.
But in Scroggins and Malley's (2010) analysis of reentry programs, the need
for childcare appears woefully unmet. "No more than 20% of programs in a
given area provide this service" (p. 154), although more programs offered
parenting skills courses. Very few programs provided general health care
and less than 50 percent of programs in any given area provided counseling
and mental health services, both of which are concerns for returning sisters.
More programs offered substance abuse treatment, however, but the type of
treatment provided is unknown. At least one program in each given area was
found to offer housing and transportation services, but most could only serve
a small, limited number of participants. "Among the programs in our sample,
employment and job training are generally the most readily available of all
services" (p. 157), as these services were offered by at least five programs in
any given area. However, the majority of educational programs focused on
helping women to pass the General Educational Development test (GED),
which is a service offered in many prisons. However, according to Erzen
(2017), many "cash-strapped prisons" eliminated prison-sponsored GED programs and depend solely on faith-based volunteers to meet inmates' needs in
this way. Finally, in regard to social support, a significant number of reentry
programs offered assistance with life skills and friendship building, a need
which the authors determined was likely to be adequately met. Therefore,
according to the study, most "currently available reentry programs do not
sufficiently meet the needs of postincarceration women" (p. 160).

As it is methodologically difficult to evidence empirically how women's
reentry needs are or are not met, and therefore to determine best practices in
women's reentry, there is a significant body of literature grounded in years of

research and experience, as well as theory, that offers a different perspective on how to care for women in reentry. First, scholars advocate for gender-responsive programming that recognizes not only the unique pathways of women into prison but their unique pathways out as well. Second, research indicates the importance of treatment for co-occurring disorders. Third, over the past ten years, mentoring has come to be considered a cost-effective means of caring for and assisting returning sisters.

Gender-Responsive Reentry Programming

As evidenced above, women's concerns and needs, along with the barriers they face when reentering society, are similar to and yet quite distinct from their male counterparts'. Just as gender-responsive programming is essential within prisons, it is also a requisite part of successful transitional and reentry programming. According to Covington and Bloom (2006), the barriers women face during reentry often require them to utilize and navigate multiple organizations that provide isolated or partial services, each with its own set of requirements and demands. Moreover, many helping professionals and volunteers address the needs of returning sisters in both an isolated and a sequential manner which negates the complex interconnections among reentry concerns (Berman, 2005). Gender-responsive reentry services necessitate the provision of wraparound or holistic services, implemented along a continuum of care, by culturally competent providers (Berman, 2005; Covington & Bloom, 2006; Holtfreter & Morash, 2003; Morash, 2010). Yet wraparound services that offer a continuum of care require partnerships. According to Berman and Gibel (2007),

> Institutional corrections and community supervision agencies need to join forces with public and private community organizations to ensure that the community support is available for women to successfully fulfill their criminal justice system obligations, and achieve successes that will ensure that they do not return to prison. (p. 164)

More about how such partnerships can be formed will be addressed in chapter 4, but for now it is important to understand why wraparound services are so essential to women's successful reentry.

Holtfreter and Morash (2003) evidenced the need for wraparound services when they conducted an analysis of the risks and needs of 402 female returning citizens in the state of Minnesota. They used cluster analysis to arrange participants in groups based on commonly shared risks and needs, and the risks and needs identified in the study were exactly those already addressed above (i.e., employment, substance abuse, parenting, recidivism, etc.). Yet the study's findings indicated that the group at greatest risk for recidivism, which constituted one-third of the sample population, demonstrated significant need related to substance abuse, mental health, and children, as well as employment and education. This cluster included more African American and Hispanic participants than the other clusters, which means these returning sisters were also likely forced to contend with the effects of racism and other oppressions on a daily basis. The authors noted that the participants' risk of recidivism, in combination with their diversity of needs, indicated the tremendous need for "wrap-around services that organize access to a great many different program elements tailored to each woman, or programs that are very holistic in providing many services at one source" (p. 152).

Gender-responsive services require collaboration with community-based service providers who enter the prison prior to an inmate's release in order to conduct assessments and provide services (Berman & Gibel, 2007). Establishing a relationship inside is an essential element of gender-responsive service as it fosters trust, increases the likelihood that a woman will follow up with the organization upon her release, and maximizes the woman's time behind bars. This is particularly important for women as they typically serve shorter sentences than men (Berman, 2005; O'Brien & Lee, 2006). In an evaluation of the ReConnections program, a "one-stop shop" on the South Side of Chicago, O'Brien and Lee (2006) found that gender-responsive services require concrete assistance. At the time of release, women need identification, gate money, transportation, an adequate supply of medications, a supportive case manager or mentor in the community, and a detailed and structured schedule that can be followed for the first week (Berman, 2005). Female returning citizens also benefit from receiving technological training for things that may have changed during their incarceration, such as the need to use credit-like cards for transportation and various social supports. Although this list may not seem extensive, it is far more comprehensive than what most returning sisters are afforded. Finally, female returning citizens benefit from setting concrete goals and tracking steps toward their completion, provided it is not done prematurely or in a way that overwhelms (O'Brien & Lee, 2006). People of faith and congregations can play an important role in implementing gender-responsive services. According to Berman (2005),

> Community-based agencies, faith groups and others can be important allies both to the individuals being released and to the institutions. They can serve as a necessary bridge and offer services that women need but that the institution is not structured to provide. (p. 26)

As previously noted, outcome research on reentry programs is problematic as the intended outcomes of gender-responsive programs should be far more holistic than a reduction in recidivism, which renders empirical inquiry a challenge. Nevertheless, it is important to recognize the research that has been done on gender-responsive reentry programs, such as *Moving On: A Program for At-Risk Women* (Van Dieten, 2010), which significantly lowered rates of future arrests and convictions among female returning citizens (Duwe & Clark, 2015; Gehring, Van Voorhis, & Bell, 2010). Moving On is a twenty-six-session, curriculum-based program grounded in gender-responsive strategies as well as relational theory, motivational interviewing, and cognitive behavioral theory. Each session lasts one-and-a-half to two-hours, and sessions occur once per week. Sessions address topics such as relationships, negative self-talk, problem-solving, and assertiveness.

Gehring, Van Voorhis, and Bell (2010) examined the effectiveness of Moving On among 190 female probationers (not parolees) in comparison to a matched group. Even when those who did not complete the entire curriculum were included, rearrest rates were significantly lower at eighteen months for the treatment group (11%) than for the control group (21%). Conviction rates were also significantly lower at eighteen months for those in the treatment group (9%) than for the control group (16%). Furthermore, rearrest rates were higher for those who did not complete the program as opposed to those who did.

Duwe and Clark (2015) also conducted a study investigating the effectiveness of the Moving On program, and employed more rigorous, powerful research methods than Gehring, Van Voorhis, and Bell (2010). Duwe and Clark examined recidivism rates among those who participated in the program during two distinctive periods, one in which the program was implemented with high fidelity and the second during a period when the program was implemented with lower fidelity. When implemented with high fidelity, participants in the Moving On program were significantly less likely to be rearrested and reconvicted as compared to those in the matched sample who did not participate in the program.

Co-occurring Disorders

As indicated in chapter 1, abuse of drugs and alcohol are higher among female than male inmates and among those outside, with an estimated 47 percent to 62 percent of sisters inside qualifying for a substance use disorder (Mumola & Karberg, 2006; Tripodi & Pettus-Davis, 2013). Moreover, approximately 80 percent of sisters inside with substance abuse disorders have co-occurring mental health disorders (COD; Johnson et al., 2015). Given the prevalence and the distinctive needs of female returning citizens with COD, concerted attention is needed to care for these women and ameliorate the deleterious impact of COD on the women themselves, their families, and their communities. This is especially true as "female offenders with COD have greater aftercare needs but are less likely than women with substance use disorder alone to complete substance use aftercare programs" (Johnson et al., 2015, p. 418).

Johnson et al. (2015) conducted a study with 14 individual providers, including discharge planners and directors of reentry service programs, who served returning sisters at a single state prison and aftercare network. According to the providers, sisters inside with COD are a vulnerable population, and their needs during reentry are distinct from women who only suffer from substance use disorders as well as from men. Providers identified numerous triggers that cause depressed women with substance use disorders to relapse, such as: unhealthy romantic relationships, a lack of family modeling, a history of trauma or exploitation, family responsibilities and life stressors, discontinuing medication, and more. Although providers indicated that they cannot accurately predict who will and who will not relapse, they identified factors that seem to decrease women's risks. "Getting older, going back to supportive situations, distancing themselves from substance using or criminogenic peers, and having a feasible plan for post-release treatment are good prognostic indicators" of remaining sober (p. 424).

According to the providers who participated in the study, supporting returning sisters with COD requires establishing relationship with a service provider while still incarcerated and continuing that relationship following release (Johnson et al., 2015). That provider should then be available to the returning sister within twenty-four to seventy-two hours following her release in order to provide and be able to offer "assistance with managing multiple social service agencies" (p. 416). Providers shared significant concerns regarding the threats to well-being that female returning citizens experience as the result of unhealthy and unsupportive relationships. Therefore, returning sisters with COD need support from sober individuals, such as sponsors or mentors, and to establish a relationship with a mental health professional in order to address relationship, family, and self-esteem issues. Finally, returning sisters with COD need help establishing "realistic expectations for the difficulties of recovery/life skills" (p. 421).

Women reentering society following incarceration are often challenged to change "people, places, and things," which for many means ending unsupportive and unhealthy relationships and seeking better, sober social support. Social support is an important component of recovery and overcoming substance use disorders. In addition, many women with co-occurring disorders (COD) experience major depressive disorder (MDD), for which social support is also a helpful intervention. According to Johnson, Williams, and Zlotnick (2015), returning sisters with COD are at significant risk for relapse during the first days following release, a risk that is exacerbated by being around substance-abusing friends and family. Returning sisters whose sobriety is threatened are more likely to reach out to people with whom they have established relationships rather than strangers, and they often experience barriers to transportation and phone access. Based upon this knowledge, the authors conducted focus groups with female inmates in order to develop the Sober Network IPT intervention.

Sober Network IPT is a cell phone-based intervention for female returning citizens with COD. "Sober Network IPT works to buffer women against . . . relapse by actively working with them to have positive, reliable, familiar sources of sober support, including professional treatment services, in place before they leave prison" (Johnson, Williams, & Zlotnick, 2015, p. 332). The Sober Network IPT cell phone connects returning sisters to a prison-based counselor for three months as they work to develop sober community resources. It also connects them to other sober resources, including crisis lines and sober family members. Participants in the Sober Network IPT intervention also participated in twenty-four in-prison group therapy sessions wherein they learned how to develop a sober network and other relationship skills.

Sober Network IPT cell phones were given to eighteen female returning citizens with co-occurring disorders in two states (Johnson, Williams, & Zlotnick, 2015). Treatment started in prison, as referenced above, and returning sisters spoke to their prison-based counselors an average of twenty-two times during the first three months of their release. Although the study participants did not significantly increase their sober networks between the time of release and the end of three months, they did experience significant improvement in their drug/alcohol use and depressive symptoms between the baseline period and three months following release. Analysis revealed that female returning citizens value "familiar, continuous therapeutic relationships" (p. 344). Participants experienced their prison-based counselors as caring, nonjudgmental, dependable, and persistent. And finally, when returning sisters struggled during reentry, their instinct was to withdraw. They highlighted the importance of counselor-returning citizen confidentiality and the need they had to speak freely about their cravings to use and the challenges faced.

In a related study, Johnson et al. (2013) identified seven "recovery facilitators" among returning sisters with co-occurring substance use and major depressive disorder: the receipt of sober support; the avoidance of known relapse triggers; the experience of being sober in prison or the fear of additional incarceration due to relapse; the receipt of treatment in prison; feeling motivated and confident in one's ability to remain sober; an increase in self-awareness and an emphasis on self-care that was learned in prison; and housing and employment. The Sober Network IPT program and the findings revealed by Johnson et al. (2013) offer important implications for individuals and churches seeking to support returning sisters. The barriers and needs identified by the authors, as well as the relatively simple intervention employed, offer a wise, recommended practice for faith-based mentors as well as individuals and congregations seeking to support returning sisters.

Mentoring

When the National Reentry Resource Center (NRRC) was established under the Second Chance Act (SCA) in 2008, a block of grants was awarded to mentoring programs for adults and juveniles reentering the community following incarceration. Beginning in 2011, a smaller number of grants were also awarded to mentoring programs focused on the promotion of responsible parenting by returning citizens. Between 2009 and 2015, 147 of the 719 total grants awarded through the Second Chance Act focused on the provision of adult mentoring services (The Council of State Governments Justice Center, 2016b). The emphasis on funding mentoring programs resulted from over a decade's worth of research demonstrating the positive social, behavioral, and academic impact that mentoring can have on at-risk youth (Cobbs Fletcher, 2007). Funders hypothesized that mentoring aids returning citizens by providing them with trusting, consistent, and nonjudgmental relationships in a way that would facilitate navigating the barriers to reentry and managing related frustrations (Bauldry, Korom-Djakovic, McClanahan, McMaken, & Kotloff, 2009). The goal of most mentoring programs and relationships is to offer returning citizens support and a positive role model. However, research demonstrating the efficacy of mentoring relationships with female returning citizens is still in its nascent stage (Umez, de la Cruz, Richey, & Albis, 2017).

Research on the Ready4Work reentry program, a "partnership of local community- and/or faith-based organizations to provide ex-prisoners with targeted case management, employment services and mentoring," offers some insight into the efficacy of mentoring (Bauldry et al., 2009, p. 20). For example, returning citizens who are older, or are female without minor children, or who express greater religiosity, are more likely to participate in mentoring relationships (Bauldry et al., 2009). Mentoring relationships seem to be most effective when established pre-release (Bauldry et al., 2009). Although correlational rather than causational, returning citizens "who met with a mentor at least once were twice as likely to obtain a job as were those who were not mentored" (Bauldry et al., 2009, p. 15). Furthermore, those returning citizens with a mentor secured jobs more quickly and were more likely to retain those jobs.

Based upon interviews with fifteen participants in a Ready4Work program who opted not to participate in a mentoring relationship, Bauldry et al. (2009) identified barriers to the successful cultivation of a mentoring relationship. For example, some participants viewed mentoring as something for youth only and not a resource that they, as adults, would need. Some felt that all of their time and effort should be focused on securing employment. Some felt overwhelmed by the many demands and obligations they faced and did not feel they had the time to participate. Some were reticent to discuss their lives with strangers. Some were dubious regarding the motivations of mentors affiliated with faith-based organizations, suspecting that there was an ulterior motive. In addition, in a study conducted on the mentoring component of the Ready4Work program, Bauldry et al. (2009) found that most mentoring relationships were quite brief, with 68 percent lasting three months or fewer and 89 percent lasting just six months or fewer.

Researchers and practitioners also advocate for the use of peer-mentoring services for returning citizens, wherein successful returning citizens serve as mentors to women coming home. Welcome Home Ministries in San Diego County implemented a peer-mentoring program in which successful graduates of the program serve as mentors/case managers (Goldstein, Warner-Robbins, McClean, Macatula, & Conklin, 2009). The relationships begin prior to the mentee's release from prison and, upon release, the mentee is met at the prison and welcomed into a program that addresses co-occurring disorders and offers wraparound services. According to a study of forty-four returning sisters enrolled in the program, there was a "77% reduction in the rate of recidivism measured over a 12-month period postrelease. In addition, a large percentage of women are able to participate in outpatient psychiatric and substance abuse programs, become educated, and find housing and employment" (Goldstein et al., 2009, p. 312).

For the past fifteen years there has been overwhelming consensus that the government alone cannot facilitate the rehabilitation of the millions of men and women behind bars and reentering community, and that partnerships with community programs and faith-based organizations are imperative. As noted throughout the book, churches and people of faith need to work toward abolishing the prison industrial complex by expanding prison ministry beyond bars. Many of the programs with a mentoring component are supported by faith-based organizations, and faith-based mentoring is an important way that people of faith can support returning citizens. According to Johnson (2011), there is a deficit of mentors in pre- and post-release programs, and churches have an important role to play as they are both volunteer-rich and compelled by Christ to meet this need.

For example, Court Services and Offender Supervision Agency for the District of Columbia (CSOSA) began a Faith-Based Initiative in 2002, with mentoring as one of the initiative's central components. CSOSA partnered with faith institutions to connect returning citizens to mentors in order "to build strong moral values and provide positive role models for the men and women returning to our communities through coaching and spiritual guidance" (CSOSA, n.d., para. 4). CSOSA mentors assist returning sisters by connecting them with faith-based resources. Research suggests that the mentoring relationships influence positive outcomes including fewer parole violations, fewer positive tests for drug use, and less recidivism/rearrest (CSOSA, n.d.). Programs like this are replicated throughout the country, and assistance and guidelines for establishing mentoring programs are readily available (Cobbs Fletcher, 2007; Umez et al., 2017).

RELIGION AND REENTRY

What is the role of religion during reentry? Prior to this book's publication, research on the spiritual and religious experiences of returning sisters was scant. This book examines such experiences in order to posit recommendations for revised praxes of care that expand prison ministry beyond bars. Below is a brief overview of existing faith-based reentry services, the efficacy of such programs, and their benefits and perils.

As evidenced in chapter 1, many sisters inside do indeed "find God" in prison. Finding God often results from the way addiction caused sisters inside to feel sick and tired of being sick and tired. Finding God may result from the experience of incarceration itself as prison causes many sisters inside to feel broken and ashamed. Finding God can be correlated with the psychological, cultural, and social dynamics of life behind bars as such experiences oftentimes compel sisters inside to appeal to and pray to the God of their understanding, and to seek out positive, spiritually grounded people. Therefore, finding God inside of prison leads many sisters inside to be open to or to seek out faith-based reentry services.

Formal and informal faith-based reentry services have existed for centuries, although prior to the research grounding this book, little was known about the spiritual and religious experiences of returning sisters. Yet, as previously mentioned, there is great ambiguity and little consistency regarding what constitutes a "faith-based program." Some faith-based programs are "faith-saturated" and others seem to be predominantly secular in name and practice (Mears, 2007). Moreover, there is "no master list of faith-based reentry programs and no single agent responsible for tracking faith-based reentry efforts at either the federal level or across the 50 states" (Willison, Brazzell, & Kim, 2011).

In an effort to clarify some of this ambiguity, the Urban Institute conducted an exploratory study intended to determine what defines a faith-based program and how faith "works" in these programs (Willison et al., 2011). Willison et al. (2011) used factor analysis to analyze the characteristics of faith-based programs and cluster analysis in order to group the participant programs within a typology. Eighty-five percent of the forty-eight programs surveyed self-identified as "faith-based," and this designation was claimed more often by programs affiliated with the Abrahamic traditions (Christianity, Judaism, and Islam; others preferred the term "spiritually-based"). However, less than half of the programs reported an affiliation or association with a religious community. Nearly 75 percent of the programs agreed or strongly agreed "that program commitment to clients is based on religious beliefs or conviction. A similar percentage (73.2 percent) reported that spiritual principles or religious beliefs formed the basis for the program's model" (p. 3). Yet despite this fact, program activities were not overwhelmingly religious. The activities rated as most important to the programs were largely secular, such as helping clients to create a support system, rather than faith-based, such as prayer or the study of sacred texts. The top five services offered included "ministry/spiritual development (85 percent); life skills training (83 percent); mentoring (81 percent); aftercare/reentry services (79 percent); and employment services (73 percent)" (p. 4). In addition, it is interesting to note that 42 percent of the programs surveyed received government funding and 83 percent received funding from religious institutions. This study helped to clarify what faith-based programs are and how faith "works" in them by deducing the programs' identities, missions, vision, and staff had an explicit faith component. Faith-based programs were not frequently affiliated with religious communities (i.e., churches) and religious transformation or conversion was overwhelmingly not required (Willison et al., 2011).

Why are faith-based reentry services important? First, faith-based reentry services are essential because "decades of research document that religiosity or religious commitment is associated with reductions in delinquent behavior and deviant activities" (Johnson, 2011, p. 175; see Appendix D). Religion acts as a protective factor against crime and delinquency. This is true even when religion is defined simply by church attendance (Johnson, 2011). Although a causal relationship has not been empirically demonstrated, it seems that regular church attendance increases one's social network and promotes a sense of belonging. Churches often instill a sense of civic responsibility, morality, and concern for others. These factors then lead to a reduction in harmful or criminal actions. Moreover, not only does religious participation reduce destructive behavior, but it likely contributes to or increases prosocial behaviors. Research shows that "religious commitment is a source for promoting or enhancing beneficial outcomes like well-being; hope, meaning, and purpose; self-esteem; and even educational attainment" (Johnson, 2011, p. 182).

Second, faith-based reentry services are important because even though religion may increase desistance and reduce recidivism, many returning citizens do not seek out the sanctuary of a church following release. More will be said about this in chapter 4, but it is not enough for congregants to sit in the pews and proclaim radical hospitality to returning citizens. Churches need to be proactive in connecting with returning citizens to offer a network of care and support. Seeking out a faith family during reentry is often experienced as another task in an already overwhelming list of demands. Yet, according to Johnson (2011),

> The decision to bypass the church is a recipe for disaster–effectively separating former prisoners from the support they would absolutely have to have in order to live a law-abiding and productive life in the free world. Without connections to the church, ex-prisoners will not have a mentor to hold them accountable, and they will not have access to the vibrant networks of social support that exist in so many congregations. (pp. 157–158)

Returning citizens need a network of support comprised of caring individuals who can help them to overcome the barriers of reentry and become an integrated member of community in a way that many have not experienced before.

Third, rehabilitation does not occur by faith alone. Many Christians believe that sisters inside need Christ. But far too often they overlook returning sisters' needs for housing, transportation, mentoring, and support. The spiritual conversion or renewal that happens for a significant number of inmates is encouraging, but it is not a panacea for the barriers they will face as returning citizens. Returning citizens, as shown throughout this chapter, need tangible, material assistance in addition to spiritual support. Churches and faith-based programs are in a unique position to address their needs in a holistic manner. Ultimately, the spiritual growth that occurs behind bars will not continue if returning citizens face the overwhelming demands of reentry alone.

There is, however, a paradox inherent in the provision of faith-based reentry services. That is, the government alone cannot adequately provide for the needs of returning citizens, nor can faith-based reentry programs (Erzen, 2017; Johnson, 2011). Since President George W. Bush established the White House Office of Faith-Based and Community Initiatives in 2001, now renamed the Office of Faith-Based and Neighborhood Partnerships, the federal government aimed to create more effective partnerships with faith-based organizations. These efforts were increased with the passage of the Second Chance Act in 2008. "Resource-strapped policymakers and criminal justice practitioners are increasingly turning to the faith community to help meet the multiple needs of the roughly 700,000 individuals released annually from the nation's prisons" (Willison et al., 2011, p. 1). Despite the benefits of faith-based reentry services, the government should not support such programs to the detriment of programs that meet the needs of returning citizens from minority or no faith backgrounds. According to McRoberts (2002),

"Protective measures, then, should ensure that ex-offenders are not herded against their will into church programs, but they should also ensure that existing secular programs are not starved to support church-based ones" (p. 10). This issue will be further addressed in chapter 4 when we examine how faith-based organizations can partner with the government to effectively meet the needs of female returning citizens.

Another dilemma in the provision of faith-based reentry services is that there is little scientific evidence supporting the efficacy of such services, which is due, in part, to the methodological problems inherent in research of this nature. For example, in order to demonstrate the efficacy of faith-based reentry programs, rigorous research practices require that such programs evidence success in comparison to an alternate situation. That is to say, faith-based reentry programs should show that they are more effective at reducing recidivism than no treatment at all, than "'business as usual' (i.e., the de facto set of services that released prisoners may typically access)" (Mears, Roman, Wolff, & Buck, 2006, p. 354), or than a comparable program that is not faith-based. However, this approach to demonstrating efficacy is problematic given that many faith-based programs employ "secular" interventions, such as cognitive behavioral therapy, that may not have a faith component and are already an evidence-based treatment. Research on the efficacy of faith-based reentry programs entails "considerable methodological problems, including a lack of random assignment, no use of controls or comparison groups, self-selection biases, and limited measures of impact" (Mears et al., 2006, p. 359). Moreover, the research that is available, despite its methodological flaws, is conflicting, with some studies evidencing the positive outcomes of faith-based programs (O'Connor, 2005) and other studies showing no difference in recidivism rates between the treatment group and a matched sample (Johnson, Larson, & Pitts, 1997).

As previously stated, an overdependence by the government on faith-based organizations to provide reentry services is problematic (Erzen, 2017; Johnson, 2011). Additional research is needed to evidence the efficacy of these programs as evidence-based practices are preferable, and tax-payer dollars should ideally be spent on "what works." In addition, "there exists a level of funding and bureaucratic entanglement at which church-state cooperation becomes state domination and coercion" (McDaniel, Davis, & Neff, 2005, p. 166). In order to uphold separation of church and state, faith-based reentry programs may capitulate to state demands in a way that ignores or even violates their central values and doctrines. Finally, adherents of minority religious traditions, and even Christians, may experience marginalization or oppression as the result of such programs. For example, in Texas and Minnesota, two states that implemented Prison Fellowship Ministries' InnerChange Freedom Initiative, volunteers who wished to assist inmates were required to sign a faith statement proclaiming "the life-transforming power of Jesus Christ" and the inerrancy of the Bible, which resulted in the exclusion of many motivated volunteers (McDaniel et al., 2005, p. 175). The quagmire is that religious groups should not be required to renounce or overlook the central tenets and doctrines of their faith in order to help inmates and returning citizens, and yet prison staff and inmates alike should not be forced to believe in or practice a religion in order to be employed or receive rehabilitative services. As referenced in Appendix C, this danger was made quite public when a federal judge ruled that the InnerChange Freedom Initiative program in Iowa "coerced inmates into adhering to Christian beliefs and doctrines" (Mears, 2007, p. 32). According to McDaniel et al. (2005), religious programs and doctrines function in a coercive manner when they are the only means of rehabilitation offered to brothers and sisters inside. For example, "American inmates of the 19th century who wished to 'better themselves' during their incarceration were offered the Bible or nothing at all to achieve their goals" (p. 176).

Nevertheless, Christians and people of faith need to understand the spiritual and religious experiences of returning sisters and create careplans and programs to aid them. According to Johnson (2011),

> We are in need of a plan where coordination and collaboration are central, where the goals of the reentry model are realistically available, where the specific elements of the plan are replicable in any community, and finally, where the plan is affordable and does not add new costs to already overburdened correctional budgets. (pp. 200–201)

Project Sister Connect addresses this need by providing a model for justice-seeking spiritual support for returning sisters.

SUMMARY

Justice-seeking spiritual support for returning sisters requires understanding their immediate needs as well as the barriers they face to successful reentry as described in chapter 2. Project Sister Connect addresses these experiences by enacting the Two Feet of Love in Action through both charitable works and social justice. Part II of *Women Leaving Prison* examines returning sisters' spiritual and religious experiences during reentry and details a call for revised prison ministry praxis in Project Sister Connect.

Part II

UNDERSTANDING AND TRANSFORMING REENTRY: SPIRITUALITY AND SISTERHOOD

Chapter 3

Faith Beyond Bars

*Returning Sisters' Spiritual and
Religious Experiences during Reentry*

Understanding the spiritual and religious experiences of returning sisters requires elevating their voices which are too often silenced. To accomplish this goal, two qualitative research studies were conducted that employed interpretative phenomenological analysis (IPA), a research methodology that is "concerned with understanding personal lived experience and thus with exploring persons' relatedness to, or involvement in, a particular event or process (phenomenon)" (Smith, Flowers, & Larkin, 2009, p. 40). Chapter 3 presents the findings from the two qualitative investigations grounded in semi-structured interviews with nineteen returning sisters and five faith-based mentors. Chapter 3 reports how returning sisters made meaning and sense of their spiritual and religious experiences during reentry. It demonstrates how they understood God and God's role in their reentry, the types of spiritual and religious support they did and did not receive from individuals and congregations, the ways their beliefs both helped and hindered their reentry experience, and their experiences with faith-based mentors. Chapter 3 also details faith-based mentors' experiences with returning sisters and highlights their observations on their sisters' spiritual and religious experiences. Chapter 3, in dialogue with the wisdom of chapters 1 and 2, serves as the basis for Project Sister Connect, the model for revised prison ministry praxis posited in chapter 4.

The methodology employed in the two qualitative studies is detailed in Appendices A and B, and the findings are reported below. The first study conducted with returning sisters resulted in the generation of three superordinate themes: God and reentry; church and reentry; and faith-based mentors and reentry. The lived experiences of returning sisters' are further elucidated by the second study's findings wherein faith-based mentors shared their perspectives on returning sisters' spiritual and religious experiences.

THE SPIRITUAL AND RELIGIOUS
EXPERIENCES OF RETURNING SISTERS

Table 3.1 provides an overview of the first study's findings and details how the emergent themes were organized into the three superordinate themes.

Superordinate Theme: God and Reentry

Returning sisters shared extensively about their understandings of and relationships with God during reentry. Four emergent themes were generated based upon the interviews conducted with the nineteen study participants. The emergent themes related to participants' understandings of God and God's ways, their experiences relating to God during reentry, their understandings of how God, reentry, and recovery are related, and their lived experiences of faith during reentry.

Emergent Theme: Understandings of God's Nature and God's Ways

Whether or not one believes in or adheres to a religious tradition, each study participant has a religious location (Greider, 2015) and therefore a unique understanding of and relationship with or to God. Although not all participants identified as Christian (see Table 0.1 in the Introduction), all nineteen participants spoke about God, God's nature, and God's ways, which resulted in the generation of five codes. Table 3.2 reports the five codes that contributed to the generation of the emergent theme, understandings of God's nature and God's ways, and provides a statement made by a study participant that illustrates each code.

God's omnipotence. Many participants stated explicitly that "God is in charge." Participants expressed the belief that God has a reason for everything,

Table 3.1   Findings

Superordinate Theme	Emergent Themes
God and reentry	Understandings of God's nature and God's ways
	Experiences relating to God during reentry
	God, reentry, and recovery
	Lived experiences of faith during reentry
Church and reentry	Church support during reentry
	Relating to Church folk
	The search for Church
	Barriers to Church participation
Faith-based mentors and reentry	Lived experiences in faith-based mentoring relationships

Source: Copyright 2018 by Author.

Table 3.2 Understandings of God's Nature and God's Ways

Emergent Theme	Codes	Excerpts
Understandings of God's nature and God's ways	God's omnipotence	"God is in charge and He has the final say so. He shows us all around."
	God's providence	"I do believe there are experiences whether it be prison, incarceration . . . whatever . . . it's always God working in your favor."
	God is in adversity	"I think God puts the same situation in your life until you get it right. It's a test, because we don't have the patience to go through it."
	How God responds	"He made sure that everything I prayed for I got . . . My release, parole, everything. He just made it all happen for me."
	Being obedient to God and getting out of God's way	"I know that God is great and he has the final say so. And I'm just so happy to say that I no longer put my hands in stuff. I move out of my own way so that He can lead the way."

Source: Copyright 2018 by Author.

which enabled them to put their trust in God's omnipotence. As Shawna succinctly stated, "God is in charge and He has the final say so. He shows us all around. His handwriting is everywhere." This belief and this way of relating to God provided Shawna with a sense of comfort. She continued, "It's just a wonderful feeling when you can get to a place where you know that God is in charge. And that when we are worried about what's going to become, He's already worked it out." Andrea shared a similar perspective on God's omnipotence. Andrea explained how God's power is revealed in both blessing and hardship. According to Andrea, God took the lives of family members who enabled her addiction, specifically her parents, her brother, and her son, in order to make her stronger. Andrea spoke at length about her son who, at age eighteen, was shot eight times and survived, but at age twenty-one was tortured and murdered. Looking back at that experience Andrea said,

I was upset and mad with God. "Why would you take him?" He didn't take the person that did what they did to him, and tortured him, and kidnapped him, and threw his body out there . . . but I still feel like, just by me being raised that way, that our life's already planned. . . . He take people for reasons, and that's why I know He took my loved ones.

Trina's understanding of God's omnipotence was a bit different from other participants' in that she believed both in God's power and humanity's free will. She stated, "I know that God has a path for me already I have to follow. I know I have free will. I also know that He saved me from the pits of hell." Yet even still, after being in and out of jail and prison since 1995, Trina viewed her free will as related to God's plan. She continued, "I think that He had to let me do all I did and get to where I had to get to before He would have my eyes to actually be opened where I could see that it was a better way that always has been there." Participants' perspectives on God's omnipotence are further revealed below in relation to their understandings of God's providence and what results when one is obedient to God and lets God take the "driver's seat."

God's providence. The majority of participants expressed how God does everything for a reason, and many spoke about God's providence: not only is God omniscient and all-knowing about the future, but God cares for and guides God's creation to the best possible future. As noted in chapter 1, many participants expressed the belief that God caused their incarceration for a reason. For example, Andrea was pregnant and abusing drugs, and from Andrea's perspective, God put her in prison to save her baby. She stated,

That's why I said I got locked up . . . I believe that God had a reason for that . . . because I was pregnant. He knew if I left out there and got that money, then I would have probably messed her [the baby] up, or something else, or someone else.

I asked Andrea if she saw that as the purpose of her incarceration even when she was in prison, or if that was the meaning she made of her experience in hindsight. She shared how she prayed to get out of prison, believing that there was a better place for her, but that she "stayed in the room, read my Bible, and prayed that when ready for me to go, He'll be ready for me to go. He'll let me out." Andrea also shared her belief that God put people in her daughter's life to take care of her during Andrea's active addiction, and that even today God continues to guide her life. She stated,

I know that God has a reason for everything. He's still holding onto me with all that I done been through. Long as I keep doing what I'm doing, He's gonna keep His hands on me . . . I might have to do the foot work, but I know He's the one who has the power.

According to participants, not only does God do everything for a reason, but God sees our future. Shawna was addicted to drugs and had prayed for a change. Prior to her incarceration, she got clean and considered her prayers answered. She was working at the time, and soon realized that without a drug habit she had a little extra money. She developed what she called an addiction to money, which led her to maintain her sobriety but begin selling drugs. She said,

> So I began to sell. Don't matter what you do with that stuff, there's no good to it. . . . So I guess [my incarceration] was God's way of saying, "You prayed to get clean and now you're going to do this? No you're not!"

It was not "the addiction of using, it was the addiction of making the money" that landed Shawna in prison. Yet God saw her future and made it possible for her to enter a residential transitional program upon her release from prison. Shawna said,

> God can see what we can't see. The unknown He knows. So was I headed back that way [toward drugs]? Perhaps, maybe I was. And He just said, "No. I'm not even going to allow you to even get mixed up in that stuff again."

As Shawna said, because God saw her future, God made a way for her to enter a residential reentry program and to continue her healing journey.

Rochelle also shared how through God's providence God meets returning citizens' needs during reentry. For Rochelle, God's provision was mediated through "a little girl that lived, slept in the cell across from me." Rochelle was in her cell, voicing to another sister inside her concerns about release. She did not have a place to go to and she did not want to live with any family members. The "little girl" told her about a reentry program and gave her the phone number. Rochelle called, set up an interview, and was accepted.

> So that was God. . . . He knew I was worried because I had prayed on it. And then the girl spoke to me and gave me their number. And then they accepted me. And I said, "Oh God! You are really awesome!" You know He started manifesting everything that I was asking for. . . . So everything that I've asked for, whether it's small, minute, or great, He's given it to me.

Lisa also spoke about God's providence and recounted how God had taken care of her. Lisa had a history of addiction and, in order to support her drug dependence, she engaged in prostitution. She believed that God started preparing her for her recovery and a life with God long before she got clean, and that God cared for and protected her all along the way. Lisa shared,

> Every time I went to the clinic I had a different venereal disease. I'm just glad today I'm not HIV, and I don't have AIDS. And you know, maybe part of that

was believing in God and sticking with God. Every time I lay with somebody and they tell me they was clean, somebody had to believe in me and know that I had a future ahead and that this day that's here today has came. It was coming . . . this is what God prepared me for a long time ago and it was just waiting. But until I started believing in something other than other people, it wouldn't have never happened.

God is in adversity. As evidenced above, numerous participants' expressed the belief that God does everything for a reason and that through God's providence God leads returning sisters toward their greatest good. Participants also explained, however, how God sometimes uses adversity or hardship in order to incite growth and strength. Recall, for example, the way Andrea believed that God took her son and permitted his murder to put a stop to the way her son enabled Andrea's addiction and to help make her strong. Similarly, Rochelle expressed the belief that God caused her to stumble in order to make her strong. She said, "He's got me through all of this. And He's not finished, because He's still putting stumbling blocks in my way to step over, you know, to help me . . . to see how I'm going to handle it." I asked her for an example of a time when God caused her to stumble in order to help her, and she talked about when she was denied disability benefits. Feeling defeated, she shared her feelings with a friend who referred her to someone that could help her to appeal her case. She also mentioned it to a case manager at her reentry program, who referred her to the same gentleman her friend had mentioned. Rochelle viewed the experience of being denied disability benefits as God putting a stumbling block in her way, but then saw God's providence in the fact that two separate individuals referred her to the same resource for help in appealing her case. Shanice was in prison twice and also shared how God is active in adversity but uses it for good. She stated, "I think God puts the same situation in your life until you get it right. It's a test, because we don't have the patience to go through it."

As noted in chapter 1, given the high percentage of returning sisters with substance use disorders, past and present, changing people, places, and things can sometimes make reentry easier. Lisa, however, returned to the same neighborhood where she used to get high. At the time of the interview, Lisa was living in a residential transitional program, but prior to her incarceration she was sleeping in a truck parked right down the street. She viewed her ability to stay clean in the same neighborhood where she got high to be God's work and God's ability to make her stronger in the face of adversity. Lisa stated,

I got high in this same neighborhood and it's the same neighborhood I'm recovering in. I'm not on probation. Nothing is holding me here. I'm here on my own. So that's how God holds me. Any time I walk out this door and walk down to that corner store, and people not approaching me because they see that I want better for myself. That's God working. Because some people don't even have that choice. And some people that get clean as soon as they walk out that door somebody else see them they wanna get them high. So you know, that's how God walks me through. He helped me get clean in the same neighborhood I used in.

Lisa went on to explain how God continues to keep her strong and never abandoned her. She referenced the famous Footprints prayer and thanked God as she's now able to walk on her own.

How God responds. As evidenced above, the majority of study participants expressed belief in God's omnipotence and providence even in the midst of adversity. In addition to explaining God's nature, participants also explained God's way of being. Specifically, they shared how it is that they experience God's response to requests for help and assistance. As mentioned above, Trina believes that God is in charge, but also believes that she has free will. In the midst of her addiction, God "took care of me even when I didn't believe that I could take care of myself." But in Trina's mind, she was the one who, with God's help, initiated her recovery. She stated,

When I finally did that [asked for help] with an open heart, He got to see in my heart. Because they say He knows anyway. I think when I finally said, "My God, I can't do this no more," then He was ready to show me another way. A way that had always been there had I chose right.

God was there, ready and waiting to help her to heal from addiction, when Trina asked for it.

Shanice shared how God gave her everything she had asked for while incarcerated, but following her release she fell prey to temptations. Shanice had a year to serve in prison and contemplated taking sleeping pills to "numb out" and pass her time. But instead she decided to stay in her cell, read the Bible, and pray. And as a result, God acted "favorable." She said, "He made sure that everything I prayed for I got. . . . My release, parole, everything. He just made it all happen for me. I lost sight of that once I got out. I started doin' what I wanted to do again." As previously stated, Shanice had no reentry plan and knew in advance that she would return to her boyfriend's house and to a life of drugs and alcohol. Nevertheless, from her perspective, when she was being faithful, God answered her prayers favorably and gave Shanice everything she prayed for.

Finally, Shawna and Malea both noted how although God always responds to prayer, God also has a sense of humor. While incarcerated, Shawna repeatedly heard from other inmates about a particular reentry program. She went to see the case manager in prison who, upon hearing her background, referred her to the same reentry program. Shawna then went to a reentry event inside the prison and the first person she met was a representative of the same reentry program. In recounting this story, Shawna stated, "God does have a sense of humor, doesn't He?" Malea also saw the humor in God's omnipotence and providence and the way God responds to prayer. At the time of Malea's first incarceration, she was a "straight dope dealer."

> I didn't get addicted until the second time around. I tried the product and was off to the races. I didn't realize the addiction until the third time [in prison]. Always through that, I always leaned on God for help. When you call out, watch what you ask for. He's got a funny way sometimes. [God said,] "Okay. I'm gonna help you. Let's get you back here [in prison] and get yourself together."

Malea went on to say that "it was time for me to sit." She'd leaned on God throughout her years of dealing and doing drugs, but she never figured God would put her back in prison to heal her. She found the irony of that to be amusing and indicative of God's humor.

Being obedient to God and getting out of God's way. Around half of the study's participants indicated that receiving God's providence requires being obedient to God and letting God lead the way. Tammy, who was in and out of jails and prisons twenty-five times, said she would not have successfully completed parole if she didn't have "some faith that there's something down the end of this road if I do the right thing. You can call it what you want. I call it God. . . . So every time I did the right thing, and kept praying, everything fell in place." Chelsea also spoke about the need to be obedient to God. She shared how the residential reentry program where she lived at the time of the interview was a "blessing." She continued,

> I feel like He gave me that and in return I don't use drugs. I don't hang out with the same negative people. I've changed my ways. . . . He opened the doors for me and in turn I gotta do my part. I gotta show up every day and do what I'm supposed to do.

According to Chelsea, she used to have a "no consequence type of attitude," but she now believes that "I have to answer to God." Being obedient to God not only means choosing right behavior, as Tammy and Chelsea illustrated, but allowing God to take the lead.

Martha shared an elaborate metaphor of what it means for her to get in the back seat of the car and allow God to take the driver's seat. Martha was addicted to heroin and after four years in prison she knew she needed help learning how to lead a life free from addiction. So she prayed to God and God made a way for her to participate in residential treatment upon her release from prison. She said,

I used to cry and I'd talk to God and I told Him what I want and stuff. And He started putting stuff in motion. And I got in the backseat and let Him start driving the car for me. And stuff just started working for me.

She went on to share how God can't take you where you need to go unless you "stop driving the car" and let God get in the driver's seat.

Emergent Theme: Experiences Relating to God during Reentry

With a sense of how participants understood God's nature and ways, we now turn to examine how participants related to God during their reentry experiences. Table 3.3 reports the six codes that contributed to the generation of the emergent theme, experiences relating to God during reentry, and provides a statement made by a study participant that illustrates each code.

Table 3.3   Experiences Relating to God during Reentry

Emergent Theme	Codes	Excerpts
Experiences relating to God during reentry	Desire to know God or a higher power	"My spirit within myself that knows that it's something greater, someone greater, and I yearn for that connection. Regardless of how much pained up I am I still want that connection."
	I need God	"I wouldn't have been able to get through what I've gotten through if it wouldn't have been for God. I dare not give that to man, not at all. You've gotta have a higher power."
	God is working in me and supporting me to put my life back together	"He's [God's] the one that's got me through everything I've been through, you know, good or bad."
	Gratitude to God	"I'm just so thankful that I have a higher power, that I was given the opportunity, a second chance, to be here."
	Giving up on God during reentry	"After so many incarcerations and so many tries of getting it right, you kind of give up [on yourself and God]."
	Blaming God	"'Man. He's supposed to help me out.' Then I'm like, 'Well why is He not helping me out when I go to prison?'"

Source: Copyright 2018 by Author.

Desire to know God or a higher power. First, participants shared how they desired a relationship with God, and particularly not "someone else's God," but the "God of my understanding." In many ways this finding reflects the fact that sixteen of the nineteen study participants had histories of substance use and addiction and, at the time of the interview, many were involved in twelve-step programs like Alcoholics Anonymous (AA) and Narcotics Anonymous (NA). Participants expressed a desire to know God and to maintain close relationship with God. For example, Deborah was raised in the Baptist faith and her grandmother made sure she went to church every Sunday. Deborah shared how prior to her incarceration she "had thoughts about God, I always knew there was a God, but I wasn't that big on it." While in prison she went to church sometimes "to get more understanding." I asked her what made her want to know more and she replied,

> They say there's a hell and a heaven. I don't wanna do down. I'm not sayin' that I'm goin' to hell because you can change your life to be better. I just wanna know God for me. Because if it had not been for God I wouldn't be where I'm at today.

Prison also gave Treva the opportunity to get "back to my road to finding God, finding my higher power. It put me in better touch with God and having more time to sit down to further know Him." Treva shared how she was raised in church and knew God, but it wasn't until she was incarcerated and then released that she was able to get "to know Him on a more personal level." Danielle also shared how she has

> always yearned to have a spiritual connection with God. Even in my addiction I went to church. Even if I was high. Even if I had to do the drugs in the bathroom of the church. I was determined to let God know that I'm here. I love you. Please, start loving me.

Danielle recounted the many times she'd been raped and "pained up" and how she questioned where God was in those experiences. Yet during her reentry, she continued to seek that deeper connection with "something greater, someone greater . . . regardless of how much pained up I am."

Finally, participants also expressed how that deeper spiritual connection has to be with the God of your understanding. According to Deborah, "You knew your parent's or your grandmother's God, but you gotta get to know God for you." Sandra also recognized this, and prison and reentry enabled her to begin establishing that connection with the God of her understanding. She said, "I did learn to get a God for myself, not my mother's God, but my own God." Prison and reentry have also helped Trina to realize how she was "worshipping a God my mother and them knew" and to begin "to learn Him for myself." She stated how during her incarceration she was engaging in misconduct that resulted in her getting

> more time than I was facing from the get go. And I just had to call on something greater than myself. To please help me because I couldn't help myself no more. So I don't know if I found the one [the God] of my own or decided to draw back on the one that I was raised with, which I'm trying to learn Him for myself. But I do know there's something greater than me.

Trina was trying to learn who God was for her based on her desire to "call on something greater than myself."

I need God. Like Trina, other participants shared how both in prison and during reentry they needed God or a Higher Power, and they warned about what can happen if you start taking God for granted. Treva had been out of prison for just two months at the time of our interview. She reflected on the role God had played in her life and the importance of having a higher power. She stated,

> I know God is in my life. I feel God in my life. I feel the difference inside of me because if it had not been for that I wouldn't be where I'm at today. I've had a lot of trials and tribulations, and I know that I couldn't have got nowhere—I wouldn't have been able to get through what I've gotten through if it wouldn't have been for God. I dare not give that to man, not at all. You've gotta have a higher power. I know that there is a God.

Trina also shared the importance of God in helping her to transcend trials and tribulations in life, in prison, and in reentry. She stated, "I needed something greater than myself to help me through this process. I could not do this by myself." Tammy's need for God was grounded in the need to depend on another source of strength and power. She explained how this is particularly helpful when in prison:

> Spirituality, even in the prison system, can be a source of power. Because some things we as humans, not even in our own strength, can some things get done. They have to be power and it has to come from somewhere.

And for Tammy, that source of strength comes from her higher power. Shanice also shared how she could not navigate the reentry journey without God and God's guidance. She said,

> I need Him to do it. I can't do anything without Him. I have to deal with my issues, whether I want to or not, and that helps me knowing that He's gonna be

behind me doin' everything possible to help me. The only thing He can do is guide me. We have choices. Right, wrong, left, yes, no. You choose, and I had to have faith to choose the right one to know that He's gonna be behind me in every choice that I make. The right choice.

But when Shanice was released and things started to work in her favor, she "put Him on the side. 'Okay, God. I got this.'" She shared her mistaken conception that "I didn't need Him anymore, and we always need God. I was like, 'Okay, God got me through that [prison]. Okay, I got this [reentry]. I'm gonna get a job.' But nothing ever works out without Him." It was clear from participants that the need for God or a higher power is not left at the prison gate.

God is working in me and supporting me to put my life back together. Participants shared their sense that God was at work in their lives offering unwavering support and helping to put their lives back together following incarceration. As Treva stated,

> God was at work with me when I was in [prison]. God was at work with me when He brought me here. God has been at work with me long time before I even hit [the state] . . . I know God is in my life. I feel God in my life. I feel the difference inside of me because if it had not been for that I wouldn't be where I'm at today.

As previously mentioned, Lisa compared God's action in her life with the Footprints prayer. She commented that God was always walking along beside her and "He didn't abandon me, you know, and I'm able to walk on my own now." She attributed the fact that she did not contract HIV despite her unsafe sexual practices to her unwavering faith in God and to God's unwavering support of her. "I just say never underestimate the powers of God. You understand me. And what He can do. Just because you don't see, believe, or touch Him, you know, He still works." Rochelle echoed God's steadfast support when she stated, "He's the one that's got me through everything I've been through, you know, good or bad. You know I lean on Him a lot for everything. Even before I make decisions I pray on it. So God has been very good to me." And because of this participants, like Trina, shared how "everything that had been stripped down from me, God has slowly put back in my life again."

Gratitude to God. In response to participants' need for God and God's unwavering support, participants expressed gratitude to God. As noted above, Trina was working to differentiate the God of her mother and her childhood from the God of her own understanding. And as she worked that process during reentry, she expressed her profound gratitude to God for what God has done in her life. She said,

I know that God has a path for me already I have to follow. I know I have free will. I also know that He saved me from the pits of hell. So I look at it like, why can't I go and worship who I think that I understand every Sunday? And as I go every Sunday I learn more about Him, and I'll come to understand what it is and who it is that I'm worshipping . . . I have Sunday to just kick back and say "thank you," to the God that I worship. "Thank you, Jesus oh Lord, for giving me your grace and your mercy and allowing me to even make it to church on Sunday."

Treva also expressed tremendous gratitude to her higher power. She recounted how overwhelmed she can be by her gratitude and the fact that some nights it prevents her from sleeping and moves her to tears. She said,

> I'm just so thankful that I have a higher power, that I was given the opportunity, a second chance, to be here. With all that I've been through, I'm thankful to have made it out whole, with my mind, with my limbs . . . I'm very grateful to my higher power, and I would like to do everything that I can do to prove that I'm grateful.

Detailed above are four ways that participants related to God that are overwhelmingly positive. However, participants' relationships with and experiences of God during reentry were not entirely helpful. Participants shared times when they gave up on God during reentry and blamed God when they did not feel God's support and care. Giving up on God may, for some, be part of a larger process of spiritual growth, but it is important to present returning sisters' experiences of both spiritual consolation and desolation.

Giving up on God during reentry. Danielle and Shanice both spoke poignantly about how they gave up on God and the loss of faith they experienced during reentry. When Danielle was released from prison, she wasn't "ready to be clean." She was angry with herself because she'd gotten "the information to stay clean . . . the information on how to live life on life's terms," but after her release she "rolled in the street. I did what I had to do since I was very young." Danielle reflected upon how she "pick and chose" when she "wanted God to be there" for her. She said,

> It's only when I needed something or you know wanted something at that time. I'm being honest. You know because I got to a point whereas though God ain't going to work for me anyway, 'cause I done lost my boys [both her sons were murdered]. I been out there all them years on drugs and all that stuff done happen. So I figured what's the use. After so many incarcerations and so many tries of getting it right, you kind of give up.

Danielle was caught in the revolving door of incarceration. She was frustrated with herself and the struggles she experienced trying to get clean. She was angry at God that both her sons were murdered while she was locked up. And even though she changed people, places, and things following her release, found a new church community, and went to worship every Sunday, her relationship with God was ambivalent at best.

As previously mentioned, even while in prison Shanice knew she would start drinking and drugging with her boyfriend upon her release. And even though she'd been reading the Bible and praying during her incarceration, she "lost focus" and started "worrying about other things" when she went home. Shanice shared how this should not have happened because "when you believe in God, you believe in God. Most people don't lose your faith like that, but for me, it was hard." She recounted how her prayer life and engagement with scripture changed incrementally. She went from a devout practice every morning and every night to not

> praying at all. Then I stopped reading my Bible in the morning. I'm gonna read it at night. He understands. I stopped reading my Bible at night. It's like a trickledown effect . . . I still had faith, but without the practice, faith is no good.

Shanice had not been part of a church family since the 11th grade, and she thought she didn't need a twelve-step community. At the time of the interview Shanice was sober and had decided to get clean on her own accord. She had resumed reading the Bible and praying twice a day and, as others reported earlier, being obedient to God and disciplined in her practices was important to her. She noted, "I have to stay on this track in order to get where I need to be. I mean no ifs, ands or buts. This is what it is."

Although Rochelle's experience of faith during reentry did not mirror Danielle's or Shanice's, she did observe how many returning sisters find God behind bars and "forget all about the Lord" when released. She stated,

> You got a lot of people that when they get locked up they find God. Because they want God to do this and do that for them. But as soon as they get released, and they get back out on the streets, they fall back to their old ways. And God is no longer a preference for them. They forget all about the Lord. You know. So it is what it is.

Yet in Rochelle's mind, churches have a role to play in returning sisters' amnesia about the Lord, because people go to church for the wrong reasons and preachers preach "all the wrong things." We will return to further explore Rochelle's perspective about this below.

Blaming God. As previously mentioned, many participants understood their incarceration as being God-ordained and expressed gratitude for the way God used prison to help them. Shanelle was the only participant in the study to blame God for her incarceration, but her experience, though isolated, is worthy of mention. Shanelle did not identify as Christian or a member of any religious tradition, but as noted in chapter 1, when in prison she started "going to church. I sang on the choir. I was doing Bible study. It was good. It was really good." She did those things because even though she was "mad at God" and questioned "Why is He doing this to me?", she saw how "happy" other inmates were when they went to church, "like something really touched them." But Shanelle never seemed to be able to deal with her anger and her anger toward God. She recalled,

> I just had thoughts like, "Why God always make . . .," well, I do bad things, but then I was like, "Man. He's supposed to help me out." Then I'm like, "Well why is He not helping me out when I go to prison?" or something like that. Then I get mad.

Shanelle reported that when good things started happening to her, her belief in God was strengthened. She shared her belief that God does everything for a reason, and her desire to know more about God. But as the interview ended, I had the impression that Shanelle's spiritual disciplines evidenced a certain amount of magical thinking about how God would reward her for her practice if she just followed the rules.

Emergent Theme: God, Reentry, and Recovery

The above section elucidated how participants experienced God during reentry. As sixteen of the nineteen study participants had self-identified substance use disorders, they spoke at length about their intersecting experiences of God, reentry, and recovery. Table 3.4 reports the three codes that contributed to the generation of the emergent theme, God, reentry, and recovery, and provides a statement made by a study participant that illustrates each code.

Table 3.4 God, Reentry, and Recovery

Emergent Theme	Codes	Excerpts
God, reentry, and recovery	God changed me	"I was a drinker at the end. I would still be out there doing that. I thank God that he changed me."
	God sustains me	"That's my God. I'm telling you. 'Cause I don't know how, but He made sure I found a way."
	"Church Ain't Gonna Keep you Clean"	"Church ain't gonna keep you clean. I'm telling you. It's not . . . You gotta address this disease too."

Source: Copyright 2018 by Author.

God changed me. All sixteen participants with histories of addiction referenced God's role in their addiction and recovery. Some participants explicitly stated how God changed them. As previously mentioned, Andrea believed that "God has a reason for everything." In the midst of her addiction and numerous afflictions, she believed that

> He's still holding onto me with all that I done been through. . . . He has changed my anger issues towards people. I don't lash out at them like I used to . . . I was a drinker at the end. I would still be out there doing that. I thank God that he changed me.

Malea also attributed the change in her addiction to God and God's way of answering her prayers. Malea was incarcerated four times and was trapped in prison's revolving door. Malea shared how, after being released from prison for the third time, she prayed to God saying, "I can't do this [addiction] anymore. Do what it is you gotta do. Change my thought process. Change whatever it is you gotta do. I can't do this anymore." And she laughed a bit as she told how God changed her life rather suddenly. "He helped me alright. He kicked my door in. 'Let's go [she was arrested].' I wasn't mad. I wasn't angry. I did it to myself. I just need You to clean me up so I can keep moving forward." Andrea, Malea, and other participants struggling with addiction during their reentry identified ways that God enacted change in their lives and changed them in a way that set them on the road to recovery.

God sustains me. Numerous study participants spoke about how God sustained them on the road to recovery following their release from prison. For example, Desiree's addiction was not to a substance, per se, but to the lifestyle of running the streets. She made a promise to God, saying, "God, whatever, I could be broke on my last penny. I will not hit these streets again. And He tested me in that area. He have placed me in the position to be broke." Desiree felt tested by God and tested by Satan as well. "Satan knows how to get to me too, because he knows my weakness. He knows what gets me off track." But through it all, God sustained her. She shared how every day she prays, "'God, please give me the strength not to go backwards.' And day goes by I get through it and it gets easier and easier. The tests get easier and easier."

As previously mentioned, following her release from prison, Chelsea had to spend one week living at her mother's, in a house where her family was actively using drugs and in a "horrible" neighborhood. When I asked her how she was able to stay clean in the midst of such circumstances, Chelsea responded, "That's my God. I'm telling you. 'Cause I don't know how, but He made sure I found a way." Lisa was also living in the same neighborhood where she used to get high, as noted above. She explained how God protected her and "holds" her so that she can navigate the neighborhood and remain sober. She stated, "I believe God is the only person that can keep you through the struggles."

"Church ain't gonna keep you clean." Sandra was the only participant to offer this observation, and although hers was an outlying experience, it bears mentioning. As noted in chapter 1, while in prison, Sandra had a faith-based mentor, went to church, sang on the choir, and participated in four years of religious education through the Evangelical Training Association. She shared how she learned about God and the Bible, but did not really "internalize it." Sandra served six years in prison, and just three days following her release she relapsed and began using drugs. Based on her experience, Sandra bluntly stated, "Church ain't gonna keep you clean. I'm telling you. It's not. You can do all that, but it ain't gonna keep you clean. You gotta address this disease too, along with God, finding God and your understanding." Sandra had to "tap into what's going on . . . even though it's hard finding that out, but you gotta find out what's going on in the inside to make you wanna get high in the first place. I needed therapy. I needed medicine. Psychiatric medicine." Sandra saw a psychiatrist in prison, received a diagnosis of depression, and was put on psychotropic medication. She never received therapy, but she recalled how the psychiatrist "always ask me, 'Do you believe in God?' I said, 'Yeah.' 'Cause they know that helps, too. They know. The psychiatrist know that." Yet, according to Sandra, the fact that she never understood what was at the root of her addiction meant that taking medication, believing in God, and going to church "ain't enough to keep you clean."

Emergent Theme: Lived Experiences of Faith during Reentry

With an understanding of how participants viewed and related to God, and how they experienced God during reentry, it is important to now uncover how participants lived their faith during reentry. Table 3.5 reports the three codes that contributed to the generation of the emergent theme, lived experiences of faith during reentry, and provides a statement made by a study participant that illustrates each code.

Individual vs. communal faith. Chapter 1 evidenced how some study participants preferred individual over corporate faith practices during their incarceration. Similarly, a portion of participants differentiated their experiences of individual and communal faith practices following their release from prison, and highlighted the importance of individual faith practices that keep one spiritually grounded over and above participation in religious communities. More will be said below about why and how returning sisters participate in religious communities. But for now, it is important to evidence how participants' individual experiences of faith were meaningful in their reentry. After years of not participating in worship in prison, Rochelle's friend took

Table 3.5   Lived Experiences of Faith during Reentry

Emergent Theme	Codes	Excerpts
Lived experiences of faith during reentry	Individual vs. communal faith	"A lot of people, they say, 'Oh. You need to go to church,' and this, this, and that. God is in the midst of you wherever you go. So that's a bunch of blah, blah, blah."
	Worshipping during reentry	"That's my God. I'm telling you. 'Cause I don't know how, but He made sure I found a way."
	Returning citizens' perspectives on faith	"Church ain't gonna keep you clean. I'm telling you. It's not . . . You gotta address this disease too."

Source: Copyright 2018 by Author.

her to a worship service inside in the Seventh Day Adventist tradition, and Rochelle found a faith home behind bars. But following her release, Rochelle preferred to practice her faith individually. She shared,

> A lot of people, they say, "Oh. You need to go to church," and this, this, and that. God is in the midst of you wherever you go. So that's a bunch of blah, blah, blah. Because if you have your faith, and you have still time and moments to yourself, and you talk to Him, He is there. He's everywhere you are. I could be walking down the street and be talking to the Lord. I'm always praising him, too, because I always sing, "Jesus" [singing]. Wherever I go. If I'm just thinking about God and I just want to give him that praise, I sing, "Jesus" [singing].

Rochelle practiced finding God in all things and praising God in her daily walk. Like Rochelle, Sandra also prioritized individual over communal faith. As previously mentioned, she was the only participant to differentiate the concepts of spirituality and religion. Sandra stated,

> Spirituality, for me, is something that's within, and how I can look to my God in Jesus for support and relief that I know everything will get better. I try to use that. My faith and stuff to help me get through these trying times. Religion is just something like going to church. Taking communion. Stuff like that. Just doing the ritual. You know what I'm saying? That's fine, because it's good to go to church and commune with everybody. That's just not it. That's just not what it's all about.

Shanice also shared about the centrality of her individual faith practices. She had not been part of a faith community since childhood, but she said that her faith disciplines and practices are "the most important thing . . . then the coping skills come, but I have to have faith in God. I have to practice and keep—that's never-ending. That's never-ending." When Desiree first left prison, she went back to the church of her childhood. More will be shared about this below. But after a while, she distanced herself from the church and stated how now, "I support myself spiritually." She continued,

> I listen to my gospel music. I don't read my word but I pray on a consistent basis. Even when I'm on my quiet time I meditate. I cry. I still cry even though . . . sometimes I still feel like I'm institutionalized a little bit. . . . It's hard to explain, you know, from trying to let go what you used to be and trying to change.

Participants' individual faith practices, their spiritual disciplines, were meaningful even when, for various reasons, communal faith practices were not.

Worshipping during reentry. Although some participants preferred to engage in individual over communal faith practices, many found going to worship and practicing their faith in communal contexts during reentry to be particularly meaningful. Numerous other participants, however, identified barriers they faced in attending worship during reentry, a fact that will be explained in greater detail below. But what are the worship experiences of returning sisters? First, for Trina and Sandra, their motivation for attending worship during reentry was different than what it had been. Trina shared how as a child she participated in church because "that was what I [was] supposed to do. I went because that's, you know, what everybody else in the family did." Following her release from prison, her motivation was different. "Now I go because I like to go . . . I like to have my soul filled with some kind of food other than the food that's on my table." For Sandra, going to church during her reentry was "not about what I do." She continued,

> It's about me being a better person and believing that God loves me no matter what . . . It's not about all that showy stuff. It's not about works. . . . It's just me turning my life over to God. . . . It's just being a better person. It ain't about trying to get nothing out of it. Praying to God so I can get a job. Praying to God so I can get a house. I don't do that no more.

Trina participated in a reentry program that restricted her worship attendance for a while. But when she graduated to the next phase of the program and was able to worship at her family's church on Sundays, it "felt good." She stated,

> I was so glad when I get to go when I got to phase two and I could do church. And I didn't care that I hadn't been there in two years or so. I didn't care that the last time they seen me I was skin and bones [due to addiction]. I didn't care nothing about that. I wanted to worship a God that I'm trying to learn.

Worshipping at her family's church means Trina gets to see her father and her nieces on a weekly basis as they serve, respectively, as security and ushers. As evidenced above, some participants preferred to engage in individual faith practices and others preferred the communal experience; however, whether participants practiced their faith individually or communally, they shared perspectives on finding the right faith home, which will be elaborated on below.

Returning citizens' perspectives on faith. Participants not only shared about their experiences living their faith, they also offered insights into their perspectives on faith and its role during reentry. Shanice, as mentioned above, felt the need to participate in faith practices because they facilitated positive coping, and she is dedicated to learning how to cope without drugs. Her faith, however, was in its infancy and she needed the support of a faith community during reentry. If you recall, Shanice lost her focus and lost her faith during reentry. She shared how a faith-based reentry program could have helped her reentry experience. She stated,

> My faith would have been stronger [in a faith-based reentry program]. You send a person out there that's learning to read the Bible, starting to believe in some stuff, and you send them out into the wilderness. They disappear. . . . We don't tend to wait for the long picture, because it's too long. We don't see it. So our faith dies.

Shanice needed a faith community and to experience God through others. For Tasha, her faith helped her to cope and to be honest with herself during her reentry. She shared how her faith helped her

> on a personal level. Mentally. And how I just refuse to let it get the best of me. I just trust and I have faith that you know I'm, in due time, things will work themselves out and I can only do the best that I can in the space that I'm in. And it helps me continue to be really honest with myself in terms of, well, you know, you could have did better . . . I'm able to do that I think because I'm spiritually grounded and I know how important it is to be accountable and responsible for my actions and to be honest with myself.

Greater detail and thicker description of participants' perspectives on faith will be posited below when examining their experiences of and with churches.

Superordinate Theme: Church

The returning sisters in this study spoke at length about their negative and positive experiences with churches and the types of support they did and did not receive from congregations. Two emergent themes were generated based upon the interviews. The emergent themes related to participants' experiences with their "family church" and, for one participant, a church that was willing to meet her on the street.

Emergent Theme: Church Support during Reentry

With an understanding of participants' lived experiences of God during reentry, we now turn to examine participants' lived experiences of churches during reentry. Participants shared about their experiences with their family's church as well as the "church of the streets." For example, some participants had long-term, even lifelong, relationships with a "family church," the church where their grandmother, father, cousins, or other family attended. Desiree was raised by her grandmother. She was brought up in an urban Baptist church, and her grandmother made sure she was an active member. Desiree sang in the choir and participated in a liturgical dance ministry while growing up. When Desiree was sent to prison, her grandmother shared her experience with some members of the church and requested their prayer support. But Desiree did not receive any contact from church members during her incarceration. She recounted,

> They didn't even send me no letter. They didn't even send me no money for nothing . . . I think that's what made me, when I came home, and when I did get back into church, I didn't allow that to hinder me or hurt me from still going back to church.

Initially following her release from prison, Desiree returned to the same church, the church of her childhood, despite her disappointment that they did not support her during her incarceration. She started singing in the choir again, but she felt as though she could not be her true self there. Whereas she used to speak her mind, she felt that she had to "keep my mouth closed. Moreso stay humble. When I got to say something just bite my tongue." She said, "they don't understand the mentality that I still have a little bit, you know, from being incarcerated." As the months following her release passed, Desiree found herself no longer going to church. She stated,

> I kind of shied away now. It's like moreso I don't want to be involved with that church no more. It just, it broke me a little bit. . . . Because I needed them at that moment [during her incarceration] and they wasn't there.

Shanelle's experience mirrors Desiree's in that her family's church, the church she grew up in, was not there for her during her incarceration. Some of the congregation knew about Shanelle's incarceration from her uncle who was an elder, but "they just told me tough love. Like they made me do tough love. Like no support." But after she was released from prison, Shanelle went back to worship there. At that time, there were

two older ladies that was in the church. I guess they seen me grow up. So yeah
they did help me. . . . Like make sure that I had a ride to church. Make sure that
I was okay like being in the halfway house. Like make sure, not money-wise,
but just come and check on me and make sure me and my son was alright.

But Shanelle did not feel comfortable talking to them or sharing with them
about her experience. "It's a big trust issue. I always think about what other
people's going to think about me or judge me."

Becky also returned to her family's church following her release from
prison. During her incarceration, one of the pastors and a couple of the members wrote her letters and "said I was welcome to attend afterwards [after her
release]." Because she was released on house arrest, Becky had to get special
accommodation from her parole officer to attend worship and the pastor willingly wrote on her behalf and welcomed her back. But a year after her release,
and regular attendance at her family's church, Becky accepted an invitation to
attend another fellowship. "One Saturday night she called me and I got up and
went to her church. Well, let me tell you. This pastor was a recovering addict.
Amazing. Amazing. I had never felt that way before. I went out giving my
whole life to God." For a while she attended this church on Saturday evenings
and her family's church on Sunday mornings, but eventually she decided that
she needed to move on and go where she was being "filled." More will be
said below about the significance of the pastor's past addiction in Becky's
decision to make this her faith home.

Unlike any other participant, Lisa received radical hospitality and support from a Christian congregation. Her story is lengthy, but deserves significant attention. Prior to her incarceration in prison, Lisa went to jail. She
recounted,

I went to jail. I did some time. When I came out of jail I was living in a truck.
The truck just so happened to be across from the church. At that time I was
going through a lot of hallucinations and stuff like that, because I have mental
health issues. And they used to be on the outside of the truck watching, you
know. And they would come over there and I wouldn't talk to them, but they
would put food, and bottles of water, and stuff on top of the truck while I was in
there. . . . And they would stand across the street, sometimes they come outside
the church and have service in front of the lot . . . church people never gave up
on me.

Lisa shared how the church's material support began to grow into spiritual
support.

The people in the church got me a mattress . . . and they would always bring
me the food and clothes and stuff, and one day I went over there and I asked for

a Bible. I just so happened to be getting high at that time, and I took all of my drugs with me because I didn't want to leave them behind. And I went in the church, and I asked for a Bible. And I went in the bathroom, and I was sniffing my stuff, and I just so happened to read the Bible and stuff and I got more into the Bible because I didn't understand. So it just made me read more, you know, and go a little further in to it.

The church continued to support Lisa while she was living in the truck. She got to know the church leaders and the members, but at times she was "embarrassed to go into the church." I asked what made her embarrassed to go, and she answered,

Because I would sit down and talk to them in church crying, and then right after church I would go down to the corner and start prostituting. And they would see me. You know when I see them, I just turn my head or start humming or something. So yeah it was kind of embarrassing because people start believing in you and then, you know, when you don't have no outlet or nothing, you understand, you don't do nothing but let people down and stuff. You know, but you have good intentions, and they just believed in me. Now today they're like, you know, my fans.

At the time of the interview Lisa accepted that the church folk were her "fans." In part this was because they stood by her after the incidents she recounted above, during her incarceration in prison. "When I was locked up, they wrote me. They sent me the pamphlets. The books. You know they sent me money when they could, so I could get things. But they made sure I always had religious pamphlets and stuff to read and stuff and books." And following her release from prison, the church continued to show her care. "They got me a phone so I could be able to get some things done while I was in here [a transitional program] so they said I wouldn't have no reason to come back to the streets." Lisa explained why she thinks the church was so caring and supportive to her. She said,

I believe a lot of people in them, in the church, was just like me at one time. So they wasn't just on the inside looking out, you understand, they was on the outside looking in at theyself. They feel like somebody else pulled them out the rut. I was just somebody else that they helping out like somebody helped them. Sometimes you gotta share your blessings and that's what they did.

Lisa assumed that the sixty or so members of that congregation and its leaders could relate to her and could see their own story in hers. This directly relates to the next emergent theme: how study participants related to church folk, and vice versa, during reentry.

Emergent Theme: Relating to Church Folk

Participants spoke extensively about how they experienced both connection and disconnection with churches and the people in the pews. They explained the fear they had of being judged, what they did to "save face," and the role that recovery played in their relationships with church folks. Foremost, the way that participants could and could not relate to the people in the pews had a significant impact on whether or not they sought out a faith family following their release from prison. As Desiree shared above, she did not feel she could be herself in the church of her childhood and felt she had to keep her mouth shut. She felt that the congregation did not understand her "mentality" that resulted from her incarceration experience, and eventually she stopped attending. Tasha also felt a disconnect with the members of the Moorish Science temple.

> Maybe they had that experience because they went to prison 20, 25 years ago. Or maybe they had that experience because their brother or husband had went to prison. But I don't feel like the women in the temple really get me and where I'm at. And it's not like I'm looking for no special attention or nothing, but just maybe some acknowledgment just to say that, you know, we get it where you are, that's where we're going to meet you at.

One of the biggest factors that caused Tasha to feel disconnected and misunderstood was that the women of the temple repeatedly asked her to

> join committees and go on certain trips and do this. And, it's like, sounds exciting, really great. I'd love to be involved, but do you have any idea what I'm dealing with right now, like for real? Do you stop and think that maybe you should try and come and help me do some of the work I'm doing instead of trying to help me do the work that you're doing?

Tasha explained how overwhelmed she was following her release from eighteen years in prison and the barriers to participating in the Moorish Science community that she faced. More will be said about her experience below. But even after Tasha began to feel more established and less overwhelmed, her experience was that the women of the temple had no interest in "uplift[ing] people" and that "we're not on the same page."

It's frequently argued that returning citizens may not seek out churches for fear they will be judged for their past sins. Following her release from prison, Latrise participated in a residential rehab program at which time she went with another "young lady" to a church "around the corner. And they had an awesome service. And I thought it was going to be the hardest thing in the world to do." I asked Latrise why she thought it would be so difficult, and she said,

Probably because the way I see the church, or the way I see the churches that I went to in [another state]. I felt like I would be judged or that no one would befriend me. That I would be emotionally and spiritually a mess.

Latrise was pleasantly surprised that her assumptions and fear of judgment were unfounded. Danielle, however, also feared judgment by church folk.

The churches look at you like you's a junkie, and you know, they don't even ask why you were in prison or what led to your imprisonment or none of that. They just straight judge you. And I thought the only person that's supposed to judge us is God.

Despite her perception that churches judge you, Danielle continued to go to church throughout her addiction. Prior to her incarceration, Danielle found a church in her neighborhood.

It's a Baptist church and I loved it so I would go high, sober, whatever. I still went every Sunday. And on Wednesday, we had Bible study. And I plan on going this Sunday since I'll be off black out [in the residential treatment program]. I miss it too. I can't wait to get back there.

I asked her if the church knew about her incarcerations, to which Danielle stated, "That community know everything about me. But it's like they didn't judge, cause it's a lot of people in that church are recovering addicts or people that was in prison."

Latrise also took comfort in the fact that fellow congregants had histories of incarceration and/or addiction. Perhaps the grace that permitted congregants to acknowledge their adverse experiences was bestowed by the church's pastor, because "the pastor himself, he had a rough background . . . I had seen a picture of him, back in the day, and oh my goodness. And I was like, 'I thought I looked rough! He looked real rough!'" Participants seemed to gravitate to churches where congregants and/or religious leaders shared about the adversity and affliction they had experienced. As Becky illustrated above, she left her family church to go to a new church where the pastor was a recovering addict and integrated his experiences within the sermons. Becky shared how even when she does not attend worship in person, she listens to his sermons online.

I can sit there and listen to that sermon 50 million times and every time get something different out of it. He really relates it to his drug use. Like he said, when God set him down into rehab, he had a choice. He had a choice to follow Jesus, to change his addiction and decide no against it. Then that allowed him to fall in love with God.

In explaining why church members continued to support Lisa when she lived in the truck, when she was prostituting, when she went in and out of prison and jail, Lisa stated that they could relate to her and could acknowledge that at some point someone else had also "pulled them out the rut."

Not all participants, however, wanted churches to know about their backgrounds. Trina's father worked security in the church. And even though the church had seen her looking rough, she did not want to share her story with them because her father is "a real private man."

Treva also preferred not to share details of her background with her new church community. She explained that "just about everybody in church is broken souls. Church is a hospital for broken souls." At the time of the interview, Treva had recently started going to a very small congregation of just five or six women. The fellow congregants knew that she was living in a transitional program for women, but she did not want to share with them about her experiences of addiction and incarceration. She explained, "Everybody would like to be looked at like you're not damaged goods. It is what it is. I'm 51 years old. I'm not gonna be pure as the white-driven snow. Nobody is." Given that Treva was the youngest woman in the congregation at age fifty-one, she assumed the other congregants would not assume she was "pure as the white-driven snow." She figured in time they would get to know the hardships one another faced in the past, but she preferred to "save face" until they knew one another better.

Emergent Theme: The Search for Church

Participants offered insights into what they are seeking in a faith family or what it is that keeps them in church. They explained the importance of seeking out a small church as well as a church that lives its mission. As evidenced above, some participants' search for church ended when they found a congregation or a pastor who had also experienced the adversity of addiction and/or incarceration. Relating to church folk was an important dynamic in participants' decisions to participate in or to leave a church community. Participants also shared other important factors in their search for church. Some participants explained their desire to participate in a small church family. Recall Treva who, as mentioned above, had just joined a small congregation that had about five or six members each week at worship. There was something about a small congregation that met her needs better. Treva shared how after worship everybody engages in fellowship. She said,

That's what we do after church. Everybody sits around the table. We all sit down, and we talk, and we eat like family. I like that especially coming from where I came from with my background, being out there in the streets, and da da da da da. Family's broken. Coming out of jail. You need that close knitness. And that was just what I needed.

Andrea shared Treva's preference for a small faith community, although she had worked for three years as a housekeeper at a megachurch before she was fired for her alcohol use. She explained how she knew the leaders and the community of that church so well, and that she still sometimes watches their worship service on TV. But following her incarceration, rather than go to a church of 7,000, Andrea said she wants a smaller church.

> I really don't care for the big, big churches. I like the more intimate ones, where the preacher know you, and he—you can go to him, talk to—you see him next Sunday, "Hey, Andrea! How you doing this Sunday?" says something like that.

Andrea questioned how the pastor of a church like the one she had cleaned, with 7,000 members, could remember the members and keep tabs on their lives.

For Andrea and Treva, the church's ability to "be there for you" was contingent upon its size. A small church made them feel a sense of communal support. For Sandra, the need for community was not predicated on the size of the church, but the way the church lived out the Christian mission. Sandra grew up in the church, going every Sunday, singing in the choir, and serving on the usher board. Her mother was the associate pastor of that same church when Sandra went to prison, but no one from the church reached out to her. When I asked Sandra what it meant to her that the church did not reach out to her despite her mother's standing, she said,

> What it meant to me is that's not a church I wanna go to anymore. You know what I'm saying? Because I know some churches do reach out to you, 'cause it was churches that came to the prison. That's in the Bible. They look out for prisoners, widows, and children. Their outreach is not like that. They go to nursing homes and stuff like that. They don't go to extremes, to the trenches to get the people that really need that.

Sandra shared how she would prefer to attend a church that lives the Christian mission by engaging in outreach. "Shelters and prisons or warring in the streets. Getting the prostitutes and all that. I like stuff like that. That's what I want in the church." But at the time of the interview, Sandra was not going to church. Like many other participants, Sandra faced significant barriers to church participation.

Emergent Theme: Barriers to Church Participation

Participants' inability to relate to church folk and their desires for a particular kind of church family can function as barriers to church participation. Participants named other dynamics that function as barriers in their desire and/or ability to participate in the life of a congregation. Table 3.6 reports the three

Table 3.6   Barriers to Church Participation

Emergent Theme	Codes	Excerpts
Barriers to church participation	Overwhelmed	"I was so busy and overwhelmed with trying to rebuild my life."
	Misunderstood	"My grandmother always told me I want to see you at church, but she doesn't know deep down inside how I feel about that church."
	Working weekends	"I'm looking for a church home. Still, I gotta find the time to work."

Source: Copyright 2018 by Author.

codes that contributed to the generation of the emergent theme, barriers to church participation, and provides a statement made by a study participant that illustrates each code.

A glimpse into participants' perspectives on and encounters with churches, as detailed above, reveals how many participants failed to feel supported and cared for by congregations during their incarceration and reentry experiences. Participants' stories were especially poignant when the church of their family and/or the church of their childhood failed to show them care. This functioned for many participants as a barrier to their desire to participate in a church community.

Participants also noted other barriers that prevented them from cultivating a church home. As Tasha stated above, she was overwhelmed during her reentry and found that the women of the temple wanted more from her in terms of time and resource than she was able to give. She said, "When I came home, like for the first year I didn't attend because I was so busy and overwhelmed with trying to rebuild my life and public transportation." They just did not understand where she was at in her reentry process and what it meant to return from prison after eighteen years inside.

Desiree also felt misunderstood by church members. As recounted above, following her release she returned to her grandmother's church, the church of her childhood, but she eventually stopped going when she felt as though she could not be herself and they did not understand the impact of incarceration on her mentality. When Tammy first released from prison she did begin participating in the life of a church. But when she got a job, her work schedule prevented her from attending every-other-Sunday. Pretty soon, she just stopped going all together. Deborah, who also worked every other weekend, found that she tried to go to church when she could, but work often got in the way. Sandra expressed a desire to find a church home. She said,

Right now I'm looking for a church home. Still, I gotta find the time to work. On Sunday mornings, I have home group [NA meeting] on Sunday mornings at 10. Churches usually start 11, something like that. Or maybe I could find one with an early morning services at 7:30. I haven't found a church.

As previously mentioned, Becky was released on house arrest. Because she was able to get support from her family church and her parole office, she was able to attend weekly worship. However, this experience is likely not shared by all returning citizens released on house arrest as many returning citizens may not have a relationship with a local church and not all local churches would be so supportive.

Superordinate Theme: Faith-Based Mentors and Reentry

Interviews with nineteen returning sisters revealed their lived experiences of God and church during reentry. The interviews also uncovered how they experienced faith-based mentors. Participants completed a Demographic Form (see Appendix A) in which they were asked whether or not they had a relationship with a faith-based mentor during their incarceration or reentry experiences. Nine of the nineteen participants indicated that they had a faith-based mentor. However, conversation with participants revealed that only two of the nineteen participants had faith-based mentors who had been assigned through a mentoring program and who met with them individually on a regular, ongoing basis. It is important to note, also, that the two inmates who had faith-based mentors served four and six years in prison. The remaining seven participants who indicated that they had a faith-based mentor did engage in mentoring relationships, but they were much more informal. For example, two participants had numerous faith-based mentors with whom they met in small groups through their participation in the Kairos program inside and their weekly prayer and share group (see Appendix C). Two other participants had mentors that were informally arranged, were not part of a mentoring program, and with whom they did not engage in ongoing, one-on-one meetings. And three participants considered a faith-based volunteer to be a mentor, but those volunteers entered the prison as part of faith-based programs, such as a Bible-based life skills course, and did not meet with the participants one on one.

As noted in chapter 2, for more than a decade the federal government has focused on the provision of mentoring services as a means of benefitting inmates and, specifically, returning citizens through the initiatives of the Second Chance Act. Yet only two of the nineteen study participants engaged in formal, faith-based mentoring relationships. And, upon their release, one of the two returning sisters never connected with her faith-based mentor, and the other returning sister connected with her mentor just once. Nevertheless, given the priority placed on mentoring by the government, and the benefits it can offer (as evidenced in chapter 2), it is important to uncover participants' lived experiences with faith-based mentors whether the relationships were formally defined or not. The experiences and perspectives of Danielle, Sandra, and Tasha are helpful in illustrating the diverse ways the returning sisters in this study related to faith-based mentors.

Emergent Theme: Returning Sisters' Lived Experiences
in Faith-Based Mentoring Relationships

Danielle was one of two study participants who participated in a formal faith-based mentoring program. She was assigned a faith-based mentor through a mentoring program coordinated through the prison chaplain's office. Danielle had asked to be assigned a faith-based mentor because, as she said,

> I just knew I need to learn how to, just, how can I put this? She [the faith-based mentor] had information that I needed to better me. That's pretty much the way it was. It wasn't because it was through Chaplain [last name] or because it was spiritually-based or faith-based. It was because I knew this woman knew how to succeed as a woman and I didn't. And I wanted to learn, to learn how to do that.

I asked Danielle if her faith-based mentor was able to help her to do that, to which she replied,

> No. She probably would have, she was in the process of it. She was willing to help me actually go to school and everything. She was going to get me the computer. But I had, it's like, I don't know. I failed for so long. I kept blocking my own blessings. I would mess it up before they could mess it up. You see what I'm saying. So that's basically what happened. It's this thing like, they gonna have you. They gonna string you along.

I probed further, trying to understand what Danielle meant by how she "kept blocking [her] own blessings" and her concern about how "they gonna string you along." Through the conversation, Danielle's root concerns about the relationship were revealed when she eventually said, "I think I wanted her more of a mother than as a mentor. And she wasn't. So I discarded it like okay." I asked Danielle what she was looking for in a mother figure and she said, "Love. Time. You know." And she started to cry. I asked Danielle if her mom was around at the time of her incarceration to which she replied, "My mom's still around. But not me."

When Danielle was released from prison she went home on house arrest. She met with her faith-based mentor once, who she described as "a good Christian woman," but the relationship "fizzled out" after that. She said,

"My mother is my mother and I can't replace her no matter how hard I try. And how hard I've tried." Although Danielle was clean when she was released from prison, she went home on house arrest and it was not long before she relapsed and was sent back to prison. At that time, the chaplain's office reconnected her with her faith-based mentor. She explained,

> When I went back to prison, she became my mentor again. . . . She gave me another chance. I gave her another chance. We gave each other another chance. But I was still looking for that mom. . . . But she was so sweet. She really wanted the best for me. I just needed to want it for myself and I didn't at the time. I wanted, I don't know what the hell I wanted. I wanted a mom. I wanted to be better out there, but I felt as though if that, if my mom was there things would get better. You get what I'm saying? Moms are supposed to teach you these things and protect you. And you know everything I learned I learned on the street. And that sure ain't how to be a lady [laughs].

Danielle's relationship with her faith-based mentor ended during that incarceration even though she wanted and needed a mentor. She wanted to learn how to live life like a "lady." She wanted to learn the skills and Christian values that the mentor knew. But she continued to "block [her] blessing" even after receiving a second chance.

Sandra also had a faith-based mentor who she met during her incarceration with the intention of receiving reentry support. Sandra shared,

> I had a mentor that came once every Sunday. . . . They came and visited us to see what we was doing. . . . She talked to me. I would talk to her about what was going on. Then she helped me deal with some stuff the way the Bible would deal with it and stuff. 'Cause it was Christian. They was Christians and stuff. It was real supportive. No financial stuff. It was just real supportive. Someone I could talk to. 'Cause I didn't get a lot of visits either. It was good.

Sandra met with her faith-based mentor on a regular basis and knew that the relationship would continue following her release. But that did not go exactly as she had planned. She shared,

> They was gonna help us on the outside. When I came home . . . my mother had died while I was in prison. I had two minor children still at the house, living with my stepfather. When I came home, I didn't even connect with her [the faith-based mentor]. It wasn't her fault, it was mine. I didn't connect with her.

As previously stated, Sandra was only home for three days before her drug use resumed, she was put out of the house by her stepfather, and she entered a rehab program. That ended the relationship with her faith-based mentor.

As previously mentioned, after serving eighteen years in prison, Tasha started working in reentry services. She shared both her lived experiences with, and her perspectives on, faith-based mentoring. During her incarceration, Tasha had relationships with two individuals, one through the Moorish Science temple and another through a Christian church, whom she considered faith-based mentors. They did not meet with her regularly or on an individual basis, but they did strengthen her faith and provide her with material support that enabled her to take correspondence courses while incarcerated. Although these individuals contributed significantly to Tasha's experiences behind bars and beyond, her perspective on the concept of faith-based mentoring was not positive. She said,

> I think it's a bunch of propaganda. I know [the government] says they have a mentoring program. I was never assigned one, and I requested for one when I first came home. I didn't like press the issue or nothing but, and I'm not saying that it's not being done, but not on the scale that people think it is. Just like everything else people say they're doing stuff that they're not really doing. But on paper it looks really great. How can you prove it? . . . It's not real. I can assure you. I know a lot of people on supervision and they do not have faith-based mentors. And I specifically requested one when I came home, just to see what would turn up. Nothing happened.

Tasha's experience requesting a faith-based mentor, in combination with her status as a government employee in reentry services, renders her perspective disconcerting.

FAITH-BASED MENTORS' LIVED EXPERIENCES IN FAITH-BASED MENTORING RELATIONSHIPS

Given participants' limited experiences with faith-based mentors, along with the government's and churches' emphasis on providing this type of spiritual care and support, I interviewed five faith-based mentors in order to understand the lived experiences of mentoring and their perspectives on the spiritual and religious experiences of female returning citizens during reentry. The research questions driving this study were reported in the book's Introduction and the methodology can be found in Appendix B. The data derived from the interviews was extensive, and what is presented below is a small subset of the overall findings. Insights from this study will also be used in chapter 4 as they influence Project Sister Connect, the model for revised prison ministry praxis. Table 3.7 presents the faith-based mentors, the number of years they served as faith-based mentors, and the number of returning sisters they had mentored.

Table 3.7   Faith-Based Mentors

Participant	Number of Years Served as Faith-Based Mentor	Number of Faith-Based Mentees Mentored
Karen	1.5	2
Eunice	2.5	1
Melanie	5	More than 20
Rachel	8	3
Sharon	7	"About 30"

Source: Copyright 2018 by Author.

As noted above, the nineteen returning sisters who participated in the first study had a diversity of experiences engaging with faith-based mentors. The same is true of the five faith-based mentors who participated in this second study. Table 3.8 presents the superordinate and emergent themes that were generated by participants' insights into and perspectives on their experiences.

The relationships between the faith-based mentors who participated in this study and the women they mentored all began during the mentee's incarceration, prior to her release from prison. This section focuses only on the faith-based mentors' experiences in reentry mentoring.

Emergent Theme: Mentoring a Returning Sister

First, participants described their lived experiences mentoring returning sisters. Sharon had mentored "about 30" female returning citizens and posited how they tend to fall into three categories: (1) "There's some that will just email you and talk to you on email" or Facebook; (2) "Then there's the ones that are kind of—you don't hear from them unless they need something and

Table 3.8   Faith-Based Mentors' Lived Experiences in Faith-Based Mentoring Relationships during Mentees' Reentry

Superordinate Theme	Emergent Themes	Excerpts
Faith-based mentors' lived experiences in faith-based mentoring relationships during mentees' reentry	Mentoring a returning sister	"I pray with her. I listen. I give her a chance to talk. And vent. And just share her story of where she is in her life and how God is helping her."
	Returning sisters' spiritual and religious experiences	"She's still holding on. I think [her faith] has really grown, and she has seen that God is faithful to her."

Source: Copyright 2018 by Author.

then they call you"; and (3) "The ones that just regularly keep in contact with you—they wanna keep in touch because they wanna keep themselves in that loop if you will."

The other four participants' experiences reflect the typology Sharon presented in many ways. Karen's mentee represented the first category: Karen and her mentee were in regular communication, but only via text message, and the type of support Karen provided was strictly emotional and spiritual, not material. During the mentee's incarceration, Karen and her mentee corresponded regularly by mail. Written communication was at the core of their relationship, and this continued following her release, but via text messaging rather than letters. Although they had discussed getting together in person, Karen was prayerful about it and "the Lord told me no . . . He said no. I listened. I've learned to do that."

Eunice's mentee represented the third category: Eunice and her mentee spoke on the phone "maybe every other week" and they got together every month or two. Eunice said, "I talk to her maybe every other week, and I never ask a lotta questions. I just say, 'How are you? Everything going okay?'" Prior to her release, Eunice gave her mentee the number to her home phone. But in the process of changing service providers, the number was changed, and her mentee had no way to reach Eunice. Rather than letting the relationship end, the mentee contacted the prison chaplain, who contacted the director of the faith-based mentoring program, who contacted Eunice to see if she would be willing to give her mentee a working number. Eunice saw that as "positive" and an indication of their relationship's strength. Sharon and Melanie, the two participants with the most mentoring experience, spoke about returning sisters who seemed to represent the second category in Sharon's typology, but these relationships were short-lived and/or sporadic.

Communication and contact between faith-based mentors and female returning citizens differed depending on numerous factors and did not always fit neatly into Sharon's typology. Rachel, for example, faced a unique barrier in trying to maintain relationship with her mentee. Rachel's mentee was released from prison into a work release program under community supervision. This occurred five months prior to my interview with Rachel. Although her mentee was no longer under the jurisdiction of the prison, according to the pastor in charge of the prison ministry at Rachel's church, Rachel was not permitted to call or visit her mentee until the pastor received the approval of the prison chaplain. Rachel continued to write to her mentee, but said "it's a little mind-boggling" that they could not speak on the phone or visit since they visited throughout her incarceration. But, as she stated, "I don't want to do anything to jeopardize my position in the prison ministry so I can't go without Rev. [last name] saying it's okay."

Additional research into the barrier Rachel faced proved insightful. Although I was unable to locate anything in writing, I was informed by a faith-based volunteer in the state where Rachel served that when a returning citizen is released from prison under community supervision, the state no longer permits faith-based volunteers to continue the mentoring relationships outside the prison unless special dispensation is received (N. Stockbridge, personal communication, October 27, 2017). Sharon and Rachel served as faith-based mentors in the same state, and Sharon received special dispensation from the chaplain at the women's prison to continue her mentoring relationships with more than thirty women following their release. Rachel, however, had not been granted this permission and was stuck waiting for five months while her pastor tried to work with the prison chaplain to enable Rachel and her mentee to meet in person and/or talk on the phone. After four years of walking alongside her mentee inside the prison, Rachel was stymied in her ability to support her during a crucial phase of her reentry.

Although the nature of mentor-mentee contact varied, all of the faith-based mentors interviewed provided spiritual and emotional support to their mentees, and many also offered material support. Rachel was a previous State Department employee and had served sixteen months in federal prison on conspiracy charges. She viewed her own incarceration as God's way of preparing her for prison ministry. Based on her own experience, she knew the importance of feeling loved and having someone to talk to. She used her experience to guide the way she mentored. She said, "You need to vent to someone. You need someone to try to understand you. And a lot of those women are actually in need of someone to just show that they love them." Rachel explained how her mentee's family was not very supportive and how her mentee's mother passed away during her incarceration. Therefore, in Rachel's mind, it was even more important to offer her mentee spiritual and emotional support. She stated,

> I pray with her. I listen. I give her a chance to talk. And vent. And just share her story of where she is in her life and how God is helping her. And encouraging her to stay faithful to the Lord because I know that if she allows Him to, He can turn her life around.

But as important as the spiritual and emotional support were in Rachel's opinion, she also felt called to start a clothing bank for returning sisters. She stated, "I'm going to use my garage to actually house clothing and then as the churches contact me, then I'll give the church clothing of what sizes the individuals need." Although Rachel sought to meet the material, emotional, and spiritual needs of her mentee, her own experience taught her to engage in ministry *with*, rather than ministry *to* or *for*, sisters inside and returning sisters. Rachel knew the value of being in solidarity with returning sisters.

Sharon also shared about the emotional and spiritual support she provided; in addition, there is one form of material support that Sharon provides to all the returning sisters she mentors: undergarments. "I'll take you out and buy you some underwear. I always buy underwear because that's something that ain't nobody getting no used. I'll buy you underwears and bras 'cause you need that and you didn't get it inside." Sharon was adamant that the mentees recognize that the undergarments she provided are from God. She said, "It's not coming from me. It's coming from God and don't abuse what He's [giving you]." Sharon warned that faith-based mentors need to be cautious in the type and amount of material support they provide because returning sisters may manipulate mentors, a topic we will return to below. Sharon stated,

> You have to be really careful because you can't just shower them with stuff because some of them will use it to sell it 'cause they're still playing. They're not serious. Some of them will look at that like a Christmas day and start buying stuff that's really not appropriate.

In addition to spiritual, emotional, and material support, Melanie also provided referral resources to a female inmate who was soon to be released. As part of a faith-based mentoring program, Melanie facilitated a biblically based life skills course inside the prison for any inmate in the mentoring program who wanted to attend. One participant had been incarcerated five times. She came to Melanie prior to her release and told her that she was "scared" and that she didn't "want to come back this time." Melanie shared how the female inmate was ill-prepared for reentry, and she knew this given the revolving door of incarceration in which she had been trapped. The soon-to-be-released sister inside told Melanie, "You know? There's not a lot of people here that I can talk to about this." As Melanie said to me,

> There were so many people that were doing long sentences where she's been in and out five times. She said, "People really don't want to hear from me." It's tough. You've had your opportunity. You've come. You've gone. You've come. You've gone. I don't want to hear it. She said, "I can't really talk to people about this, but I'm really scared. I'm really scared. I don't want to come back."

Moreover, the sister inside was not eligible for any reentry coordination services because she was going to be released without parole. Melanie compiled information about transitional programs, gave it to her co-mentor, the faith-based mentor who was assigned to the sister inside, and worked with the mentor and the chaplain to schedule an in-prison interview for the sister inside with a residential reentry program.

Sharon also helped to provide returning sisters with important resources and, in her case, it was the resource of employment. Sharon owned a drug and alcohol testing company and in her seven years of prison ministry she employed five returning sisters, some part-time and some full-time. I asked Sharon how she knew a returning sister would make a good employee and what qualities she looked for. Because Sharon participated in numerous faith-based ministries inside the prison, including Kairos, she came to know many sisters inside well and was able to observe them intimately over a period of time.

> When I see the way you act when you don't think anybody's watching you tells me a lot. I mean, we all fall. We all have our, whatever, but I'm just saying, you can preach it out of your mouth but then you turn around and it's a whole different thing. Just the interaction with other inmates. There's a lot of things that tell me you're real or you're not real and there's quite a few that put on a good front.

Not all the women Sharon hired succeeded. "One of them, I gave a job and she started using drugs and wound up going back in. She went in twice since. It happens." Sharon explained how she knows the cycle of addiction, however, and would have worked with this woman to help her get clean if that was her desire. She shared how the woman was "declining,"

> Then I called her in and I said, "Okay. Here's the come to Jesus moment." I said, "This is the time to admit what you did because I'm fixing to do a drug test. So we can get it all out now, but your grace account's empty." I said, "You will get no more so you can admit to me what you did. I'm gonna do a drug test to see that you're telling me the truth. After that, if you do it again, you're done." Of course she fell off the wagon and so she was fired, and it was within a matter of three weeks she was back in jail.

Despite the risks of relapse and recidivism that returning sisters face, Sharon noted that she's willing to give "the right" returning sisters a chance because if they can't come up with the money they need, "What do you think somebody's gonna do? They're gonna go right back to what they did to make money."

Sharon and other faith-based mentors spoke about the potential for returning sisters to "abuse" or "manipulate" both faith-based mentors and churches.

> If they say something like, "Well I need clothes," and I'm like, "Well my church does a clothes closet. If you give me your sizes, they'll bring in a gently used whatever. Give me a wish list." If they're like, "Oh great, that's wonderful," I'll say, "Look. I'll buy you underwear 'cause you want that new, but your clothes, give me that size." And I just see how they respond. If they're like "Oh, that would be wonderful," then I know they're serious.

If not, they are likely "scamming." Sharon shared a story about a returning sister who complained about having a "stupid flip phone." Thinking that the woman should be grateful for what God was providing to her, Sharon said, "Tell me about it. Compare this flip phone to the one you were using when you were inside." Sharon recounted many stories in which she used sarcasm to keep it real with inmates and remind them to stay humble before God.

Karen was also on guard against being manipulated by her mentee. "Because sometimes incarcerated people ain't always tell the truth. Part of that is the reason they're there. She [Karen's mentee] had a real sweetness about her. Then I saw the other side, too." The faith-based mentoring program in which Karen participated had strict rules about gift-giving. Mentors were not supposed to give gifts until after six months of being in relationship, after which point a gift valued at $10.00 could be given at Christmas and on birthdays. Karen did not adhere to this rule and she ended up giving her mentee money to buy things at the commissary, shipping her packages when the prison permitted, and buying her a TV. But by the time her mentee was released, Karen had set stricter limits on the type of material support she would provide. Karen stated, "She's smart. She's college-educated. She knows how to shake you down for money." Karen learned the difference between ministry *to* and ministry *with* sisters inside and returning sisters, and therefore upon her mentee's release, she was careful to be in a relationship grounded in solidarity. Following her mentee's release, Karen and her mentee both initiated communication with one another and, as noted above, exchanged text messages on a regular basis. "Because I care about her. I still pray for her all the time. I just had to put the brakes on the money."

Rachel served as a faith-based mentor to a woman who had been in and out of prison. Because of her recidivism, the mentoring program decided to assign the inmate two mentors to provide her with necessary support during her incarceration as well as upon her release. In explaining why the woman had been assigned two mentors, Rachel stated,

> She's a strong-willed person. . . . She's the type of individual that can be manipulative. So you have to watch out for her and be able to detect that. . . . She was telling me the situation of how she returned this time when I met her. And it was because she was in a halfway house and she stated that the caretaker there or the facilitator actually struck her. But I know and I was told that she was more of a violent type of individual and didn't want to follow instructions. And she's the one that initiated this disagreement.

Rachel continued to mentor her for four years during her incarceration, writing to her monthly and visiting her at least twice a month. Moreover, she continued the relationship following her release, but is waiting for the prison chaplain's permission to do more than write letters.

Emergent Theme: Returning Sisters' Spiritual and Religious Experiences

Sharon served as a faith-based mentor to over thirty female returning citizens who had participated in the Kairos program inside. In walking alongside returning citizens during their reentry journey, Sharon realized how different places and different environments can serve to nurture or stymie returning sisters' faith and spiritual resilience. Sharon talked about the difficulties returning sisters face when forced to return to an environment that does not nurture their faith.

> It's really a case by case thing . . . some of them go into an environment where just because of the nature of where they had to go, their spiritual side is not being fed . . . Sometimes you go into a place where you don't have any control over where you go or you have to go back to family and nobody in your family's saved.

Sharon recognized how returning sisters frequently experience few choices about where they reside following their release, and therefore may find themselves with people and in places that do not support them spiritually. For this reason, Sharon explained how she made herself available to returning citizens around the clock. She stated,

> If you need anything, if you call me up at three in the morning to say, "I need you to come pick me up 'cause I'm about to do something crazy," I'll be there and I'll pick you up. I'll pray you through it and I'll do whatever I can to help you.

Eunice mentored a woman who also faced "challenges" in her living situation, and her ability to manage the situation evidenced to Eunice her ability to "hold on" to her faith. Eunice explained how her mentee had to move out from her cousin's house as it was not helping in her reentry. Her mentee did not explain what was going on in her cousin's house, but she told Eunice, "Too much drama's going on in here. I need to get out of here. This is not good for me." According to Eunice this showed "wisdom" and evidenced the woman's faith. "She's still holding on. I think [her faith] has really grown, and she has seen that God is faithful to her. You do what you have to do and call on Him." To Eunice, her mentee's wisdom to leave an unhealthy living situation showed her ability to hold on to her faith and call on God for help.

Rachel also mentored a returning sister who showed spiritual strength in her ability to "hold on" to her faith. As previously mentioned, Rachel's mentee had been in and out of prison five times. Five months after her last release, Rachel said,

> She's still out and I give all the glory to God because I do believe that she wants to remain out. I can't say that I've seen her grow spiritually because when I met her I thought she was very spiritually connected to the Lord. She prays a lot and gives her testimony. I really feel that if she keeps that up that she'll be fine.

Rachel's mentee, despite her past recidivism, was able to "hold on" to her faith.

Rachel's own incarceration and reentry experiences were likely influencing her perspective on her mentee's experience. As previously mentioned, Rachel was charged with conspiracy when working at the State Department and she served sixteen months in federal prison. In reflecting on her mentee's spiritual and religious experiences, Rachel stated,

> Even when I look at my situation, just one little minute wrong decision could change your entire life. And you really, to make it through that journey, you really have to be spiritually inclined and stay that way. Because I could have gave up. I could have said I can't do this. Even now. When I think of employment, I could say, "You know what? I'm tired. I can't keep going through this." But I have to keep telling myself, you know, if God carried me through that He'll give me a way to make it through this. . . . At one time I used to say it takes a strong individual to make it [in reentry]. But it's not about being a strong individual. It's about being strong in your faith and know that the Lord will take care of you. If you don't have that, then you give up.

Rachel's own reentry experience and the struggles she faced in trying to stay strong in her faith likely influenced her assessment of her mentee's spiritual journey and her faith that her mentee will be able to "hold on."

Karen believed that her mentee would be able to "hold on" to her faith and the "spiritual growth" that occurred during her incarceration, but she was concerned that her mentee's "mental health issues" might get in the way. Karen explained how during her incarceration her mentee

> was a believer. She read the Word. . . . She was very receptive to that. She went to church programs at the prison. She talked about the classes that she took, faith-based classes that she took that she really enjoyed. I did see some spiritual growth in her, in the way she talked and the scriptures we would share.

But Karen seemed concerned that despite her spiritual growth, her mentee may face challenges that she would struggle to overcome. "She's a smart lady. She just has mental health issues."

Sharon explained how she was able to tell if someone was rehabilitated by their faith, if it seemed like they could "hold on" to their faith during reentry, or if they might be spiritually at risk. Returning sisters who are spiritually rehabilitated "have a good spiritual support system. And if Kairos really effected a change, they want to give back." Sharon continued,

The ones that are genuinely true, they want, like I said, when I needed to bring witnesses in, they came right in. I can call them to speak, give testimony at a Kairos team meeting to tell these new team members what the impact of Kairos is. They want to do things. They volunteer at soup kitchens. They will do things to help shelters, women's shelters.

According to Sharon, the desire to give back and show care to others served as evidence of a "conversion" and the returning sisters' ability to "hold on" to the faith.

Faith-based mentors shared about their mentees' faith and spirituality as well as their religious practices. They spoke about whether or not their mentees attended church and what that meant in their reentry journey. Eunice mentored a woman who was incarcerated for twelve years. During that time, the female inmate's pastor and his wife visited her "faithfully." Eunice said, "I was shocked that they stood by her all this time." Eunice invited her mentee to attend her church following her release, even though she said she was "not trying to push church down her throat, but you need that, that foundation." But her mentee said she planned to go back to her own church, the church with the pastor who stood by her during her incarceration.

Sharon's perspective on the importance of attending church during reentry differed from Eunice's. She explained the approach she takes with her mentees who do not have a church from prior to their incarceration. Sharon stated,

You have to go pick them up and bring them to church and make them. . . . First of all, think about people on the outside feel walking into a new church. You feel awkward. Now imagine you've been locked up, so you already feel awkward in society. . . . They sure ain't gonna walk into a church by themselves. . . . They need somebody to pick them up and say, "Come on. You can come to church with me," and invite them to church. That is critical.

Sharon felt strongly that mentors should "bring [mentees] to church and make them [go]." She stated that they need help to walk into a church. Yet she also shared the story of one of her mentees who had been in and out of prison twelve times. When she was recently released, she went to a city where she had never lived to participate in a reentry program and to change people, places, and things. Sharon explained how she sought out a church home.

She's very active in church, you know? She found a church, she just found one, it was there, walking distance. Cause she was only—when she first got out, she was only allowed to walk, and she [could] only go a three block radius. There was a church the next block over and that's the one she went to. . . . That's even a bold, ballsy—when somebody takes it upon their self to walk to a church, that's somebody that's seeking the Lord. Because they're not just complacently sitting there and got to be picked up. They're actually yearning and looking and searching.

SUMMARY

The findings from the two qualitative studies evidence the spiritual and religious experiences of returning sisters. The findings illustrated how female returning citizens understand God's nature and God's ways of being, how they relate to God and the role of faith in reentry, and how they experience the church. In addition, nine of the nineteen participants shared about their experiences in relationship with a faith-based mentor. Findings from the second study conducted with faith-based mentors served to strengthen understandings of returning sisters' spiritual and religious experiences and offered insights into faith-based mentoring relationships. The wisdom revealed by participants' lived experiences, in correlation with the wisdom revealed in chapters 1 and 2, serves as the foundation for the development of Project Sister Connect, the model for revised prison ministry praxis and justice-seeking spiritual support posited in chapter 4.

Chapter 4

Project Sister Connect

Rather than reinforcing the abuse and oppression so many returning sisters experienced during childhood, as adults, and as the result of the prison industrial complex, Project Sister Connect is grounded in practices of radical acceptance, connection, and righteous indignation in the face of structural injustices, as exemplified in the ministry of Jesus. Based upon the wisdom shared by returning sisters and reported in chapter 3, as well as the wisdom revealed through the literature in chapters 1 and 2, chapter 4 presents Project Sister Connect, a model for revised prison ministry praxis that facilitates women's successful reentry by enacting the Two Feet of Love in Action. The model includes the provision of charitable works, one of the two feet, through the development and implementation of a sisterhood that addresses returning sisters' holistic needs. In addition, the model entails striving toward social justice, the second of the two feet, by advocating for criminal justice reform at structural and super-structural levels. Prior to presenting the framework for Project Sister Connect, the importance of this call for revised prison ministry praxis is briefly reiterated.

THE PROBLEM

Over two million Americans are presently behind bars in state and federal prisons and county jails, and each year approximately 650,000–700,000 individuals return to their communities facing numerous barriers to successful reentry (Kaeble & Glaze, 2016; Willison, Brazzell, & Kim, 2011; U.S. Department of Justice, n.d.). In addition, there are 820,000 people on parole and an estimated 3.6 million on probation (Wagner & Rabuy, 2016). Although recidivism rates are difficult to determine, best estimates indicate that nearly two-thirds of released prisoners are rearrested within three years (National Institute of Justice, 2014). These staggering statistics evidence how structural injustices and oppressions can usurp the growth experienced behind bars of many inmates, and also expose the failure of the criminal justice system to rehabilitate many others.

The Church's Response

As indicated in the book's Introduction and in chapter 1, thousands of Christian congregations and people of faith engage in prison ministry. They offer worship experiences and Bible studies to inmates behind bars with the aim of evangelism and leading prisoners on the pathway to Christ. These ministries are vital and serve to evidence God's love for all God's children; regrettably, they most often overlook the 700,000 men and women who are released from prisons each year. The Christian imperative to care for prisoners too often stops at the prison gate. According to Johnson (2011), ministry inside the prisons is perceived as simpler and safer, and less messy and complex.

Congregations often avoid providing the care so desperately needed by returning citizens during reentry by attempting to become "welcoming churches" or "Stations of Hope" (Healing Communities, n.d.; Nolan, 2004). Many well-intentioned churches focus on becoming places where returning citizens can participate in worship and feel welcomed and not judged. For example, Nolan (2004) noted that "fear of rejection by their hometown church is one of the greatest fears many Christian inmates experience as their sentence comes to a close and they prepare for their return home" (p. 5). The returning sisters interviewed in this study did voice concerns that churches would judge them for their pasts. Nolan and others addressed the fear of rejection by creating a "welcoming church" that embraces returning citizens by fostering a sense of inclusion that lets them know God's love. Such efforts are not "bad" or "wrong," they are simply inadequate. Recall, for example, how only four of the nineteen participants in this study returned to their family's church or the church they attended before their incarceration; moreover, just two of the nineteen participants chose to intentionally seek out a new church family. Participants noted numerous barriers to regular engagement with a church including their fear of judgment, but also their experiences of being overwhelmed, misunderstood by church members, and the competing demands on their time. Reentry ministry necessitates meeting returning citizens where they are rather than requiring them to conform to the church, even when the church is a welcoming community. Reentry ministry requires meeting returning sisters' holistic needs—needs related to education and employment, substance abuse and mental illness, poverty and relationships—that cannot be addressed simply by participating in worship.

Participating in the life of a congregation can be an important factor for some returning sisters, but it cannot be the key to unlocking the provision of faith-based support. "Welcoming churches" inadvertently tend to maintain the prison industrial complex rather than abolishing it by doing little to change unjust laws and policies regarding mass incarceration, ignoring how structural injustices impact returning citizens, and failing to enact *both* charitable works *and* social justice, the Two Feet of Love in Action.

In addition, the majority of reentry ministries are predicated on the belief that crime results from individual immorality (Dismas Ministry, n.d.; National Benevolent Association, n.d.; Nolan, 2014; Prison Fellowship, n.d.-c). For example, Nolan (2004), a leader in the Prison Fellowship movement, stated that "crime is, at its root, a moral and spiritual problem, and breaking free of criminal attitudes and behaviors requires a spiritual transformation" (p. xvi). Models for reentry ministry that support this perspective then aim to rehabilitate and transform criminals into spiritually grounded, morally upstanding citizens. The problem with this approach is that it is narrow in its reach and intends only to serve returning citizens who are interested in "getting religion" (McRoberts, 2002, p. 5). In addition, reentry ministries that view the primary cause of incarceration as moral failure, and thus fail to see how structural injustices and the prison industrial complex impact inmates and returning citizens, implicitly support a "boot straps" mentality that views barriers to reentry as individual obstacles that can be overcome through prayer, right belief, and right action. The Christian church needs models of prison ministry that view crime as more than moral failure and that recognize the complex systemic factors that contribute to women's incarceration. In addition, the Christian church needs models of reentry ministry that enact the Two Feet of Love in Action by working toward the transformation of hurting people as well as broken systems.

The Government's Response

In 2001, President George W. Bush established the White House Office of Faith-Based and Community Initiatives and made it abundantly clear that the government alone cannot meet the needs of inmates or returning citizens (Johnson, 2011). The establishment of the Office of Faith-Based and Community Initiatives, along with the passage of the Second Chance Act, evidenced government efforts to harness the power of faith-based reentry services. Erzen (2017), however, criticized governments for failing to address the needs of returning citizens and opting instead to leave the task to faith-based organizations, thus creating an unjust overdependence. The impetus for the government's dependence on faith-based organizations was not the result of empirical data evidencing the efficacy of such programs; rather, it was financial. Erzen recounted two poignant examples of this. First, when the state of California was ordered by the U.S. Supreme Court to release 30,000 prisoners in 2011, rather than reallocating state funds to meet the prerelease and reentry needs of the soon-to-be returning citizens, the state allowed this vacuum to be filled by faith-based programming, or not to be filled at all. Second, "In 2003, Ellsworth Correctional Facility in Kansas cut its GED program in half and eliminated the substance-abuse program, but opened a Prison Fellowship ministry" (Erzen, 2017, p. 164). As previously mentioned, faith-based programs like Prison Fellowship's InnerChange Freedom Initiative cannot operate on government funds due to the separation of church and state. Therefore, the facility's decision to reduce and eliminate programs so sorely needed by inmates resulted in the state passing the bill to the church.

The Need for Partnership

Many conservatives argue that faith-based organizations are best suited to care for returning citizens because crime is a moral failing that requires rehabilitation through spiritual transformation. The government, however, cannot eschew its responsibility to returning citizens, and thus to society, and leave churches to fill the gap. Many liberals argue that the government is best suited to care for returning citizens because it was the government's War on Drugs and unjust sentencing laws that resulted in the prison industrial complex and the incarceration of millions of Americans. Churches, however, cannot deny their responsibility to returning citizens by assuming that if they are welcomed, they will come. Collaboration and leveraging the collective capital of both the government and faith-based organizations is likely the only way of effectively addressing this epidemic. Yet the failure of government and faith-based organizations to effectively establish partnerships can be summarized in one word, according to Johnson (2011), *"prejudice"* (p. 193). Faith-based organizations think that government and academic institutions are prejudiced against people of faith and religious institutions, and governments and academics are concerned that saving souls is the sole goal of prison ministry.

It is time that such prejudices are faced head-on and that partnerships between government and faith-based organizations are established in a manner that leverages the best of what each has to offer. Toward this end, intermediary organizations, such as United Way, Goodwill, and Catholic Charities, can play an important role in bridging the gap between government and faith-based organizations. Any congregation seeking to expand its prison ministry beyond bars can implement Project Sister Connect, the model for revised prison ministry praxis posited below. Yet because systemic change depends upon church-state partnerships that hold each entity responsible for meeting the needs of returning citizens, Project Sister Connect will be more successful long term if supported by intermediary organizations and implemented by local congregations. The importance of partnerships and the role of intermediaries will be revisited following the presentation of Project Sister Connect.

PROJECT SISTER CONNECT

Project Sister Connect is the fruit of the exercise in practical theology endeavored in chapters 1–3. Critical correlation or dialogue between the lived experiences of returning sisters (chapter 3) and social scientific scholarship (chapters 1 and 2) resulted in the generation of wisdom that undergirds this model for revised prison ministry praxis. Project Sister Connect is a model of ministry intended for use by concerned citizens, people of faith, and congregations who desire to meet the needs of returning sisters in a manner that is justice seeking, spiritually integrated, empowering, and gender responsive.

Two Feet of Love in Action

Abolishing the prison industrial complex requires dismantling the structural injustices that oppress and entrap women prior to, during, and following incarceration. This will not occur if Christians simply focus on meeting the material needs of returning sisters. Therefore, as previously stated, Project Sister Connect aims to engage the Two Feet of Love in Action by extending justice-seeking spiritual support to returning sisters as well as working to eliminate the structural injustices that ensnare them during reentry. Therefore, one step of Project Sister Connect is to provide charitable works through the development and implementation of a sisterhood, a model of spiritual support presented in greater detail below. The other step entails striving toward social justice by advocating for criminal justice reform at structural and superstructural levels. This means working to eradicate high recidivism rates and the structural injustices that result from the prison industrial complex. Enacting the Two Feet of Love in Action is a key step for addressing the barriers plaguing returning sisters at the micro level as well as at the structural and superstructural levels of their ecological contexts.

Underlying Assumptions

Prior to presenting the model for revised prison ministry praxis, it is imperative to identify three underlying assumptions. First, as a methodology, practical theology encourages the examination of sacred text and tradition in addition to social scientific wisdom. *Women Leaving Prison* took a unique approach by viewing the lived experiences of returning sisters and faith-based mentors as sacred and evidence of the continuous revelation of God's wisdom and love. Numerous books and articles offer biblically based and theologically grounded perspectives on prison ministry that fail to elevate the voices of returning sisters and listen for how God may be speaking truth through their lived experiences. This book offers a corrective to this one-sided approach and, instead, considers women's experiences themselves to be a sacred text.

Second, Project Sister Connect recognizes that individuals from various faith traditions, as well as individuals outside institutionalized religion, desire to help and to serve returning citizens. Therefore, although Project Sister Connect requires the sponsorship and support of a Christian church, sisters who engage in this ministry can be of any or no faith. Concerned citizens are encouraged to serve in the sisterhood, and all sisters must respect one another's relationship to religion. Moreover, returning sisters are not required to be Christian or to profess Jesus as their Lord and Savior. They should, however, be seeking spiritually integrated care and support. The relevance of this ministry to female returning citizens outside the Christian faith is distinctive given that the vast majority of faith-based reentry services require a profession of faith. Moreover, serving the needs of all returning citizens, regardless of faith, is essential if the supporting congregations are to develop meaningful partnerships with government.

Third, any model aimed to empower returning sisters necessitates a gender-responsive approach to care. Project Sister Connect recognizes that the needs of female returning citizens are markedly distinct from their male counter-parts'. As detailed in chapter 1, the backgrounds and demographics of female inmates and returning citizens, along with their unique pathways to prison, necessitate services and interventions that reflect the gendered nature of their experiences. If women are to be successful in reentry and avoid recidivism and prison's revolving door, pre- and post-release programs need to address women's unique needs and experiences (Galbraith, 2004). Gender-responsive support during reentry requires the provision of wraparound or holistic services, implemented along a continuum of care, by culturally competent providers (Berman, 2005; Covington & Bloom, 2006; Holtfreter & Morash, 2003; Morash, 2010). For example, it was noted in chapter 3 how returning sisters often need treatment for substance use disorders and, for many sisters, treatment for co-occurring mental illness. In addition, they need to explore the relational precursors and outcomes of their substance use and mental health problems, including experiences of past victimization and abuse. As with any supportive relationship, maintaining confidentiality is essential and not doing so can jeopardize the relationship and the success of Project Sister Connect. The sisterhood is expected to keep any and all information shared by the returning sister confidential unless permission to share is granted or requested by the returning sister. Trust and confidentiality are vital for justice-seeking relationships intended to promote healing and wholeness.

Enacting Charitable Works through the Sisterhood

As noted above, one step of engaging the Two Feet of Love in Action involves assisting returning sisters via charitable works. Project Sister Connect does this by developing and implementing a sisterhood, a community of spiritual support for returning sisters. Toward this end, the sisterhood utilizes aspects of existing ministries that are, anecdotally, already known to be effective.

Building on What Works

As noted in chapter 2, despite governmental efforts to determine what works in reentry and to privilege evidence-based practices, it is methodologically difficult to verify best practices in female reentry. Based upon the available literature, it appears that care is most effective when it is gender-responsive, attends to women's co-occurring disorders, and entails a mentoring component. Two models of ministry offer insights for enacting these best practices.

First, Stephen Ministry is a one-on-one caregiving ministry that was developed in 1975 to train laity in the provision of spiritual care and support to fellow congregants (Haugk, 1984). The name was derived from the ministry of Stephen, who in the book of Acts was tasked with offering care in a manner now central to the Christian faith. Trained Stephen Ministers typically provide one hour of care, once a week, to an assigned care receiver. To date, more than 600,000 individuals have been trained as Stephen Ministers and are serving in over 12,000 churches throughout the world (Stephen Ministries, n.d.). Project Sister Connect borrows from this model by training laity to provide individual spiritual care and support to a female returning citizen who, much like care receivers in Stephen Ministries, is experiencing transition. The uniqueness of Project Sister Connect is that individual care providers, called sisters, perform a specific role or function and act as part of a larger team. Despite the vast numbers of Stephen Ministers and care receivers, no controlled outcome studies have been conducted on the effectiveness of the ministry (Tan, 2013). Moreover, despite the popularity of Stephen Ministry, there is no evidence in the literature that it is or was used with female returning citizens.

Open Table is another model of ministry that trains laity to help individuals seeking to effect change in their lives. In the Open Table model, volunteers join together to form a Table and enter into a year-long relationship with an individual experiencing poverty. "The Table members, together with the individual or family being helped establish goals, accountability, develop an overall plan and implement it" (Open Table, Inc., 2017a, p. 1). The Open Table model is based on the Wraparound Process and is in the nascent stages of demonstrating empirically validated efficacy (Open Table, Inc., 2017b). Project Sister Connect draws upon the Open Table model in that each individual caregiver, or sister, functions in a distinctive role. In addition, the sisterhood in Project Sister Connect operates in many ways like a Table with the intention of providing wraparound services. Building upon the success of Stephen Ministry and Open Table, Project Sister Connect utilizes aspects of these two models in order to meet the three best practices in female reentry outlined above.

The goal. Project Sister Connect is a model of reentry ministry wherein a sisterhood of five to seven women partner with and empower a returning sister as she navigates the vicissitudes of reentry by forming connections and facilitating spiritual support. In solidarity with the returning sister, the sisterhood helps her to overcome the structural injustices that function as barriers to successful reentry by providing spiritual, psychological, and material support. The goal is not only to positively impact the life of the returning sister, but to remove her from prison's revolving door, thereby reducing the likelihood of recidivism in a way that directly impacts the effects of the prison industrial complex.

The sisterhood. Depending upon the distinctive needs of the returning sister, the sisterhood is comprised of five, six, or seven women, or sisters, whose mission is to support the returning sister in her reentry. Each sister occupies one of the following roles: spiritual companion and coordinator, referral resource, phone friend, goal auditor, technology and career counselor, twelve-step sponsor (if needed), and parent-child advocate (if needed). All sisters in the sisterhood covenant to support the returning sister for one year following her release from prison, although the role of the spiritual companion and coordinator is more involved and requires a longer commitment. The role and function of each of the sisters is described below. These positions do not require specialized training or a particular degree. However, the goal is to recruit women with a degree of competence in the role they will fulfill but who also possess the passion and heart to walk alongside the returning sister in solidarity as she attempts to meet her goals in various life domains. Based upon the desire of many returning sisters to talk with others who have experienced reentry, and the motivation many successful returning sisters have to give back and help others, the phone friend and the twelve-step sponsor are two roles that could be successfully fulfilled by appropriate returning sisters. Figure 4.1 details the sisters that comprise the sisterhood. As members of the sisterhood walk together, their faith journeys will likely be enriched.

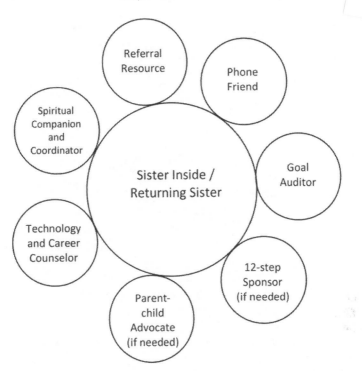

Figure 4.1 **"The Sisterhood of Project Sister Connect."** The Sisterhood of Project Sister Connect is comprised of five to seven support sisters who perform specific tasks to assist the returning sister by ameliorating the barriers she faces to successful reentry. *Source*: Copyright 2018 by Author.

The spiritual companion and coordinator. The spiritual companion and coordinator has the greatest responsibility within the sisterhood. This sister establishes the relationship with a sister inside, a female inmate who will soon be a returning sister, through a process outlined below. She is responsible for writing to and visiting the sister inside on a regular basis in order to establish a relationship and, eventually, to conduct a strengths-based assessment, a process also explained below. As spiritual companion, this sister engages in a "special form of friendship that offers a space of freedom in which we can be honestly ourselves and explore our deepest spiritual longings" (Stewart-Sicking, 2016, p. 28). For some sisters inside, these spiritual longings may fit neatly within the Christian tradition and may be enhanced by the study of sacred scripture. For other sisters inside, they may identify as part of another religious tradition, as part of no religious tradition, or their spiritual and religious beliefs and practices may be more eclectic and "cafeteria style." Regardless, the spiritual growth that can often occur inside needs to be nurtured and supported by a spiritual companion. Becky, one of the participants in the study grounding this book, shared how the returning sister "needs to have someone to contact. She needs to have someone that could do that role with [as spiritual companion]. Once you start that spiritual journey you're reminded how it relates to addiction and so much more." If such spiritual support is not provided, the returning sister may "lose focus" and lose faith, as described by Shanice in chapter 3.

The spiritual companion and coordinator is also required to be an active member of the supporting congregation. The responsibilities of the supporting congregation are detailed below, and it is the job of the spiritual companion and coordinator to serve as a liaison between the sister inside and the wider church family. She may request prayers on behalf of the sister inside; with permission, she may share updates on the sister's status and anticipated release date; and she solicits support for the sister inside from the congregation, for example via letters and birthday cards. When the sister inside is released, the spiritual companion and coordinator invites her, as she is now a returning sister, to participate in the life of the congregation. Participation in the life of the supporting community is encouraged, but it is not required. If the returning sister wants to participate in worship or in other activities and ministries, the spiritual companion will work with other members of the congregation to provide transportation and resources required for the returning sister's full participation.

As spiritual companion and coordinator, this sister is also responsible for recruiting women to fulfill the other four to six roles in the sisterhood. These women may be recruited from the supporting congregation, but they may also be recruited among concerned citizens in the wider community. The spiritual companion and coordinator is in charge of establishing the sisterhood, coordinating their training, and serving as a liaison between the inside sister and the sisterhood prior to the release of the sister inside.

Prior to her release from prison, the spiritual companion and coordinator works with the sister inside to secure housing. This might be in a transitional or reentry program, it might be in the home of a friend or family member, or it might be with a member of the congregation. However, the spiritual companion and coordinator helps to solidify a plan for stable shelter during reentry that enables the sisterhood to then help the returning sister focus on other pressing needs and concerns. In addition, the sister inside and the spiritual companion and coordinator work together to establish a structured schedule for the returning sister's first week outside. For inmates who are not released to a program, this structured schedule is essential for easing the returning citizen's transition between the rigidity of prison time and the fluidity of time outside (Berman, 2005).

Referral resource. The sister serving as the referral resource is responsible for amassing a detailed and expansive guide to community resources.

Numerous reentry guides featuring local resources across areas of need can be found online for many major cities and urban areas. Counties also frequently publish resources online to assist returning citizens. Once the spiritual companion and coordinator conducts the strengths-based assessment (a process detailed below), the referral resource should seek to establish direct relationships with personnel working at the organizations relevant to the returning citizen's needs. She should be prepared to make referrals prior to the release of the sister inside as well as during her reentry. As evidenced in chapter 2, female returning citizens greatly benefit from the provision of wraparound services. The sister serving as referral resource is responsible for functioning as a liaison with community organizations in order to provide wraparound care for the returning sister; however, all of the sisters collaborate to support this process.

The referral resource is also responsible for helping the returning sister to acquire health insurance. Changes in the Affordable Care Act will significantly impact if and how returning citizens are eligible for health insurance. However, at present, sisters inside, if eligible, can sign up for Medicaid coverage while incarcerated although they cannot receive coverage until they are released. If sisters inside are not eligible for Medicaid, they have a sixty-day special enrollment period following their release in which they can purchase health insurance through the marketplace without waiting for the annual open enrollment window. Applying for health insurance is a complex process requiring a significant amount of documentation and paperwork. Even still, many returning citizens will find they are unable to secure affordable coverage, yet another structural injustice plaguing many returning citizens. The sister serving as referral resource plays an important role in helping the returning sister to pursue all available options. This is especially important given the behavioral health and medical needs experienced by many returning citizens. As Sandra noted, even returning sisters who received some guidance inside about reentry need someone to walk alongside them. She stated,

A lot of them [returning citizens] don't know what to do when they come out, even though they have reentry in there. I had that in there. Reentry, job readiness, all that. Financial. The same stuff I'm taking here. When you come out, sometimes that stuff go right out the daggone door.

The referral resource in particular, and the sisterhood in general, empowers women to recall and utilize the information they may already possess about successful reentry and to garner the resources necessary to support that process.

Phone friend. Access to a cell phone can be a critical component in reentry as it helps to connect returning citizens to supportive family and friends as well as prospective employers. As detailed in chapter 2, the Sober Network IPT was a cell phone based intervention used with female returning citizens with co-occurring disorders (Johnson, Williams, & Zlotnick, 2015). Project Sister Connect modifies this program in order to assist returning sisters in connecting with the sisterhood and, when relevant, using the phone as a tool to support sobriety and obtain employment. One of the key financial contributions of the supporting congregation is the provision of a cell phone that is loaned to the returning sister immediately upon her release. The phone numbers of everyone in the sisterhood are programmed into the phone. The returning sister is permitted to use the phone for one year after which the number can be transferred to a new contract for which she is responsible. The phone friend plays a unique role in that she is responsible for texting or calling the returning sister every day for the first thirty days following her release. If she does not receive a response from the returning sister within twenty-four hours, she notifies the other sisters. The phone friend should be available to receive calls as much as possible, although the returning sister is encouraged to call anyone in the sisterhood for support as needed.

Tasha and Sandra, two participants in the study grounding this book, both spoke about the importance of having a phone friend, a fact corroborated by the literature (Johnson, Williams, & Zlotnick, 2015). Tasha explained the significance of having someone to listen to you during reentry when she said, "'Cause a lot of people in reentry don't have somebody that's really listening to them and hearing what they're saying. And really looking at them and seeing them." Sandra spoke about the benefit that comes when you can count on one person to be there for you every day. She said, "If I was coming home today, what would make a difference is maybe having somebody for the first 30 days . . . take them new places and stuff like that. Have somebody that would be with you for the first 30 days. Like my sponsor." Although the phone friend is not responsible for transportation, she is responsible for being a consistent, day-in, day-out presence in the returning sister's world.

Goal auditor. As was noted in chapter 2, female returning citizens benefit from setting concrete goals and tracking steps toward their completion, provided it is not done prematurely or in a way that overwhelms (O'Brien & Lee, 2006). Based upon the strengths-based assessment conducted by the spiritual companion and coordinator (a process described below), the goal auditor works with the returning sister to establish short-, mid-, and long-term goals. These goals may be small, like spending twenty minutes studying for the written driver's test, or large, like regaining custody of a child. The goal auditor helps the returning sister to establish attainable goals and to audit progress toward their completion. The goal auditor and the returning sister meet weekly, either by phone or in person, to assess progress and revise goals as needed.

Technology and career counselor. Many returning sisters need help ~~~~~ ing technology, a competence that is often required for securing employment as so many job applications today must be completed online. The technology and career counselor helps to guide returning sisters in technological training including basic computer literacy, and for things that may have changed during their incarceration, such as using credit-like cards for transportation and advances in cell phone technology. Recall Desiree, a participant in the study grounding this book, who was incarcerated for two and a half years, yet upon release struggled to understand the "new" smart phone technology.

The technology and career counselor also supports the returning sister, when relevant, in seeking employment. As noted in chapter 2, many returning sisters have limited employment histories. Moreover, they face numerous barriers to employment as the result of their time behind bars. The returning sister and the technology and career counselor can work together to create or to strengthen her resume, to navigate the challenges of the online job application process, and to practice interviewing skills. The technology and career counselor can help the returning sister to discern the type of employment that meets her skills, but also what she feels to be her calling. If additional education or training is required, the technology and career counselor can help the returning sister to research opportunities and make application.

Parent-child advocate (if needed). Given the prevalence of sisters inside who are mothers to minor children, the parent-child advocate occupies an important role in the sisterhood for returning sisters with minor children. As evidenced in chapter 2, reintegrating with children following incarceration is often more challenging than returning citizens expect. This is true for myriad reasons, such as the strain of navigating "the system" and the interpersonal dynamics that often arise with extended family or others responsible for childcare during the mother's absence. The role of the parent-child advocate will differ greatly according to the returning sister's circumstance; however, possible functions of the advocate include working with the returning sister to seek legal guidance if she lost custody of her children and is seeking to regain it; accompanying the returning sister when visiting her children under foster care or the care of an extended family member; helping the returning sister to plan outings with minor children who are or are not in her custody; connecting the returning sister to parenting support groups such as Parents Anonymous; assisting the returning sister in locating appropriate daycare or childcare, if needed; or listening to and supporting the returning sister who regains custody of her children and is struggling to fulfill her obligations as mother. As reported in chapter 2, according to Scroggins and Malley (2010), the childcare needs of returning sisters with minor children are woefully unmet. Therefore, these are just a few of the important functions that the parent-child advocate may fulfill.

Twelve-step sponsor (if needed). If the returning sister is in recovery, regardless of the addiction, or if she is the adult child of an addict/alcoholic, she may decide, through consultation with the spiritual companion and coordinator, to seek the support of a sister who functions as a twelve-step sponsor. This can happen in a variety of ways and is the most malleable role in the sisterhood. For example, some sisters inside continue relationship with outside sponsors they had prior to their incarceration. In such cases, the sister inside could choose to invite her sponsor to participate in the sisterhood. She may also choose not to, perhaps to further diversify her network of support. If the sister inside does not have a sponsor, once she is established in a twelve-step fellowship, she may decide to seek out a sponsor. Inviting that individual to participate in the sisterhood is optional but encouraged. As explained above, the sisterhood is comprised of five-to-seven sisters, each with a designated role and responsibility, who work together to address the psychological, emotional, material, and spiritual needs of the returning sister. Although formal training is not required, there are numerous training opportunities that sisters may find helpful.

The Training

As stated above, working with an intermediary organization such as Catholic Charities would enable access to government funding and support in a way that could facilitate expanded training opportunities. However, as churches work to develop the sisterhood and implement Project Sister Connect before such partnerships are established, there are numerous free and low-cost training opportunities that can strengthen the sisterhood and enhance the ability of each sister to fulfill her role. For example, sisters will be better equipped to meet the needs of returning sisters if they receive training in the art of motivational interviewing. Motivational interviewing is a counseling technique that can help sisters to assess the returning sister's motivation for change and, as relevant, to enact positive behavioral changes. Motivational interviewing is an evidenced-based practice that has demonstrated efficacy with many health conditions, including substance use disorders and chronic conditions like diabetes. The Substance Abuse and Mental Health Services Administration (SAMHSA) offers numerous online resources for training in motivational interviewing, including a free online training sponsored by the University of Missouri Kansas City School of Nursing and Health Studies (SAMHSA, n.d.). An introduction to the technique enables sisters to assess the returning sister's motivation for change so that the sisterhood can avoid carrying the motivation for the returning sister in a way that does not facilitate behavioral change. No matter how motivated the supportive sisters are, the success of the returning sister's reentry is predicated upon her own internal motivation and the support she receives toward achieving her own goals.

Second, if the sponsoring congregation is home to a Stephen Ministry program, the sisters participating in Project Sister Connect are advised to contact a Stephen leader to provide a workshop or a series of training sessions in the art of spiritual listening and responding that is central to Stephen Ministry. The sisterhood may also be able to receive this type of training from a Stephen leader outside the congregation or through a faculty member at a local seminary or divinity school.

Third, the sisterhood and the supporting congregation can receive training from Healing Communities or other faith-based organizations whose mission it is to support communities of faith in broadening the spiritual care they offer to include returning citizens, individuals at risk of incarceration, and their families and communities (Healing Communities, n.d.). The goal of Healing Communities is to transform congregations by de-stigmatizing incarceration and raising awareness about the plight of returning citizens. According to Stanley (2016), "Its focus is not on programs, but on perspectives" (p. 60). Therefore, the training offered by Healing Communities is focused on consciousness-raising in a way that is relevant to any supporting congregation seeking to start or expand its prison ministry.

Finally, sisters can learn from the experiences of other local reentry experts. Project Sister Connect is a model for revised prison ministry praxis that was informed by the wisdom of the female returning citizens who participated in the study grounding this book as well as the available literature. Although the model is intended to be relevant to congregations and communities across the United States, sisters will benefit from connecting with training opportunities and resources at the local level. Many local referral resources can be found online, as mentioned above. In addition, programs sponsored by county and state agencies as well as nonprofit organizations may offer training for reentry mentors and for the friends and family of returning citizens. Sisters are encouraged to participate in such trainings in order to connect them better with local and regional resources and opportunities.

Enacting the Sisterhood

The work of the sisterhood begins behind bars.

Going inside. According to Galbraith (2004), "Developing relationships with women while they are in prison must be a priority since strong and healthy relationships will be central to women's success when they are released back into the community" (p. 205). Establishing relationships with inmates during their incarceration is an essential element of gender-responsive care as it fosters trust, increases the likelihood that a woman will continue in the relationship upon her release, and maximizes the woman's time behind bars. The spiritual companion and coordinator is responsible for establishing a relationship with a sister inside who is seeking spiritually integrated reentry care and desires to participate in Project Sister Connect.

Churches wishing to expand their prison ministry by engaging in Project Sister Connect may wonder how they can establish a relationship with a sister inside. The goal is to identify a sister inside who will likely be released in six to twelve months. Some inmates time-out, or max out, and serve their entire sentence and are released without community supervision. These inmates are more likely to have an anticipated release date. However, many inmates do not know their release date and may go before the parole board annually for years on end only to be continuously denied parole. If a relationship with a sister inside is established and her release does not occur within the anticipated timeframe, surely God is at work in this relationship even if the sisterhood cannot begin its service in the timeframe previously expected.

How do congregations identify a sister inside? There is no one way to do this, and the path for each congregation will be unique. For example, many congregants have friends or relatives currently incarcerated. Seeking a referral from within the congregation can be a powerful way of garnering congregational support as it helps to de-stigmatize incarceration and strengthen the wider faith family. A second option is for the spiritual companion and coordinator to contact the chaplain at the state women's prison, explain the program, and ask for the chaplain's assistance in identifying a sister inside who is seeking spiritually integrated support that would continue through reentry. The chaplain could then serve as a liaison by connecting a sister inside to the spiritual companion and coordinator, and helping the sister inside to add the spiritual companion and coordinator to her list of permitted visitors. If the congregation has a vibrant prison ministry behind bars, a third option is to partner with a sister inside who is already participating in the congregation's prison ministry. It is important to avoid favoritism, and therefore churches may need to reflect critically on how to engage in a selection process. Finally, because Project Sister Connect serves sisters inside of any or no faith, the spiritual companion and coordinator may also connect with a prospective sister inside through volunteers serving in educational or other capacities. As evidenced in chapter 1, many participants in this study engaged in individual spiritual practices in prison but did not participate in faith-based programming or worship. The sisterhood may be able to connect with sisters inside who choose not to participate in corporate religious life by seeking referrals through educational and other nonreligious programs. Once a relationship with a sister inside is established, the spiritual companion and coordinator is then responsible for continuing that relationship, as noted above, as well as conducting a strengths-based assessment of the sister inside and assisting her in obtaining identification.

Strengths-based assessment of the sister inside. The spiritual companion and coordinator should plan to spend at least two months getting to know the sister inside through visitation and exchanging letters prior to conducting the strengths-based assessment of her needs and assets. Once a relationship and rapport are established, and the spiritual companion and coordinator knows more about the background and journey of the sister inside, the two can collaborate on conducting a strengths-based assessment. The spiritual companion and coordinator is encouraged to utilize the *Success in the Community: A Matrix for Thinking about the Needs of Criminal Justice Involved Women* that was published by the Women's Prison Association (WPA, 2018). According to the WPA (2018), "a woman's success is related to the degree that there are adequate provisions in six domains of her life: livelihood, residence, family, health, criminal justice compliance, and social connections" (para. 1). This matrix can help the sister inside to reflect upon the assets and needs she has in each of the six domains in order to move from survival, to stabilization, to self-sufficiency. After the strengths-based assessment is complete, the results can be shared with the referral resource who can begin researching how the needs of the sister inside can be addressed prior to her release. In addition, the matrix can help the sister inside to begin to articulate goals that the spiritual companion and coordinator can share with the goal auditor. A copy of the matrix can be found in Appendix E.

Obtaining identification. More often than not, sisters inside do not have valid state identification either because it expired during their incarceration or it was lost or damaged prior to or during their incarceration. Moreover, according to the Council of State Governments Justice Center (2016a), "people returning from incarceration rarely have access to birth certificates and Social Security cards, which are frequently required for obtaining state identification, and the process for procuring such documents can be daunting and costly" (p. 1). Although the process of obtaining identification differs by state, for most sisters inside and returning sisters it is complicated and arduous. Moreover, a lack of state identification impedes the ability of returning citizens to access social services and apply for jobs. Some state prisons will help inmates to obtain birth certificates and Social Security cards, but this requires that the inmate have the money in savings to cover the expense. At present, seven states will issue state identification to returning citizens who can present identification that was issued by the state's Department of Corrections (DoC), and more states need to adopt this model (Lantigua-Williams, 2016). Federal and state prisons are increasingly trying to help inmates to overcome this barrier to successful reentry, and laws are now beginning to change. The spiritual companion and coordinator needs to research and determine state laws in order to know how she can help the sister inside to obtain state identification and work to secure it prior to or immediately following her release.

Meeting at the gate. Andrea and Sandra, two participants in the study grounding this book, both noted the importance of having someone to meet you at the gate. Having someone waiting at the gate is not just about logistics and the provision of transportation. Rather, it symbolizes the support that one does or does not have in navigating the barriers of reentry. Therefore, once a release date is set, the sisterhood establishes a plan to meet the returning sister at the gate in order to welcome her home and to provide transportation and other resources. At that time, the inmate should know where she will be living based upon her efforts working with any reentry services offered inside, the spiritual companion and coordinator, and the referral resource. The referral resource is then responsible for ensuring that the returning citizen has adequate clothes, toiletries, and food, which can be donated by the supporting congregation, and an adequate supply of medication, if needed. The sisterhood then transports the returning sister to her residence and briefly helps her to get settled. The technology and career coordinator provides the returning sister with her cell phone and makes sure she is confident in knowing how to use it. The sisterhood can work with the returning sister's family and friends, if applicable, to coordinate any gatherings and to provide transportation.

The first week home. The sisterhood will walk closely alongside the returning sister for the first week following her release. This is essential because, as Tasha noted in her interview, "I think women need positive support systems . . . I think women need other women in their lives who are willing to support them unconditionally, whole-heartedly, and consistently. And meeting them where they're at on their terms." Chelsea echoed the importance of this when she noted how returning citizens need "support. They need good people in their corner that can lead them in the right way." The returning sister will be given the detailed schedule she created collaboratively with the spiritual companion and coordinator, which includes daily in-person appointments with a different sister for the first week and daily texts/phone calls with the phone friend.

Regular meetings. After completing the first week outside, the returning sister will meet with the sisterhood for one to two hours on a weekly basis for the first three months following her release. After that point, the sisterhood may decide to decrease the frequency of meetings, but only if requested by the returning sister. Weekly meetings may take place at the supporting congregation or in the home of one of the sisters. Transportation for the returning sister should be provided by a fellow sister, or fees for public transportation should be reimbursed by the supporting congregation. The weekly meetings follow a detailed agenda, which can be found in Appendix F.

A key element of the sisterhood's weekly meetings is to help the returning sister to adopt a balanced perspective of her reentry experience that recognizes her strengths alongside her growing edges and her accomplishments alongside her needs. Returning sisters benefit from a community of support that celebrates successes and offers encouragement and help in the face of barriers. As Chelsea shared, returning citizens often come home with "nothing" and lack the patience that is helpful in rebuilding one's life. She stated,

> When you [returning sister] come home you have nothing. You're starting over. You don't have many people in your life and it's all about like wanting it all like yesterday. So it's like just for them to have patience. And just know that it will come. You know. Because I feel like that's a lot of times what will get women and men locked back up or back in that negative environment. It's that they'll run out and try to get these things and rather than that I think that having patience and peace and good people surrounding them, that would just be beneficial for them.

The patience required to take small steps toward rebuilding one's life is a spiritual discipline, and it is one that can be made more manageable through the care of a supportive group of sisters.

Moving on. As noted above, the sisterhood covenants to meet and to support the returning sister for one year. However, the relationships may live on well into the future. As the one-year anniversary of the returning sister's release approaches, however, the sisterhood should make a plan for how the returning sister would like to be supported into the future. This could range from infrequent gatherings to celebrate important dates and milestones to the continuation of regular, structured meetings. The power to decide this resides with the sisterhood, and should meet the needs of the returning sister. In addition, the technology and career counselor should work with the returning sister to plan if or how she will establish her own cell phone contract. Sisterhoods are encouraged to incorporate the supporting congregation in planning a ritual or celebration to honor the returning sister's journey and success.

The Role of the Sponsoring Church

As previously stated, the sisterhood and Project Sister Connect depend upon the spiritual and material support of a sponsoring congregation. For some supporting congregations, this may be the only form of prison ministry they provide. For others, Project Sister Connect may be part of a larger prison ministry that includes the provision of other services both inside and outside the prison. Either way, the success of Project Sister Connect is predicated upon the commitment of the supporting congregation. Interested congregations need to enter into a period of prayer and discernment to determine if they are being called and guided to participate in this type of prison ministry. Prospective congregations might consider holding a Healing Communities training at their church to help the congregation to learn more about reentry and the barriers faced by returning citizens. This would help to foster the community's discernment process. Although the spiritual companion and coordinator is the only member of the sisterhood required to have membership in the supporting congregation, the support of the congregation is imperative to the ministry's success.

Congregations who choose to adopt Project Sister Connect as part of a prison ministry are required to provide both spiritual and material support. As indicated above, the spiritual companion and coordinator serves as a liaison between the sister inside and the supporting congregation. This continues after the sister is released, unless she decides to begin participating in the life of the congregation. The spiritual companion and coordinator shares prayer requests with the supporting congregation who is responsible for praying for the sister inside/returning sister as well as the sisterhood and its ministry for the duration of their journey together. The referral resource also works with the congregation to solicit donations for the returning sister upon her release, including food, toiletries, and clothing, and to identify professionals in the congregation that may be equipped to aid the returning sister in addressing particular barriers in her reentry journey. For example, the referral resource may survey the congregation to see if anyone has expertise in a particular area, for example family law, depending on the returning sister's particular needs. Financially, the supporting congregation is responsible for purchasing and maintaining the monthly fees for a cell phone to be used by the returning sister for one year. In addition, the congregation should reimburse the returning sister for any expenses she incurs using public transportation to attend weekly meetings.

How Project Sister Connect Reflects the Spiritual Experiences of Returning Sisters

Project Sister Connect was developed in response to the spiritual and religious experiences of returning sisters, as reported in chapter 3, and is intended to address returning sisters' spiritual needs in a holistic manner. Therefore, this section offers a reminder of participants' lived experiences and outlines how Project Sister Connect reflects the wisdom they shared. As evidenced in chapter 1, many of the study participants viewed their incarceration as God-ordained. Participants believed that God locked them up and sat them down to change them for the better. For the most part, participants' faith practices behind bars, whether individual or corporate, seemed to facilitate positive religious coping. Therefore, upon their release from prison, many participants reported believing that God was in charge and that God provides. Some participants saw God as active in their adversity and struggles, and they expressed the importance of obeying God and letting God take the lead. Many of the participants voiced the desire to strengthen their relationships with God during reentry and felt that they needed God. However, participants also gave up on God during reentry and blamed God for not fixing their problems. Furthermore, a number of study participants explained the importance of God in their recovery from addiction and noted how God helped them to maintain sobriety. But, as Sandra said, the "church ain't gonna keep you clean."

Participants' experiences with the church during reentry varied. A minority of participants explained how the church will be there for you, but others criticized churches for not going to "the trenches" to help returning citizens and others who are truly in need. Participants shared how they felt judged and misunderstood by church folk, especially as members of the church may not recognize how overwhelming reentry can be. Whether or not participants engaged in the life of the church seemed to be predicated on their relationships with church folk. As participants explained, people of faith with histories of addiction and/or incarceration are uniquely poised to help returning citizens to feel connected to the church. In addition, participants tended to prefer smaller churches where they could make the personal, relational connections they desired. Finally, based upon the experiences of the female returning citizens who participated in the study, faith-based mentors seemed to play a minimal, even nonexistent, role in returning citizens' reentry experiences. Therefore, how does Project Sister Connect reflect participants' spiritual and religious experiences during reentry and offer a model for revised prison ministry praxis that engages the Two Feet of Love in Action?

"We Get It Where You Are. That's Where We're Going to Meet You At."

Foremost, as Tasha stated, returning citizens seek spiritual caregivers and congregations who can say "we get it where you are. That's where we're going to meet you at." Meeting returning citizens where they are requires people of faith and congregations to leave the sanctuary. The goal of Project Sister Connect is not only to create welcoming congregations, but congregations who are, as Sandra stated, willing to "go to extremes, to the trenches to get the people that really need that." Meeting returning citizens where they are means, first, meeting them inside the prisons. In addition, it means accepting that some returning sisters will desire to participate in the life of the congregation and some will not. Some returning sisters will be Christian, and some will not.

In caring for Christian returning sisters, Project Sister Connect recognizes that, according to study participants, returning citizens find comfort in congregations comprised of folk to whom they can relate. Latrise, Becky, Lisa, and others shared the comfort they received in being able to relate to religious leaders and laity alike who themselves had histories of addiction and/or incarceration. Andrea, Treva, and others explained how they appreciated small congregations as they foster intimacy and openness wherein congregants and leaders can keep up with and care for one another. But churches are called to care for the prisoner and the returning citizen regardless of their size or the histories of their leaders/congregants. How can churches do this if returning citizens are not Christian or do not want to participate in the life of the congregation?

The Importance of Relationship and the Sanctity of Sisterhood

As indicated in chapter 1, participants spoke about the importance of relationship in fostering their faith experiences behind bars. Friends as well as faith-based volunteers helped participants to feel spiritually centered and to nurture their connection to God. Project Sister Connect is grounded in the recognition that these same spiritual relationships are needed beyond bars. Reentry for many returning citizens means transitioning from a more communal to a more individual rhythm of existence, even for those who reside in residential reentry programs. Sisters inside are used to being around others 24/7, and many female inmates benefit from the fictional families and supportive relationships they cultivated inside. Project Sister Connect helps to address returning citizens' need for "close knitness" that, according to Treva, was so important to her spirituality and faith during reentry, and to her reentry success more generally. Experiencing the close knitness of the sisterhood may increase the likelihood that the Christian returning sister will want to participate in the life of the supporting congregation, but that is not the goal. Project Sister Connect capitalizes on returning citizens' need for a "positive support system" that, as Tasha said, is comprised of "other women in their lives who are willing to support them unconditionally, whole-heartedly, and consistently." After facilitating Kairos retreats inside the prisons, and serving as a faith-based mentor to over thirty returning citizens, Sharon also indicated that the returning citizens who are successful and rehabilitated have two things in common: a good spiritual support system and the desire to give back. The support of the sisterhood evidences and embodies the love and care of God to returning sisters whether or not they are Christian and whether or not they participate in the life of the supporting congregation.

Seeking God or a Spiritual Center

Participants explained how God ordained their incarceration in order to sit them down. Sitting them down was God's way of forcing participants into the time and space they needed to get to know God better and to begin to allow God to change them. Reentry rips returning sisters out of that time and space. Therefore, returning sisters benefit from the structure and support provided by the sisterhood as they work to continue nurturing the returning sisters on their spiritual journeys.

Project Sister Connect is intended to strengthen the faith of returning sisters who, like Danielle, have "always yearned to have a spiritual connection with God" and work toward that during reentry regardless of how "pained up" she's been. Project Sister Connect is intended to help returning sisters who, like Deborah, knew their mother's or grandmother's God, but want to "get to know God for you." Project Sister Connect is intended to help returning sisters who, like Shanice, "lost sight" of God during reentry. As she stated, "You send a person out there that's learning to read the Bible, starting to believe in some stuff, and you send them out into the wilderness. They disappear." The spiritual companion and coordinator takes a lead role in helping participants to get to know the God of their understanding, to strengthen their relationship with God, and to nurture their faith and understanding if it is new or being challenged. The other sisters in the sisterhood also help to strengthen the faith of returning sisters by evidencing God's love. Loving "with word or with tongue" is important, but loving "in deed" is an equally important way of loving our neighbor and embodying God's care (1 Jn 3:17–18).

In addition, Project Sister Connect helps returning sisters who are not Christian to find or maintain their spiritual center and to live out the spiritual, religious, or humanistic values that are central to their own beliefs and orientation. As noted above, sisters participating in Project Sister Connect may be members of the supporting congregation, they may be Christians with membership in other congregations, or they may be concerned citizens or adherents of other faith traditions. Project Sister Connect is intended to strengthen the spiritual center of all sisters in the sisterhood by fostering relationships grounded in mutuality, care, and concern.

Cultivating Spiritual Community

Project Sister Connect helps to address the barriers to church participation experienced by participants. Desiree felt misunderstood by her family's church and the church of her childhood. She felt they could not understand how she'd been changed by her experience of incarceration. The sisterhood helps to ameliorate this barrier as the sisters are knowledgeable about the vicissitudes of reentry and walk closely with the returning sister to understand the uniqueness of her experience. The sisterhood recognizes that, like Tasha, many returning sisters are "overwhelmed" and are not yet able to give back to the congregation or community as they face the barriers of reentry.

The sisterhood understands the importance of employment in reentry and how many returning citizens may be employed in positions that require work on the weekend and during worship. The sisterhood creates its own weekly time of spiritual connection that reflects the schedule and commitments of the returning sister.

God's Providence Enacted through Sisterhood

Participants spoke at length about God's providence during their incarceration and shared a confidence that God would provide during their reentry. God's providence is often mediated by humanity. As St. Teresa of Avila famously stated, "Christ has no body now but yours. No hands, no feet on earth but yours" (as cited in Journey with Jesus, n.d., para. 1). The sisterhood serves as the hands and feet of God to enact God's providence in the lives of returning sisters. The sisterhood can help to sustain participants' belief in God's omnipotence and providence by meeting the returning sister's spiritual and material needs, as appropriate, in accordance with the life and teachings of Jesus. Faith-based mentors shared how they provided emotional and spiritual support to returning citizens, and how when appropriate, they offered material support, referrals to resources, and even the opportunity for employment. Project Sister Connect can evidence God's providence in a way that reflects participants' faith, understanding, and experience of God. Moreover, although it is not a goal of Project Sister Connect, experiencing God's providence will likely enrich all members of the sisterhood and nurture them on their faith journeys.

Developing Social, Cultural, and Spiritual Capital

Participants spoke about the skills they needed to navigate reentry and to live successfully outside. Some of these skills can be learned in a classroom, but many of them are taught directly and indirectly through quality mentoring relationships. Although Danielle let her relationship with her mentor "fizzle out," she was intentional about cultivating a mentoring relationship because "I knew this woman knew how to succeed as a woman and I didn't. And I wanted to learn, to learn how to do that." Project Sister Connect helps returning sisters to develop the social, cultural, and spiritual capital that is essential for a successful reentry experience. Finding employment is easier when one has a social network and capital. The sisterhood can facilitate this. Navigating unhealthy familial relationships is easier when there is someone outside the family system to offer perspective and support. The sisterhood can facilitate this. Avoiding the lure of the streets and learning how to work and live life on life's terms, in recovery, is easier when there are supportive sisters to serve as guides and accountability partners. The sisterhood can facilitate this. Moreover, Project Sister Connect recognizes that the ᴄᴀᴘᴵᴛᴀᴸ each sister needs to cultivate is distinct.

Modifying the Sisterhood

The sisterhood component of Project Sister Connect is not intended to be a universal model for reentry ministry. Rather, Project Sister Connect provides scaffolding within which supporting congregations and sisterhoods can work to best meet the needs of returning sisters. For example, sisters inside may serve thirteen months in prison or thirteen years. They may be one of numerous members of their family known to the justice system, or they may find themselves estranged from their family as the result of their imprisonment. The diverse backgrounds and prison experiences of returning citizens necessitate different forms of care and support. For example, women who served life sentences may present greater needs related to technology and employment than returning citizens who served shorter sentences; therefore, the sisterhood may consider dividing the responsibilities of the technology and career counselor between two sisters. Female inmates with histories of addiction who are trapped in prison's revolving door may face greater judgment and less acceptance from family members; therefore, the sisterhood may consider adding a second phone friend to the sisterhood to provide more daily contact with the returning sister for the initial period following her release. The spiritual companion and coordinator, in concert with the supporting congregation, is encouraged to work within the structure of Project Sister Connect to tailor the model in a way that leverages the strengths and attends to the growing edges of the returning sister, the sisterhood, and the congregation.

Evaluating the Efficacy of the Sisterhood

Project Sister Connect differs from other models of reentry ministry as it is grounded in insights from social scientific research and the lived experiences of female returning citizens. Many reentry ministries were developed in response to anecdotal data, but few result from exercises in practical theology and critical engagement with both theory and practice. This does not mean, however, that the sisterhood is guaranteed to be successful.

As noted above, determining best practices in reentry programming poses methodological challenges, especially given that reducing recidivism is typically the only benchmark of success. Nevertheless, supporting congregations need to plan how they will evaluate the efficacy of Project Sister Connect prior to its implementation. Preventing recidivism is an important goal that needs to be considered alongside a number of intended outcomes. Again, supporting congregations may wish to tailor the program's intended outcomes in order to meet the unique goals of the returning sister, the sisterhood, and/ or the supporting congregation. However, by design, Project Sister Connect is intended to prevent recidivism, support societal reintegration through the cultivation of supportive relationships, promote recovery from substance abuse, and facilitate employment (Petersilia, 2004; Vigesaa, Bergseth, & Jens, 2016).

The goals of Project Sister Connect are directly linked to the six domains of life included in the *Success in the Community* matrix that grounds the strengths-based assessment conducted by the spiritual companion and coordinator prior to the release of the sister inside (see Appendix E). Therefore, the sisterhood's efficacy is determined, in part, through the work of the goal auditor who helps the returning sister to monitor her progress toward short-, mid-, and long-term goals. The goals as well as the progress made should be documented and, as noted in Appendix F, revisited and reevaluated on a regular basis. In addition, monitoring the returning sister's progress on the *Success in the Community* matrix is a second way of evidencing the Project's efficacy. The sisterhood and/or supporting congregation may wish to establish and track progress toward other goals, yet development in these six basic domains of life is essential to reducing recidivism, cultivating supportive relationships, promoting recovery from substance abuse, and obtaining employment.

The reader may question why the spiritual growth and transformation of returning sisters is not listed as a formal goal of Project Sister Connect. The answer is both practical and theoretical. First, garnering support for reentry ministry requires sound practices in program evaluation. Measuring or evaluating spiritual growth and transformation is problematic and, some would argue, impossible. For example, returning sisters may find that their faith is tested during reentry, yet remain in lament and conversation with God in a manner similar to Job. Such experiences of spiritual struggle do not negate the possibility that spiritual growth is simultaneously occurring. Other returning sisters may exit prison and maintain the strong faith they developed during their incarceration in a way that demonstrates little spiritual growth as the direct result of participating in Project Sister Connect. Therefore, while spiritual growth may be an outcome of Project Sister Connect, it is not a goal because, as a construct, its measurement is problematic.

In addition, spiritual growth is not a goal of Project Sister Connect for theological, not just practical, reasons. Project Sister Connect is grounded in the theological belief that Christians are called to care for all returning citizens, not only citizens of a particular religious tradition or a particular denomination/church. In his ministry, Jesus served the Jews, the Gentiles, the Canaanites, and individuals from various religious and social locations; Jesus's example is one that Project Sister Connect aims to emulate. The majority of congregations that sponsor faith-based reentry programs often adopt exclusionary and narrow conceptions of the Christian tradition and what it means to be a Christian. This is due, in part, to the fact that most reentry ministries are grounded in churches and traditions that view crime as a moral and spiritual problem (Nolan, 2004). The ethic of spiritual and religious inclusion that is central to Project Sister Connect requires welcoming and caring for returning sisters from a diversity of spiritual and religious backgrounds, with a diversity of spiritual and religious destinations. For example, returning sisters may come from a non-Christian background wherein the fruits of spiritual growth may manifest differently. Given the tremendous needs of female returning citizens, it seems exclusionary and un-Christian to limit the outreach of Project Sister Connect to a small percentage of returning citizens who adhere to a narrow conception of the Christian life.

Project Sister Connect and the Role of Intermediaries

As noted above, scholarly experts in the area of prison ministry, including Johnson (2011) and Erzen (2017), argued persuasively that partnerships are the only way to engender justice-seeking spiritual support for returning brothers and sisters. One way of brokering church-state partnerships is through intermediary organizations like Goodwill and Catholic Charities. Intermediary organizations are selected by a federal agency to receive government funding, and they in turn send out a request for proposals and review applications from faith-based organizations seeking financial support for program implementation. Local faith-based organizations and congregations can submit proposals and receive government funds, funneled through and managed by an intermediary, to support their reentry ministry, provided that the reentry program does not discriminate on the basis of religion, the funds are not used to support religious activities, and any religious activities that do occur must take place at a separate time and in a separate place from government-supported programming. Intermediaries provide the opportunity for churches and faith-based organizations to engage in the capacity building that is so essential for successful reentry ministry.

Supporting congregations are encouraged to implement Project Sister Connect for a defined trial period, for example two to three years. During that time, the supporting congregation should adapt Project Sister Connect to the needs of the returning sisters served and the particular congregational and community contexts. The supporting congregation, through the work of the goal auditor and the sisterhood, diligently assesses the goals of the returning sister and is methodical in evaluating the program's success. With knowledge of the model and an understanding of its efficacy, churches are then encouraged to apply for funding through an intermediary. As repeatedly stated, viable reentry ministry requires partnership between government and faith-based organizations and, as Johnson (2011) opined, too many reentry services operate in isolation and without the capacity to build or sustain the ministry. Project Sister Connect, and any model of reentry ministry, will be more successful long-term if it is implemented by local congregations and supported by the government via intermediary organizations.

ENACTING SOCIAL JUSTICE BY ADVOCATING FOR CRIMINAL JUSTICE REFORM

Spiritual care of female returning citizens requires attending not only to the women themselves but to the unjust and broken systems that contributed to their imprisonment and erected barriers to their successful reentry. True reform requires changes at the micro level for returning sisters, which then impact their family and environment, as well as at structural and super-structural levels. The following section outlines how individual and communal care of female returning citizens can be accompanied by Christian advocacy for criminal justice reform. Abolishing the prison industrial complex is imperative and requires attending to unjust and discriminatory practices that result in imprisonment, but also those that impede the successful reentry of returning citizens and too often lead to recidivism. This section offers small, pragmatic steps to change the laws and structural injustices that impede women's successful reentry.

Addressing Structural Injustices

Improving the reentry experiences of female returning citizens requires eradicating the barriers they face as individuals, at the micro level, but also within a broken system, at the structural and super-structural levels. People of faith and concerned citizens can work to address these structural injustices by advocating for and working toward reform in three areas: residential reentry programs, substance use treatment, and employment.

As evidenced in chapters 2 and 3, women face numerous barriers to successful reentry related to housing and relationships. Successful reentry is predicated upon secure and safe housing. The vast majority of female returning citizens cannot afford to rent an apartment or purchase a home. Regrettably, establishing residence with family or an intimate partner can entail exposure to drugs and alcohol, "the streets," and/or relational discord that does not support returning citizens' desistance from crime. Given that women represent just 7 percent of the total prison population, priority has been placed on developing prerelease programs and residential reentry programs for men (Carson & Anderson, 2016). However, female returning citizens' need for housing and healthy relational support necessitates expanding the options currently available for short- and long-term, gender-specific, holistic support in a residential context. Upon release from federal prisons, 80 percent of returning citizens live in a residential reentry center (U.S. Department of Justice, 2016). However, the majority of inmates are sentenced to state, not federal, prisons. Therefore, more prerelease and residential reentry programs are needed at the state level. Concerned citizens and people of faith should visit the DoC website in their state to familiarize themselves with the prerelease programs serving female inmates. In states that lack prerelease programs for women, concerned citizens and people of faith can organize and lobby the state DoC and the state governor to prioritize establishing such programs. In states that already sponsor prerelease programs for women, concerned citizens and people of faith can volunteer in the prerelease programs to provide much-needed services to their returning sisters. Concerned citizens and people of faith can also support nonprofit and faith-based residential reentry programs. Inmates need more information about such programs, the requirements for participation, and the application process. We can volunteer to represent these organizations in prison-based reentry fairs and to disseminate information about the programs to faith-based mentors and volunteers.

Given the prevalence of substance use disorders among women in prison and female returning citizens, expanded opportunities for drug and alcohol treatment are needed both inside and outside the prison. Because federal prisons provide far more substance use treatment than state prisons, people of faith and concerned citizens are encouraged to focus their efforts at the state level. The first step is to research the type of treatment offered within the state women's prison and to advocate for employing evidence-based treatment that is gender responsive. In addition, given the prevalence of substance use disorders among female inmates, concerned individuals should identify the programs' capacity to serve female inmates and advocate for expanded coverage. Advocacy in both areas can be done by organizing to lobby the state governor and the commissioner of the state DoC. Illustrating the cost-effectiveness of drug and alcohol treatment inside, and the impact it has upon recidivism as evidenced by the literature, can be an effective means of changing politicians' hearts and minds. In addition, because female inmates will occasionally write to Narcotics Anonymous (NA) or Alcoholics Anonymous (AA) to request the support of a sponsor, if the reader is in recovery and part of a twelve-step fellowship, she can volunteer to serve as a sponsor to a sister inside. This can be the beginning of a relationship that continues through reentry.

Concerned citizens and people of faith are also encouraged to increase the availability of substance use treatment for female returning citizens. One way to do this is by supporting residential treatment facilities through both financial and human capital. In addition, both inmates and returning citizens need to know about residential treatment programs, the requirements for participation, and the application process. Volunteers can represent these programs and share information about them with churches, faith-based mentors and volunteers, and reentry coordinators inside. In addition, concerned citizens and people of faith need to create a list of the twelve-step programs, such as NA and AA that meet in the community, as well as faith-based programs like Celebrate Recovery. By establishing relationship with sponsors and leaders in these local groups, concerned citizens and people of faith can serve as a liaison between returning citizens and sources of local support.

Unjust systems that delimit employment opportunities for returning citizens also need to be addressed. There are numerous ways that concerned citizens and people of faith can ameliorate such barriers. First, the need to "ban the box" will be addressed below as it requires advocating for policy changes. But until all fifty states mandate the removal of questions about past convictions on job and housing applications, some returning citizens will benefit from getting assistance to seal their records. These laws and processes differ by state, but can, in some circumstances, enable returning citizens to prevent prospective employers from accessing their criminal record. The process and required paperwork can be arduous and confusing, and returning citizens may benefit from the help of a concerned citizen or person of faith. Another way to address the barriers of employment is to advocate at the city, state, and federal levels for an increase to the minimum wage. Given that a minimum wage does not automatically guarantee that full-time employees will be capable of meeting basic needs and achieving an equitable standard of living in a particular region and economic context, campaigns are needed that advocate for a living wage. Living wage campaigns are underway across the country and concerned citizens and people of faith can become involved in these efforts and help to mobilize others. Finally, small business owners can partner with prerelease programs and residential reentry programs to volunteer in job readiness programs and to provide employment opportunities for returning citizens. Small business owners are encouraged to research whether their state DoC already partners with local businesses, as some states provide business owners with prescreened referrals and bond the employees. In addition, small business owners should research the tax incentives they may be eligible for by providing employment opportunities to returning citizens. The Work Opportunity Tax Credit is a federal credit, ranging from $1,200 to $9,600, that businesses are eligible for if they hire a returning citizen with a felony conviction who was released from prison within the last year (U.S. Department of Labor, n.d.).

Changing Laws

Concerned citizens and people of faith are called to heal the broken systems that erect so many of the barriers to reentry faced by female returning citizens. This cannot be accomplished without changing discriminatory and oppressive laws. Legislative efforts are underway that could significantly improve the lived experiences of female returning citizens. Concerned citizens and people of faith must speak out and advocate for the rights of returning citizens on three key issues.

First, as noted above, many of the barriers to reentry can be weakened when inmates are released with proper identification. In 2016, Attorney General Loretta Lynch and the Justice Department asked the governors of all fifty states to provide returning citizens with state identification if returning citizens furnished their identification issued by the state DoC (U.S. Department of Justice, 2016). Concerned citizens and people of faith should write to their governor and legislators to encourage them to heed the directive issued by Lynch and the DOJ and to formally change the state's policy. Further instruction on how to do this can be found online through the Legal Action Center (n.d.).

Second, as indicated above, all fifty states need to "ban the box" and prevent prospective employers and landlords from inquiring about applicants' criminal history on applications for employment and housing. Over fifty local governments and nine states engaged in ban the box reforms in order to alleviate the structural and systemic discrimination experienced by so many returning citizens (All of Us or None, n.d.). Concerned citizens and people of faith are encouraged to know their city, county, and state laws and to advocate for reform both locally and at the federal level. Campaign tools and additional information can be found online through All of Us or None (n.d.).

Third, inadequate healthcare and a lack of health insurance represent significant barriers to the successful reentry of female returning citizens, especially given the chronic behavioral health and medical issues common among this population. Project Sister Connect aims to help returning citizens obtain health insurance, but the opportunity for affordable healthcare can only be made possible through progressive policies at the federal level. As indicated above, under the Affordable Care Act, inmates can apply for Medicaid and, if eligible, coverage will begin upon their release. In addition, returning citizens have a sixty-day window following their release in which they are able to secure coverage through the marketplace, although the plans differ widely by state and may or may not be "affordable." The potential repeal and replacement of the Affordable Care Act, and the cuts that programs like Medicaid and Medicare face under the Republican-proposed tax reform bill, may dramatically impede returning citizens' access to medical and behavioral health care. Concerned citizens and people of faith need to take action and advocate for the just provision of health care for returning citizens. Families USA is a 501(c)(3) that "works hard to achieve high-quality, comprehensive, and affordable health care for all Americans" (para. 1). The organization was founded in 1981 and offers detailed, comprehensive action kits online in order to guide citizens in advocating for improved health care for all.

Improving the reentry experiences of female returning citizens can only be accomplished through justice-seeking spiritual support at the micro, structural, and super-structural levels, as evidenced in Figure 0.2 in the book's Introduction. Legislative reform requires significant time and patience. Concerned citizens and people of faith are encouraged to stay informed about proposed legislation that both directly and indirectly impacts female returning citizens, to write to and meet with representatives in order to give voice to the needs and experiences of female returning citizens, and to organize with others in order to lobby for laws that enact care for returning sisters, the least among us, as though they were Christ. However, concerned citizens, people of faith, and congregations will be strengthened by recognizing that the arc of the moral universe is long, and it bends toward justice, but it does not bend itself (Sinha, 2017). Therefore, improving the plight of female returning citizens requires avoiding burnout by engaging in healthy self-care practices and finding solidarity in community.

ACCEPTING THE INVITATION

In the Introduction, the reader was invited to consider her assumptions and beliefs about prison ministry and to reflect upon why it is imperative for the church and the government to prioritize faith-based care for female returning citizens. With an understanding of the backgrounds of female inmates and their pathways to prison, the role of faith behind bars, and the numerous barriers women face during reentry, the reader was encouraged to examine how a system, which is in many ways broken, can both harm and heal. With an understanding of returning sisters' lived experiences of spirituality and religion as well as the insights of faith-based mentors, the reader was called to see both the strength and the frailty of returning citizens, and to recognize how solidarity with returning sisters can serve to evidence God's love. This chapter posited a model for revised prison ministry praxis, grounded in the wisdom of social science and lived experience, that can be implemented in an effort to extend prison ministry beyond bars and provide compassionate care for the thousands of female returning citizens that churches, people of faith, and concerned citizens too often abandon at the gate. It is my hope that the reader will be both educated and encouraged by this book in a way that calls her to be in solidarity with returning sisters and to enact that care through holistic, gender-responsive spiritual support. However, caring for individuals is not enough. Concerned citizens, people of faith, and congregations need to look beyond Project Sister Connect to extend care to the broken systems that too often fail to help those it is intended to heal.

Appendix A

Study 1 Methodology

THEORETICAL FRAMEWORK

There are numerous approaches to qualitative research. Detailing the theoretical and philosophical frameworks grounding this study, along with the process employed, enables the reader to determine the study's quality and rigor. This study was rooted in a constructivist research perspective, which maintains that knowledge and reality are continuously constructed through language, with no distinction between the knower and what is known, nor between facts and values (Duffy & Chenail, 2009). The research methodology employed was Interpretative Phenomenological Analysis (IPA), a qualitative research approach that "is concerned with the detailed examination of the human lived experience" (Smith, Flowers, & Larkin, 2009, p. 32). IPA was well suited to this study because the research questions intended to uncover and elicit deep reflection on and meaning making of personal experience. IPA

> involves detailed examination of the participant's lifeworld; it attempts to explore personal experience and is concerned with an individual's personal perception or account of an object or event, as opposed to an attempt to produce an objective statement of the object or event itself. (Smith & Osborn, 2008, p. 53)

IPA combines phenomenology, hermeneutics, and idiography (Smith, Flowers, & Larkin, 2009). Phenomenology explores the lived experience of a particular phenomenon or event, in this study the experience of reentry. Analysis of participants' experiences necessitates disengaging from the "taken for granted" world in order reflect on the details of the experience (Smith, Flowers, & Larkin, 2009). In conducting such reflection, the researcher employs a hermeneutic, a way of making sense of and interpreting the experience, that is subjective rather than objective. IPA utilizes a double-hermeneutic in that the researcher attempts to make sense of the participant's experience as the participant also attempts to make sense of her own experience. The researcher employing IPA recognizes that she brings preconceptions and assumptions to the participants' experiences that may color the interpretation. This does not give the researcher "license to claim that our analyses are more 'true' than the claims of our research participants, but it does allow us to see how our analyses might offer meaningful insights which exceed and subsume the *explicit* claims of our participants" (Smith, Flowers, & Larkin, 2009, p. 23). Finally, an idiographic approach examines the unique experiences and perspectives of each participant and explores the details of this experience, in depth, in order to create a textured understanding and description. IPA requires purposeful sampling in order to obtain this depth. IPA allows the researcher to identify and be curious about the experiences that are unique to each participant as well as the shared experiences and perspectives common among participants.

RESEARCH QUESTIONS

The following three research questions guided the study: (1) What are the spiritual and religious experiences of female returning citizens? (2) What role do spiritual and religious communities play in women's reentry? (3) How do spiritual and religious resources help or hinder women's ability to cope during reentry?

SAMPLING, PARTICIPANTS, AND PROCEDURE

The study was reviewed and approved by Loyola University Maryland's Institutional Review Board. Participants were recruited through residential and nonresidential reentry programs. I sent a letter to program staff requesting their assistance and included a flyer featuring a description of the study and the criteria for participation. I encouraged staff to share the flyer with prospective participants and to hang it on community bulletin boards. I also visited residential reentry programs to recruit participants by giving a brief description of the study during the community gatherings.

Purposive criterion sampling was employed, and female returning citizens were eligible to participate in the study if they identified as female, were over the age of eighteen, and had served time in either a state or federal prison. Snowball sampling, specifically chain-referral sampling, was also employed. Participants were invited to share information about the study with fellow female returning citizens who also met the study criteria.

Sixteen of the nineteen participants were recruited through residential and nonresidential reentry programs; the remaining three participants were referred by word-of-mouth (snowball sampling). The study's recruitment procedures resulted in a relatively large sample population that is not typical for a study utilizing IPA. IPA typically employs a very small number of participants given the danger of "sacrificing breadth for depth" (Smith & Osborn, 2008, p. 56). However, interviews were conducted and the data was analyzed over a period of two years as a means of alleviating the danger of achieving breadth over depth and ensuring the rigor in the process of data analysis. Participants' demographic and background information is reported in Table 0.1 in the Introduction.

Semi-structured interviews were conducted with participants in a public place of their choosing or, when relevant, within the residential reentry facility. Participants were asked to complete a Demographic Form (see below). The study procedures were explained to each participant and she was asked to read and sign the Informed Consent Form. The interview questions are listed below and were used to guide but not constrict the conversation. Interviews ranged between thirty-five and seventy minutes, with an average length of fifty minutes. Interviews were recorded using a digital audio recording device. The author transcribed a number of the interviews and a transcription company transcribed the rest. Transcriptions were then imported into NVivo 11, a software program used for analyzing qualitative data, and were stored as a password protected file on a secured network. Participants were sent a summary of the interview as a means of member checking. Participants were asked to contact the researcher to state if there were any errors in the summary, if any of the data in the summary required amendment, and if the participant had any additional information to add. All nineteen of the study participants engaged in the member check process, and the vast majority of participants offered no corrections, amendments, or additions to the summary. Participants were thanked for their participation in the study with a $25 Target gift card.

DATA ANALYSIS

As noted above, IPA utilizes an idiographic approach wherein each participant's lived experience, as reported through the interview, is analyzed to construct a depth of understanding. Using NVivo 11, a line-by-line analysis of the first interview was conducted using the process of horizonalization (Moustakas, 1994). Every statement or sentence was considered equally relevant until the horizon, or the meaning of the phenomenon, began to emerge (Moustakas, 1994). Themes began to emerge and codes were applied, and a codebook was constructed that was continuously revised throughout the iterative coding of all nineteen interviews. After all the coding was conducted, emergent themes were organized into superordinate themes through the processes of abstraction, subsumption, contextualization, and numeration (Smith et al., 2009). NVivo 11 was used to create an electronic audit trail of the coding as a means of enhancing the study's reliability (Golafshani, 2003). The study's findings are not intended to be generalizable.

CREDIBILITY AND AUTHENTICITY

Qualitative research does not adopt a positivist research perspective. Therefore, traditional markers of excellence, such as internal and external validity, are not relevant. Instead, this study aimed to pursue authenticity and to uphold the following markers of quality that are relevant to constructivist qualitative research methods: fairness was pursued by honoring each participant's different construction; ontological authenticity was pursued by helping each participant to better understand and articulate her worldview and experience; educative authenticity was pursued by opening participants to others' constructions; and catalytic authenticity was pursued with the intention that the analysis might stimulate or result in action (Guba & Lincoln, 1989).

The study's rigor is also enhanced through the process of bracketing. Following each interview and throughout the data analysis, I engaged in bracketing by recording memos in NVivo 11. In the memos I attempted to identify my "vested interests, personal experience, cultural factors, assumptions, and hunches that could influence" my analysis of the data (Fischer, 2009, p. 583). I wrote a separate memo after conducting each interview and added to the memo after analyzing the transcript of the particular interview.

DEMOGRAPHIC FORM

FEMALE RETURNING CITIZENS STUDY

Directions: Please fill out the following basic information.

1. Age: _____
2. Race/ethnicity: _____
3. Religious affiliation: (if Christian, please specify denomination)
   _____

4. Were you sentenced to a state or federal prison? (please circle your response)
   a) state
   b) federal
5. How many times have you been incarcerated?: _____
6. How many years did you serve in your most recent (or only) incarceration?:
   _____

7. When were you released? (please provide month and year):
   _____

8. Did you have a faith-based mentor during your incarceration or reentry? (please circle your response)
   c) yes
   d) no

SEMI-STRUCTURED INTERVIEW QUESTIONS

1. Tell me about your spiritual and religious experience while incarcerated.
   a) What spiritual or religious programs did you participate in while inside?
2. Tell me about your spiritual and religious experience after you were released.
   a) What spiritual communities, if any, do you presently participate in (i.e., Alcoholics Anonymous, Narcotics Anonymous, a church, or other spiritual group)?
3. What impact has your spirituality or faith had upon your reentry?

Appendix B

Study 2 Methodology

THEORETICAL FRAMEWORK

Like the study conducted with female returning citizens, the study conducted with faith-based mentors also employed Interpretative Phenomenological Analysis (IPA), a qualitative research approach that "is concerned with the detailed examination of the human lived experience" (Smith, Flowers, & Larkin, 2009, p. 32). IPA was well suited to this study because the research questions are intended to uncover and elicit deep reflection on and meaning making of faith-based mentors' personal experiences.

RESEARCH QUESTIONS

The following four research questions guided the study: (1) What were the participants' lived experiences of serving as faith-based mentors to female returning citizens? (2) How did participants' faith communities relate to their service as faith-based mentors? (3) How was participants' spirituality or faith impacted by their service as a faith-based mentor? and (4) What were participants' perspectives on the spiritual and religious experiences of the female returning citizens they mentored?

SAMPLING, PARTICIPANTS, AND PROCEDURE

The study was reviewed and approved by Loyola University Maryland's Institutional Review Board. Participants were recruited through faith-based mentoring programs. I sent a letter to the directors of the faith-based mentoring programs requesting their assistance and included a flyer featuring a description of the study and the criteria for participation. I encouraged the director to share the flyer with prospective participants. I also visited the quarterly meeting of one faith-based mentoring program to recruit participants by giving a brief description of the study.

Purposive criterion sampling was employed, and faith-based mentors were eligible to participate in the study if they were over the age of eighteen, Christian, involved in a formal mentoring program with a female mentee, and an active mentor during the mentee's reentry. Snowball sampling, specifically chain-referral sampling, was also employed. Participants were invited to share information about the study with fellow faith-based mentors who also met the study criteria. The study's recruitment procedures resulted in five participants, which is typical of a study utilizing IPA research methodology. Participants' demographic and background information was not collected, but specifics on their history serving as faith-based mentors was reported in table 3.7 in chapter 3.

Semi-structured interviews were conducted with participants in a public place of their choosing, such as a coffee shop. The study procedures were explained to each participant and she was asked to read and sign the Informed Consent Form. The interview questions are listed below and were used to guide but not constrict the conversation. Interviews ranged between forty-six and sixty-six minutes, with an average length of fifty-six minutes. Interviews were recorded using a digital audio recording device. A transcription company was hired to transcribe the interviews. Transcriptions were then imported into NVivo 11, a software program used for analyzing qualitative data, and were stored as a password protected file on a secured network. Participants were sent a summary of the interview as a means of member checking. Participants were asked to contact the researcher to state if there were any errors in the summary, if any of the data in the summary required amendment, and if the participant had any additional information to add. All five of the study participants engaged in the member check process, and the vast majority of participants offered no corrections, amendments, or additions to the summary. Participants were thanked for their participation in the study with a $25 Target gift card.

DATA ANALYSIS

The data analysis process employed in this study was the same as that employed in the study conducted with female returning citizens (see above).

CREDIBILITY AND AUTHENTICITY

The process of seeking credibility and authenticity was also the same as that employed in the study conducted with female returning citizens (see above).

SEMI-STRUCTURED INTERVIEW QUESTIONS

1. When did you first become a faith-based mentor and why were you interested in this particular ministry?
2. What role does your church play in your ministry as a faith-based mentor?
3. How many mentoring relationships have you participated in?
   a) When did the relationship(s) begin (i.e., when the mentee was still incarcerated, upon release, following release)?
   b) How long did the relationship(s) last?
4. Based upon your experience as a faith-based mentor, what do you think the role of spirituality or faith is for women returning from jail or prison?
   a) Can you provide an example from a mentoring relationship?
5. How has your own spirituality or faith been impacted by your ministry as a faith-based mentor?

Appendix C

Faith-Based Programs in U.S. Prisons

Ample information about the variety of Christian faith-based programs in male and female prisons is available to the reader (Barnwell, 2016; Dawson, 2015; Perry, 2006; Sullivan, 2011). Therefore, the goal of Appendix C is to highlight briefly the most well-known faith-based programs in U.S. prisons in an effort to provide concrete examples of the potential role of such ministries in inmates' religious and spiritual lives.

Prison Fellowship (PF) was founded by Charles "Chuck" Colson, a former Nixon aide, who spent seven months in prison for obstructing justice related to the Watergate scandal. Colson viewed his incarceration as God-ordained, and believed "God had put me in prison for a purpose and that I should do something for those I had left behind" (Prison Fellowship, n.d.-a, para. 5). Colson incorporated Prison Fellowship in August 1976 in an effort to offer an alternative to secular rehabilitation programs in prisons that were not considered effective. Today, 11,300 PF volunteers across the United States serve over 26,000 inmates throughout the United States by "sharing the Gospel, spreading hope, and teaching life-changing classes" (Prison Fellowship, n.d.-b, para 2.). Although PF serves wardens, inmates, and volunteers alike, its ministry to inmates is an attempt to offer inmates the opportunity for a "new future in Christ" (Prison Fellowship, n.d.-b, para. 2). This is accomplished through a variety of faith-based programs, including Bible studies, discipleship courses, life skills classes, seminary-level classes, and mentoring opportunities. According to Hallet and Johnson (2014), PF is "America's largest non-profit organization offering religious programming in prisons" (p. 672), with faith-based prison programs operating in 30 percent of all U.S. prisons and other PF programs in 86 percent of prisons (Hallett & Johnson, 2014).

Kairos Prison Ministry International offers three to three-and-a-half day retreats at men's and women's medium- and maximum-security prisons.

The ministry began in 1976 and in 2016, Kairos was active in 300 prisons and juvenile detention centers throughout the United States and abroad (Barnwell, 2016). Over 30,000 Christian volunteers, from a diversity of theological backgrounds, have facilitated structured faith-based retreats with an estimated 250,800 inmates (Barnwell, 2016). The Kairos slogan is to "listen, listen, love, love" (Barnwell, 2016, p. 3). The first step is accomplished by offering a retreat based on the "short course" in Christianity, Cursillo.

> Cursillo is designed for Christians coming from normal parish life and assumes a certain level of religious education (e.g. knowledge of the Lord's prayer). Kairos, by contrast, is designed for prisoners who are mostly not church members and indeed may be actively hostile to the church. (Burnside, Loucks, Adler, & Rose, 2005, p. 37)

After participating in the weekend retreat, Kairos residents (inmates) are invited to participate in a weekly "Prayer and Share" gathering. In contrast to programs that emphasize salvation, Kairos emphasizes agape or unconditional love. Whether inmates participate simply to get the better, often home-cooked, food or cookies, or a variety of other extrinsic rewards, the outcomes are often favorable. Schneider and Feltey (2009) conducted a qualitative study with twelve female inmates who participated in a Kairos weekend, and reported the following: "Those who took part in Kairos described it as a spiritual weekend where volunteers would come into the prison and provide unconditional love, healing, and forgiveness. The women explained that they learned to love, rather than fear, God through this experience" (p. 453). The participants for whom Kairos was a transformational experience or turning point attributed this to the role of forgiveness. They experienced God's grace through the Kairos volunteers in a way that facilitated self-forgiveness.

Unlike Prison Fellowship and Kairos, Bill Glass behind the Walls is solely focused on evangelism and bringing people to Christ through a conversion experience. Bill Glass was a college and professional football player who had a conversion experience during a Billy Graham Crusade and felt called to offer ministry inside prisons. Forty-five years ago, Glass learned the value of sharing the power of Christ with male inmates via the unique talents and testimonies of athletes, entertainers, musicians, bikers, tightrope walkers, parachute jumpers, ex-offenders, and other speakers (Colloff, 1997). Most inmates attend Glass events because they are interested in the talents of the speakers, and they do not have a faith background (J. Aten, personal communication, October 31, 2017).

The tagline for the ministry is "Evangelism on the Edge" and the Bill Glass National Training Director, Jeff Aten, referred to the ministry as an Evangelism Training Ministry (J. Aten, personal communication, October 31, 2017).

Bill Glass partners with volunteers from local churches to provide personal conversations and prayer with attendees, with the objective of helping inmates to "make a decision for Christ" (J. Aten, personal communication, October 31, 2017). The website reports the number of souls saved at each event; during 2017, Bill Glass drew on the services of 4,603 volunteers to reach 139,916 inmates and help 31,516 inmates commit to Christ (Behind the Walls, n.d.).

During the first day of the event, platform guests entertain and share their testimonies. Following the speakers, inmates join small groups to talk further about what they heard and learn more about Jesus. Local churches provide the majority of the team members or volunteers who have been trained to facilitate the small group work. Following the event, local churches and organizations such as Crossroads Bible Study provide ongoing faith education. The church volunteers are trained by Bill Glass Ministries to provide an eight-week course that they conduct in partnership with the prison chaplain (J. Aten, personal communication, October 31, 2017).

In 1997, Coloff of *Texas Monthly* interviewed Bill Glass and he shared his views about the veracity of inmates' conversion experiences. "'It's debatable if their commitments are real,' says Bill Glass, 'but that's true of people in any church'" (Colloff, 1997, para. 25). Bill Glass Ministries does not collect or maintain data regarding inmates' conversion and recidivism. However, according to Glass, "If the inmate corresponds with one of the ministry's volunteers, regularly reads the Bible, and stays nonviolent, there's a good chance that he has been saved" (Colloff, 1997, para. 25). The program's focus on encouraging inmates' commitment to Christ is distinctive and may have a strong effect on inmates as it offers the possibility of relationship with a local church that can benefit their faith journey during reentry.

TWELVE-STEP PROGRAMS

Given the prevalence of past and present substance abuse among both male and female inmates, twelve-step programs, specifically Alcoholics Anonymous (AA) and Narcotics Anonymous (NA), are commonly offered in prisons and, given the breadth and inclusivity of how faith-based programs are defined, may be considered a faith-based program. The principles of twelve-step programs are spiritual in nature. Some members find that the principles integrate well with their religious beliefs, and the program is then experienced as religious. The twelve steps are rooted in the theologically and politically conservative perspectives of the early twentieth-century Oxford Group, which purported that the suffering of addiction results from individual sinfulness, and thus it can only be ameliorated by confession, acceptance of personal responsibility, and surrender to God (Mercadante, 1996). The twelve steps today consider addiction to be a spiritual disease, and therefore a spiritual solution is required. Accepting one's limitations and turning to a Higher Power are inherently spiritual tasks in that they require one to acknowledge the powerlessness and vulnerability that accompany human finitude (Sered & Norton-Hawk, 2011). Individual responsibility, although less commonly framed in the language of sinfulness, is considered the root cause of addiction, and therefore systemic factors and social inequalities are largely eschewed.

There is very little research evidencing the efficacy of the twelve steps among women, particularly incarcerated women and women post-release (Fiorentine & Hillhouse, 2000; Kaskutas, 2009; Pelissier & Jones, 2005; Sered & Norton-Hawk, 2011). A significant amount of the literature examining the twelve steps and female incarceration is written by feminist criminologists who express concerns regarding the non-liberative and non-empowering effects of the twelve steps among a population of victimized, marginalized, and disempowered women (Combs, 2010; Sered & Norton-Hawk, 2011). For example, first, the philosophy of the twelve steps encourages self-examination in order to determine if the twelve steps are the correct intervention for any given individual struggling with the spiritual disease of addiction. However, participation in twelve-step programs is often ordered as a condition of parole and probation. Second, many women inside prison may participate in it for the extrinsic benefits. In Sered and Norton-Hawk's (2011) study conducted in a Massachusetts state prison, "AA/NA meetings typically were the only activity that offered women a regular opportunity to get out of the cells, get a free cup of coffee, and accrue positive reports that potentially allow for early release from prison" (p. 319). Therefore, participation was viewed as coercive. Third, feminist criminologists critique the twelve steps for the emphasis placed on powerlessness. This is particularly problematic for incarcerated women who often lacked any agency in abusive familial and intimate relationships.

Nevertheless, participation in AA and NA, if elective, can function as a spiritual discipline that women adopt during incarceration and can continue to practice following their release. The community fostered through the twelve steps may not be helpful to all women, as feminist criminologists portend, yet the benefits of easily identifying a community outside can be tremendously powerful.

THEOLOGICAL EDUCATION IN PRISONS

Another form of faith-based programming in prisons is religious and theological education, which is both a formal and an informal endeavor. Over the past twenty years, the number of seminaries offering theological education to inmates is continuously increasing. According to the Global Prison Seminaries Foundation (GPSF), prison-seminary partnerships are present in fourteen states and enable inmates to earn certificates of ministry as well as undergraduate and graduate degrees (GPSF, 2017a). Such programs are far more prevalent in men's prisons, but are present in women's facilities as well. They are privately funded and staffed by seminary faculty and volunteers. A few of the largest and most respected programs are described below.

With support from Oprah Winfrey, in 1995 the New Orleans Baptist Theological Seminary started a four-year, undergraduate degree-granting seminary at the Louisiana State Penitentiary, known as Angola, under the leadership of Warden Burl Cain (Fink, 2004). The program specifically targets "lifers," and graduates are equipped to minister to fellow inmates (Hallett & Johnson, 2014). Graduates of the program are frequently transferred to other state prisons to serve as "missionaries." Programs similar to the Angola Bible College were then instituted at the Mississippi State Penitentiary in Parchman, Mississippi, Phillips State Prison near Buford, Georgia (Baptist Press, 2011), and the Darrington Seminary, an extension of the Southwestern Baptist Theological Seminary, in the Darrington Unit, a maximum-security prison in Rosharon, Texas.

New York Theological Seminary, at the request of its alumni, partnered with Sing Sing Correctional Facility in 1981 to create a Masters in Professional Studies (MPS) degree program that provides interfaith theological and ministerial education to inmates serving long sentences (Erickson, 2002). The MPS is a one-year, thirty-six-credit program that was developed to educate inmates to minister to other inmates, and therefore it contains a field experience component complete with supervision. It aims to teach "all of its students how to claim and reclaim their rightful identity as valued members of society" (p. 244). Studies conducted in the 1990s indicated lower rates of recidivism among MPS alumni (O'Connor, 1996; O'Connor & Erickson, 1997). Between 1982 and 2012, more than 400 candidates completed their degree (New York Theological Seminary, 2012).

In 2011, the New Orleans Seminary began a partnership with the Louisiana Correctional Institute for Women (LCIW) to offer an eighteen-hour certificate in Christian ministry. LCIW is the only women's prison in the state of Louisiana and houses 1,100 inmates. The average maximum sentence is twenty years (Baptist Press, 2011). This was the first program of its kind. But in an effort to increase seminary programs in women's prisons, the Global Prison Seminaries Foundation (GPSF, 2017b), an organization founded by Burl Cain, hosted a meeting in 2017 that included the current director of the seminary program at LCIW as well as others seeking to implement similar programs. According to the GPSF website, those in attendance at the meeting recognized that sisters inside need gender-responsive programming. Given the number of mothers behind bars, as well as the prevalence of physical and psychological abuse among sisters inside, GPSF noted

> that the seminary leaders and teachers must be able to provide a nurturing presence outside of the traditional classroom setting to encourage healthy relationship building until the students are equipped to support each other and their families outside of prison. (para. 3)

Formal theological education provides inmates with spiritual and religious education and guidance, equips them to minister to other inmates, and endows them with a certificate or degree that can aid in employment prospects upon release. For a more in-depth analysis of the roles and functions of seminaries in men's and women's prisons, the reader is referred to Erzen's (2017) book *God in Captivity: The Rise of Faith-Based Prison Ministries in the Age of Mass Incarceration.*

FAITH-BASED PRISONS

Faith-based prisons are a distinctive type of faith-based programming as they are typically housed in separate units or facilities in which the entire prison structure is predicated upon religious values. O'Connor and Duncan (2008) likened these units to monastic communities in that they are fully steeped in religious values. They stated, "Like the regular religious services in prison, these more in-depth programs rely on a mixture of staff and volunteers, but unlike the regular services, they usually explicitly aim and purport to reduce recidivism" (p. 86). As referenced earlier, given the separation of church and state, some faith-based prison units were deemed unconstitutional, for example, when a federal judge ruled that the InnerChange Freedom Initiative program in Iowa "coerced inmates into adhering to Christian beliefs and doctrines" (Mears, 2007, p. 32). Research reveals contradicting results regarding faith-based programs' efficacy even when programs are successful in upholding inmates' constitutional rights.

According to one body of research, faith-based prisons do not appear to significantly reduce recidivism (Aos, Miller, & Drake, 2006). This assertion was supported by a study of Prison Fellowship's InnerChange Freedom Initiative (IFI) as it was implemented at the Carol Vance Unit in Richmond, Texas (Johnson, Larson, & Pitts, 1997; Johnson, 2004; Johnson, 2011). However, IFI program graduates did have significantly lower rates of arrest than the matched and comparison groups as well as lower rates of incarceration in the two years following release (Johnson, 2011). This may be correlated to the aftercare provided by the IFI program as efforts are made to partner with both parole officers and congregations to support successful inmate reentry. LaVigne, Brazzell, and Small (2007) also found that Florida's Faith- and Character-Based Correctional Institution (FCBI) for women at Hillsborough, a female facility in Riverview, Florida, did not significantly reduce recidivism rates at six- and twelve-months following release. However, the chaplain and other staff members report maintaining contact with inmates who, as a result of participating in the FCBI, have a "smoother transition back into the community" (LaVigne, Brazzell, & Small, 2007, p. 35).

Hercik (2005), in conjunction with the U.S. Department of Health and Human Services, also aimed to determine the efficacy of faith-based prisons by conducting an evaluation of the Kairos Horizon Community, a faith-based residential rehabilitation program at the Tomoka Correctional Institution in Daytona Beach, Florida. The program targets inmates and their families, lasts for one year, and "has three main goals including increasing individual accountability, family responsibility, and employability in the community" (Hercik, 2005, p. 2). This is accomplished, in part, by creating a spiritually grounded community of support and accountability, and through volunteer-led programs on anger management, financial management, life skills, and religious programming.

Hercik's study aimed to determine if the Kairos Horizon Community (1) created a safer prison environment as determined by fewer infractions and solitary confinement stays, and (2) resulted in a reduction in prisoner recidivism. Hercik conducted a quasi-experimental study with matched comparison samples. The safety of the prison environment was measured and it was found that "Kairos Horizon participants experienced reductions from baseline to all follow-up points in the incidence of discipline reports, the average number of discipline reports per month, and the incidence of segregation stays" (p. 13). Although the majority of the treatment group was not released while the study was underway,

> very few releasees were rearrested during the follow-up period (33%), and even smaller proportions were reincarcerated (8%) or had their parole revoked (10%) . . . less than half of the former Horizon participants were rearrested during the high-risk period immediately following release from prison. (p. 16)

Finally, it is important to note that, according to Hercik, the faith-based volunteers who facilitate a significant portion of the curriculum aid in inmate reentry as they offer a connection to the community and their own congregational/faith homes.

Appendix D

The Efficacy of Faith-Based Programs

Appendix D provides a brief overview of the literature examining if and why, from an empirical perspective, religion "works" as a means of rehabilitating inmates.

THE EFFICACY OF FAITH-BASED PROGRAMS

Research on the relationship between religion and crime began in earnest in 1969. Hirschi and Stark (1969) conducted a study entitled *Hellfire and Delinquency* that examined the relationship between religious commitment and delinquency in youth. A relatively small number of studies were conducted between 1969 and 2001, when the creation of the Office for Faith-Based and Neighborhood Partnerships resulted in an increasing number of published studies attempting to empirically evidence the efficacy of faith-based programs. Asking whether faith-based programs "work" is a loaded question unless "working" is defined and the desired outcomes of a faith-based program are concretized. As previously stated, the goal most faith-based volunteers have for faith-based programs is inmate spiritual transformation; however, not only is that empirically difficult to measure, but it is not necessarily the goal of correctional staff. According to the literature, faith-based programs "work," or are considered effective, when they help inmates to adjust to the prison context, create positive change in inmates' attitudes, reduce infractions and misconduct, or decrease the time to rearrest or the likelihood of recidivism.

Prior to examining the efficacy of faith-based programs, it is important to explain how this task is laden with methodological problems. One problem with the studies examining the efficacy of faith-based treatment programs is that participants most often self-select, and inmates who choose or are eligible to participate in such programs are often low-risk. In addition, inmates may participate in these programs due to extrinsic rather than intrinsic benefits. For example, it may be that participation in the program is motivated by access to food, snacks, and even drugs brought in from outside the prison (material, extrinsic rewards), rather than a desire for greater spiritual or religious well-being (intrinsic reward). Given ethical concerns in utilizing random participant assignment, most studies employ nonrandom assignment or compare inmates who volunteered to participate with those who volunteered but were rejected. Finally, the majority of studies are correlational and therefore little is known about the specific ways in which spirituality effects change. Despite such methodological difficulties, numerous empirical studies evidence the way in which faith-based programs do and do not "work," for instance in helping inmates to cope and adjust to prison culture (see O'Connor (2004/2005) for a helpful summary of the methodological problems with studies of this type and the contradictory findings regarding the efficacy of religion according to twelve empirical studies).

Religiosity and Adjustment to Prison Culture

Johnson (2011) conducted a systematic review of the literature published between 1944 and 2010 that examined the relationship between religion and crime. Johnson identified 272 studies and, although the methodological limitations of the literature were acknowledged, he determined that 90 percent of the studies demonstrated an inverse relationship between religion and crime. It is beyond the scope of this appendix to review all 272 studies. However, a significant portion of the literature examines the role of religion in influencing inmates' adjustment to prison, which is most often measured using Wright's (1985) Prison Adjustment Scale, inmates' experiences of depression and coping, and their ability to avoid misconduct and steer clear from infractions and confinement.

Religiosity and Inmate Adjustment

One of the more methodologically sound studies regarding religiosity and inmate adjustment was conducted by Clear and Sumter (2002). They surveyed 769 male inmates from twenty different prisons in twelve different states to examine inmates' adjustment to prison by utilizing measures addressing prison adjustment (the Prison Adjustment Questionnaire; Wright, 1985), depression, self-esteem, and self-mastery, and in addition by recounting the number of times inmates were disciplined for various infractions and sentenced to confinement. Although the study's sample population was comprised of inmate volunteers (an opportunity sample), the study found that higher levels of inmate religiousness were associated with higher levels of prison adjustment. However, when depression, self-esteem, and self-mastery were used as controlling variables, they mediated the relationship between inmate religiousness and adjustment. Religiousness was also directly and negatively associated with the number of times inmates were sentenced to confinement, a finding that will be explored in greater detail below. As part of this same larger study, Clear and Myhre (1995) reported the findings of a qualitative study grounded in both individual and group interviews with inmates. The authors found that religion helps inmates to adjust to prison by aiding inmates in "dealing with the emotional strains of incarceration" (p. 22) and "dealing with the deprivation of imprisonment" (p. 23).

The body of scholarship evaluating the relationship between religion and inmate adjustment is quickly becoming significant. Therefore, Schaefer, Sams, and Lux (2016) conducted a meta-analysis intended to evaluate the effect of religious programming on inmate adjustment. Fifteen studies were utilized: eleven that evaluated inmate misconduct, three that examined inmate attitudes, and one that measured misconduct and changes in belief/attitude. Twelve of the studies were quasi-experimental and three were nonexperimental. Twelve of the fifteen programs evaluated did not have an established curriculum. However, the programs included aspects of the following: Bible study, worship attendance, mentorship or spiritual counseling, church leadership training, and faith education courses.

Findings indicated that the weighted mean effect size for attitudinal shifts was −.45 and for inmate misconduct was −.15 (Schaefer, Sams, & Lux, 2016). In this case, the negative effect size indicated a reduction in criminal attitudes and inmate misconduct. The mean differences between minor and serious forms of inmate misconduct were not significant. The authors suggested that the decrease in misconduct is due to the fact that "faith-based interventions increase the number of prosocial peers to whom offenders are exposed and diminish opportunity by limiting environments conducive to offending, aiding in the development of a noncriminal identity" (pp. 615–616). This may mean that the various faith-based programs and interventions employed are, in general, equally effective in encouraging inmates to act in accordance with prison rules. This implies that an inmate's personal spirituality may be less apt to cause behavioral change than participation in a defined faith-based intervention wherein inmates benefit from the social support. Second, the greatest effect in both attitudinal change and misconduct resulted from programs with a spiritual counseling component. Therefore, the authors suggested that "faith-based programs should seek to emphasize this prosocial component in their rehabilitative efforts" (p. 616). In addition, faith-based programs/interventions that entailed a Bible study component were associated with lower rates of misconduct, but no significant change in attitude, perhaps due to the social bonds with outsiders that are formed.

Religiosity and Prison Adjustment

The majority of research examining religiosity and prison adjustment focuses on the male inmate's experience. A small number of studies examine the relationship between spirituality/religion and adjustment/coping among female inmates. For example, Levitt and Loper (2009) conducted a study of 213 women incarcerated in state prisons to understand the relationship between stress, adjustment, institutional misconduct, and degree of personal support inmates reported receiving from religious participation. Participants were divided into four categories: (1) those who did not participate in faith-based programming (n = 61); (2) those who participated in faith-based programming and reported receiving no or little support from the activities (n = 37); (3) those who participated in faith-based programming and reported receiving moderate support from the activities (n = 50); and (4) those who participated in faith-based programming and reported receiving a significant support from the activities (n = 57). Participants who reported receiving significant support from religious activities indicated fewer depressive symptoms and fewer aggressive acts and infractions than participants who did not participate in faith-based programs. Participants who reported receiving significant support scored lower on the conflict scale of the Prison Adjustment Questionnaire in comparison to participants who reported receiving no to low support from faith-based programs. Again, this highlights the importance of social bonding and support promoted by faith-based programs.

Dye, Aday, Farney, and Raley (2014) also examined the relationship between religious engagement and prison adjustment among a sample population of 214 women serving life sentences at three prisons in one Southern state. The researchers administered surveys measuring religious engagement, prison adjustment, depression, and death anxiety, which also included open-ended questions. Using multivariate analyses, Dye et al. found that "as religious engagement increases, prison adjustment improves (evidenced by lower scores on the prison adjustment scale), and both depression and death anxiety levels decrease (net of controls)" (p. 398). The relationship is not causal, as "religious engagement alone does not explain depression or prison adjustment" (p. 399); however, it seems that religious engagement helps female inmates serving a life sentence to deal with feelings of depression, which then aids in their adjustment to life in prison.

Stringer (2009) also explored how religion and spirituality function in the lives of African American mothers in prison. Specifically, Stringer examined whether religion and spirituality help "mothers cope with the negative effects of being separated from their children" and "function as tools of agency for negotiating roles and overcoming role strain" (p. 326). African American mothers whose ability to parent their children is compromised by their incarceration may experience role strain, and Stringer's study aimed to uncover if and how religion and spirituality mitigated this stress. Stringer conducted focus groups with fifteen African American mothers in a maximum-security Midwestern prison. Prior to presenting the study's findings, it is important to note that participants viewed their incarceration as the result of individual and system factors, such as addiction and poverty, but also spiritual factors. Some viewed their incarceration as the work of God (i.e., "God sat me down for a second. I was doing something wrong" [p. 334]). According to Stringer, incarcerated African American mothers use spirituality and religion to cope with their experience of role strain and their separation from their children in four ways. First, the foundational ethic of participants' morality is relational in a manner consonant with the traditional African principle of "I am because we are." Therefore, at times the mothers felt ashamed for their parental failures and at times they felt solace at the intimate connections they had with their children. Second, participants felt compelled to give their cares and concerns over to God and to focus instead on navigating their incarceration and what was within their control. Third, participants relied on informal prayers to give voice to their own concerns and situations, their concerns about their children's safety and future, and to maintain hope. Finally, participants' own faith was nurtured by their ability to pass their faith onto their children. For many participants, knowing that their children are being raised with religious values facilitated their own coping.

Religiosity and Inmate Misconduct

Many individuals, perhaps especially those of a devout faith, may assume that high rates of religiosity are correlated to lower rates of deviance or misconduct. Intuitively it seems logical that the more devoted one is to upholding, for example, the values purported in Christian scriptures, the less likely she is to commit a punishable offense. However, empirical research investigating religion and deviance, from a social control perspective, resulted in conflicting results that, at times, are counterintuitive. The findings are intriguing and vast, yet due to space constraints, only a small portion of a much larger body of scholarship is presented below.

Camp, Daggett, Kwon, and Klein-Saffran (2008) conducted an evaluation of the Life Connections Program (LCP), a faith-based, eighteen-month program specifically designed to encourage desistance from crime. The study aimed to determine whether participation in LCP related to a decrease in prison misconduct during participation in the program. The study compared

443 participants in the LCP to 1,147 comparison participants who were organized into match groups to approximate an experimental design and enhance the rigor of the study. During participation in the LCP, inmates in the LCP group were just as likely to engage in misconduct as participants in the matching group comparisons. However, inmates in the LCP were less likely than the matching group comparisons to be involved in serious misconduct. Slightly over 5 percent of inmates in the LCP vs. closer to 11 percent of matched inmates were engaged in serious misconduct during the study period. LCP participants were no less likely to engage in "nuisance misconduct," like failing to be sanitary or tidy, or being in/smoking in an unauthorized area, than those in the comparison group, suggesting that although faith-based programming may positively impact inmate misconduct, additional research is needed.

Turner (2008) examined whether an inmate's spiritual/religious beliefs and practices, as measured by the Brief Multidimensional Measure of Religiousness/Spirituality (BMMRS), influence "the number of disciplinary write ups they receive, the number of prescription drugs they use, the number of medical visits they have, and their self-reported feelings of well-being" (p. 80). Although the study's findings are intriguing, this review is focused solely on the relationship between religion/spirituality and misconduct (disciplinary write-ups). Turner's study utilized a sample of 397 male inmates and 460 female inmates at Tennessee state prisons. Based upon logistic regression with the items from the BMMRS,

> inmates described as follows are likely to have fewer disciplinary write ups: those who (1) desire to be closer to God, (2) have forgiven those who have hurt them, (3) meditate more, (4) feel less punishment from God, (5) are involved in fewer religious activities, and (6) consider themselves less religious. (p. 65)

Items five and six are, perhaps to some readers, counterintuitive, indicating that increased religious identity and involvement relate to increased misconduct. This study evidences the need for research to differentiate between spirituality and religion as two distinct constructs, given that inmates' may have deep spiritual lives and not participate in faith-based programming or they may participate for reasons of extrinsic motivation. In addition, it is regrettable that Turner did not differentiate the male and female participants in the analysis and findings.

Appendix E

Success in the Community

Success in the Community

Success in the community is about more than a job or housing, or even staying clean and out of trouble. It is about all of that, and more. Whether returning to the community after incarceration or living in the community pretrial or as an alternative to detention or incarceration, a woman's success is related to the degree that there are adequate provisions in six domains of her life: livelihood, residence, family, health, criminal justice compliance, and social connections. The other basic human need is for encouragement, support, orientation to new things, and to be recognized as valuable by others. The domains are interdependent. A viable plan must include provisions in each domain that can be reconciled with each other.

This matrix further recognizes that there are different phases of adjustment in the community: survival, stabilization, and increasing self-sufficiency. Someone may be in different phases in different domains. For example, a woman might be sober and healthy, but still homeless, on public assistance, and striving for visitation with her children.

Basic Life Areas

PHASE	Livelihood	Residence	Family	Health & Sobriety	Criminal Justice Compliance	Social/Civic Connections
Survival	Gate money Public assistance Soup kitchens, pantries Personal care kits	Shelter Family or friend Street	Find children Make contact	Continuity of medication Relapse prevention	Report to supervising authority (court, probation, parole, etc.) Comply with requirements	Receive peer support
Stabilization	Public assistance, workfare Employment/ Education Training Clothes for interviews	Transitional Residence Family or friend	Supervised visitation Get rehabilitated Trial discharge	Drug treatment and treatment of urgent health and mental health issues Counseling	Earn reduced supervision	Join support group or nurturing community Volunteer work
Self-sufficiency	Job that pays a living wage and provides benefits	One's own apartment with public subsidy, if necessary	Reunify; receive family counseling Care for others	Regular health visits paid by health insurance Ongoing support; 12 step, therapy, community activities	Satisfy conditions of supervision	Help others Contribute to community life
GOAL	Adequate money for food, clothing, transportation, and personal and family expenses	Safe, clean, affordable house that accommodates household comfortably	Reunification with children, reconciliation with family members	Physically and mentally healthy, or receiving affordable quality care including needed prescriptions	Abide by laws Live without community supervision	Healthy friendships, network of supportive adults, opportunities to give back, civic participation (voting, etc.)

WPA's programs and services aim to include provisions in all of these areas. However, funding available for needed services is too often restricted to special needs populations (like the mentally ill or people who are HIV+). Further, there are more supports for families than for single adults seeking to live on their own. In fact, it is usually most difficult to find supports for the single woman or man without mental illness, HIV, or a substance abuse problem.

Women's Prison Association • 110 Second Avenue, New York, NY 10003 • 646.292.7740
www.wpaonline.org

Figure E.1 From Women's Prison Association, Success in the Community: A Matrix for Thinking about the Needs of Criminal Justice Involved Women. *Source:* Copyright © 2018 by Women's Prison Association. Reprinted by permission of Women's Prison Association.

Appendix F

Project Sister Connect

Agenda for Weekly Meetings of the Sisterhood

1. Time for Centering (approximately five minutes): The Time for Centering is intended to center the sisterhood in the present moment and in the presence of God. It should be relevant to the returning sister's spiritual or religious journey, and therefore may include prayer, the reading of scripture or other spiritual resources, or a guided meditation. If the program is sponsored by a partnership between the government and a faith-based organization, the Time for Centering needs to occur in a time and space demarcated from the remainder of the meeting.
2. Check In (approximately thirty minutes): Each sister shares briefly, for three to five minutes, how she is doing including any highs or lows from the previous week.
3. Strengths (approximately ten minutes): The returning sister begins by sharing the strengths she demonstrated during the previous week. These strengths may be small, such as managing feelings of frustration while waiting in line, or large, such as maintaining sobriety. Each member of the sisterhood is then invited to share any strength she's seen evidenced by the returning sister during the previous week.
4. Growing Edges (approximately ten minutes): The returning sister begins by sharing the growing edges she experienced during the previous week. Again, these may be small, such as snapping at a friend, or large, such as getting in the car of a friend who was high.
5. Goals (approximately ten minutes): The goal auditor reminds the sisterhood of the short-, mid-, and long-term goals that the returning sister is working to accomplish. The returning sister provides feedback on any goals achieved and updates the sisterhood on the revision of any goals. The majority of goal auditing occurs privately between the goal auditor and the returning sister, but the sisterhood helps by serving as accountability partners.

6. Barriers (approximately ten minutes): The returning sister identifies any barriers she is experiencing in trying to achieve her goals and is invited by the sisterhood to identify any sources of support that she thinks could help to ameliorate the barriers. The sisterhood also contributes ideas on how to address barriers, and together the group brainstorms next steps.

7. Closing: The sisterhood collectively selects a prayer, a poem, or a reading that it states at the closing of every meeting. The resource should reflect the returning sister's spiritual beliefs and help to create a meaningful closing ritual. Again, if the program is sponsored by a partnership between the government and a faith-based organization, the Closing may need to occur in a time and space demarcated from the remainder of the meeting.

After the meeting ends, the returning sister can check-in with other sisters to schedule one-on-one meetings and to follow up on any suggestions made or resources offered during the meeting.

Reminder: The sisterhood is expected to keep any and all information shared by the returning sister confidential unless permission to share is granted or requested by the returning sister. Trust and confidentiality are vital for justice-seeking relationships intended to promote healing and wholeness.

References

Alexander, M. (2012). *The new Jim Crow: Mass incarceration in an age of color-blindness* (Rev. ed.). New York, NY: The New Press.

All of Us or None. (n.d.). *FAQ*. Retrieved from http://bantheboxcampaign.org/faq/#. Wfx-54ZryCc

Allport, G. W. (1950). *The individual and his religion: A psychological interpretation*. New York, NY: Macmillan.

Aos, S., Miller, M., & Drake, E. (2006). *Evidence-based adult corrections programs: What works and what does not*. Olympia, WA: Washington State Institute for Public Policy.

Arditti, J. A., & Few, A. L. (2006). Mothers' reentry into family life following incarceration. *Criminal Justice Policy Review, 17*(1), 103–123. doi: 10.1177/0887403405282450

Baptist Press. (March 29, 2011). *Female prisoners learn ministry through seminary's landmark program*. Retrieved from http://www.bpnews.net/34939/female-prisoners-learn-ministry-through-seminarys-landmark-program

Barnwell, W. H. (2016). *Called to heal the brokenhearted: Stories from Kairos prison ministry international*. Jackson, MS: University Press of Mississippi.

Bauldry, S., Korom-Djakovic, D., McClanahan, W. S., McMaken, J., & Kotloff, L. J. (2009). *Mentoring formerly incarcerated adults: Insights from the Ready4Work reentry initiative*. Philadelphia, PA: Public/Private Ventures.

Beck, A., Gilliard, D., Greenfeld, L., Harlow, C., Hester, T., Jankowski, L., Snell, T., Stephan, J., & Morton, D. (1993). *Survey of state prison inmates, 1991*. NCJ 136949. Washington, DC: Bureau of Justice Statistics.

Belenko, S., & Houser, K. A. (2012). Gender differences in prison-based drug treatment participation. *International Journal of Offender Therapy and Comparative Criminology, 56*(5), 790–810. doi:10.1177/0306624X11414544

Bergseth, K. J., Jens, K. R., Bergeron-Vigesaa, L., & McDonald, T. D. (2011). Assessing the needs of women recently released from prison. *Women & Criminal Justice, 21*, 100–122. doi: 10.1080/08974454.2011.558799

Bernard, A. (2013). The intersectional alternative: Explaining female criminality. *Feminist Criminology, 8*(1), 3–19. doi: 10.1177/1557085112445304

Berman, J., & Gibel, S. (2007). Women offenders. In M. Carter, S. Gibel, R. Giguere, & R. Stoker (Eds.), *Increasing public safety through successful offender reentry: Evidence-based and emerging practices in corrections* (pp. 159–162). Washington, DC: U.S. Department of Justice, Bureau of Justice Assistance.

Berman, J. (2005). *Women offender transition and reentry: Gender responsive approaches to transitioning women offenders from prison to the community.* Washington, DC: National Institute of Corrections. Retrieved from https://static.nicic.gov/Library/021815.pdf

Blanchard, C. (1999). Drugs, crime, prison, and treatment. *Spectrum: The Journal of State Government, 72*(1), 26–28.

Bloom, B., Chesney-Lind, M., & Owen, B. (1994). *Women in California: Hidden victims of the war on drugs.* San Francisco, CA: Center on Juvenile and Criminal Justice.

Bloom, B. E., & Covington, S. S. (2008). Addressing the mental health needs of women offenders. In R. L. Gido, & L. Dalley (Eds.), *Women's mental health issues across the criminal justice system.* Columbus, OH: Prentice Hall. Retrieved from http://www.stephaniecovington.com/articles-and-publications.php

Bloom, B., Owen, B., & Covington, S. (2003). *Gender-responsive strategies: Research, practice, and guiding principles for women offenders.* Washington, DC: National Institute of Corrections.

Boudin, K. (1998). Lessons from a mother's program in prison. *Women & Therapy, 21*(1), 103–125. doi: 10.1300/J015v21n01_01

Bradley, R. G., & Davino, K. M. (2002). Women's perceptions of the prison environment: When prison is "the safest place I've ever been." *Psychology of Women Quarterly, 26*, 351–359. Retrieved from https://doi.org/10.1111/1471-6402.t01-2-00074

Brennan, T., Breitenbach, M., Dieterich, W., Salisbury, E. J., & Van Voorhis, P. (2002). Women's pathways to serious and habitual crime: A person-centered analysis incorporating gender responsive factors. *Criminal Justice and Behavior, 39*(11), 1481–1508. doi: 10.1177/0093854812456777

Bronfenbrenner, U. (1996). *The ecology of human development: Experiments by nature and design.* Cambridge, MA: Harvard University Press.

Brown, A., Miller, B., & Maguin, E. (1999). Prevalence and severity of lifetime physical and sexual victimization among incarcerated women. *International Journal of Law and Psychiatry, 22*(3–4), 301–322. Retrieved from http://dx.doi.org/10.1016/S0160-2527(99)00011-4

Brown, M., & Bloom, B. (2009). Reentry and renegotiating motherhood: Material identity and success on parole. *Crime & Delinquency, 55*(2), 313–336. doi: 10.1177/0011128708330627

Browning, D. S. (1991). *A fundamental practical theology: Descriptive and strategic proposals.* Minneapolis, MN: Fortress Press.

Bueckert, L. D., & Schipani, D. S. (2006). Interfaith spiritual caregiving: The case for language care. In L. D. Bueckert, & D. S. Schipani (Eds.), *Spiritual caregiving in the hospital: Windows to chaplaincy ministry* (pp. 245–263). Kitchener, Canada: Pandora Press, in association with the Institute of Mennonite Studies.

Burnside, J., Loucks, N., Adler, J. R., & Rose, G. (2005). *My brother's keeper: Faith-based units in prisons*. Portland, OR: Willan Publishing.

Camp, S., D., Daggett, D. M., Kwon, O., & Klein-Saffran, J. (2008). The effect of faith program participation on prison misconduct: The Life Connections Program. *Journal of Criminal Justice, 36*, 389–395.

Carson, E. A. (2014). *Prisoners in 2013*. NCJ 247282. Washington, DC: U.S. Department of Justice, Bureau of Justice Statistics. Retrieved from http://www.bjs.gov/index.cfm?ty=pbdetail&iid=5109

Carson, E. A., & Anderson, E. (2016). *Prisoners in 2015*. Washington, DC: U.S. Department of Justice, Bureau of Justice Statistics. Retrieved from *https://www.bjs.gov/content/pub/pdf/p15.pdf*

Carson, A., & Sabol, W. (2012). *Prisoners in 2011*. Washington, DC: Bureau of Justice Statistics. Retrieved from http://www.bjs.gov/index.cfm?ty=pbdetail&iid=4559

Casey-Acevedo, K., & Bakken, T. (2002). Visiting women in prison: Who visits and who cares? *Journal of Offender Rehabilitation, 34*(3), 67–83. doi: 10.1300/J076v34n03_05

Center for Substance Abuse Treatment. (2005). *Substance abuse treatment for adults in the criminal justice system*. Treatment Improvement Protocol (TIP) Series 44. DHHS Publication No. (SMA) 05-4056. Rockville, MD: Substance Abuse and Mental Health Services Administration.

Center on Addiction and Substance Abuse. (2010). *Behind bars II: Substance abuse and America's prison population* (Source: CASA analysis of the Survey of Inmates in Federal Correctional Facilities [2004], Survey of Inmates in State Correctional Facilities [2004], Survey of Inmates in Local Jails [2002] [Data files, and U.S. Bureau of Justice 430 Criminal Justice and Behavior Statistics Reports, Prisoners in 2006]). Retrieved from http://www.casacolumbia.org/templates/Publications_Reports.aspx?keywords=prison

Chandler, R. K., Fletcher, B. W., & Volkow, N. D. (2009). Treating drug abuse and addiction in the criminal justice system: Improving public health and safety. *JAMA, 301*(2), 183–190. doi: 10.1001/jama.2008.976

Chesney-Lind, M. (1998). Women in prison: From partial justice to vengeful equity. *Corrections Today, 60*(7), 66–73. Retrieved from https://www.ncjrs.gov/App/publications/abstract.aspx?ID=176009

Chesney-Lind, M., & Pasko, L. (2013). *The female offender: Girls, women, and crime* (3rd ed.). Thousand Oaks, CA: Sage Publications, Inc.

Clear, T. R., & Myhre, M. (1995). A study of religion in prison. *IARCA Journal on Community Corrections, 6*(6), 20–25.

Clear, T. R., Hardyman, P. L., Stout, B., Lucken, K., & Dammer, H. R. (2000). The value of religion in prison: An inmate perspective. *Journal of Contemporary Criminal Justice, 16*(1), 53. doi: 10.1177/1043986200016001004

Clear, T. R., & Sumter, M. T. (2002). Prisoners, prison, and religion: Religion and adjustment to prison. *Journal of Offender Rehabilitation, 35*(3–4), 127–159. Retrieved from http://dx.doi.org/10.1300/J076v35n03_07

Cobbina, J. (2009). *From prison to home: Women's pathways in and out of crime* (Doctoral dissertation, University of Missouri – St. Louis). Retrieved from https://www.umsl.edu/ccj/pdfs/dissertation_abstracts/Cobbina_dissertation.pdf

Cobbs Fletcher, R. (2007). *Mentoring ex-prisoners: A guide for prisoner reentry programs.* Washington, DC: U.S. Department of Labor. Retrieved from https://csgjusticecenter.org/nrrc/publications/mentoring-ex-prisoners-a-guide -for-prisoner-reentry-programs-2/

Colloff, P. (October, 1997). Jailhouse flock: Using ex-cons, ex-junkies, leather-clad bikers, and magicians, Cedar Hill's Bill Glass Ministries draws prison inmates into the fold. *Texas Monthly 25*(10), 56. Retrieved from https://www.texasmonthly. com/articles/jailhouse-flock/

Combs, T. (2010). Gender-specific programs help women "break the cycle." *Corrections Today, 72*(6), 30–33. Retrieved from https://www.ncjrs.gov/App/publications /Abstract.aspx?id=256002

Cook, S. L., Smith, S. G., Tusher, C. P., & Raiford, J. (2005). Self-reports of traumatic events in a random sample of incarcerated women. *Women & Criminal Justice, 16*(1–2), 107–126. doi: 10.1300/J012v16n01_05

Court Services and Offender Supervision Agency for the District of Columbia. (n.d.). *Mentoring: CSOSA/faith community partnerships.* Retrieved from https://www .csosa.gov/partnerships/faith/mentoring-contact.aspx

Covington, J. (1985). Gender differences in criminality among heroin users. *Journal of Research in Crime and Delinquency, 22,* 329–354.

Covington, S. S. (1998). Women in prison: Approaches in the treatment of our most invisible population. *Women and Therapy Journal, 21,* 141–155. doi: 10.1300/ J015v21n01_03

Covington, S. S., & Bloom, B. E. (2006). Gender-responsive treatment and services in correctional settings. In E. Leeder (Ed.), *Inside and out: Women, prison, and therapy* (pp. 9–33). Binghamton, NY: Haworth Press.

Crenshaw, K. (1991). Mapping the margins: Intersectionality, identity politics, and violence against women of color. *Stanford Law Review, 43*(6), 1241–1279. doi:10.2307/1229039

Cullen, F. T., Wilcox, P., Lux, J. L., & Jonson, C. L. (2015). *Sisters in crime revisited: Bringing gender into criminology.* New York, NY: Oxford University Press.

Daly, K. (1992). Women's pathways to felony court: Feminist theories of law-breaking and problems of representation. *Southern California Review of Law and Women's Studies, 2,* 11–52. Retrieved from https://www.researchgate. net/publication/284292910_Women%27s_pathways_to_felony_court_Feminist _theories_of_lawbreaking_and_problems_of_representation

Dammer, H. R. (2002). Religion in prison. In D. Levinson (Ed.), *Encyclopedia of crime and punishment* (pp. 1375–1381). Thousand Oaks, CA: Sage Publications, Inc.

Dammer, H. R. (2000). *Religion in corrections: Self-instructional course.* Lanham, MD: American Correctional Association.

Dawson, K. (2015). *Kairos prison ministry: Salvation through Jesus.* Hoover, AL: Archdeacon Books.

Dismas Ministry. (n.d.). *About us.* Retrieved from https://dismasministry.org/ about-us/

Duffy, M., & Chenail, R. J. (2009). Values in qualitative and quantitative research. *Counseling and Values, 53*(1), 22–38. doi: 10.1002/j.2161-007X.2009.tb00111.x

Duwe, G., & Clark, V. (2015). Importance of program integrity: Outcome evaluation of a gender-responsive, cognitive-behavioral program for female offenders. *Criminology & Public Policy, 14*(2), 301–328. doi: 10.1111/1745-9133.12123

Dye, M. H., Aday, R. H., Farney, L., & Raley, J. (2014). "The rock I cling to": Religious engagement in the lives of life-sentenced women. *The Prison Journal, 94*(3), 388–408. doi: 10.1177/0032885514537605

Enos, S. (2001). *Mothering from the inside: Parenting in a women's prison.* Albany, NY: State of New York Press.

Equal Justice Initiative. (n.d.). *Race and poverty.* Retrieved from http://www.eji.org/raceandpoverty

Erickson, V. L. (2002). Social theory, sacred text, and Sing-Sing prison: A sociology of community-based reconciliation. In T. P. O'Connor, & N. J. Pallone (Eds.), *Religion, the community, and the rehabilitation of criminal offenders* (pp. 231–247). New York, NY: The Haworth Press, Inc.

Erzen, T. (2017). *God in captivity: The rise of faith-based prison ministries in the age of mass incarceration.* Boston, MA: Beacon Press.

Families USA. (n.d.). *About Families USA.* Retrieved from http://familiesusa.org/about

Fink, C. (May 1, 2004). Breaking into prison: A gospel invasion helps bring peace to one of the nation's most violent penitentiaries. *Christianity Today, 48*(5), 36–39. Retrieved from http://www.christianitytoday.com/ct/2004/may/4.36.html

Fiorentine, R., & Hillhouse, M. P. (2000). Exploring the additive effects of drug misuse treatment and twelve-step involvement: Does ideology matter? *Substance Use and Misuse, 35,* 367–397. doi: 10.3109/10826080009147702

Fischer, C. T. (2009). Bracketing in qualitative research: Conceptual and practical matters. *Psychotherapy Research, 19*(4–5), 583–590. doi: 10.1080/10503300902798375

Friedman, L. (Executive producer). (2013). *Orange is the new black* [Television series]. Los Angeles, CA: Lionsgate.

Galbraith, M. S. (2004). "So tell me, why do women need something different?" *Journal of Religion & Spirituality in Social Work: Social Thought, 23*(1–2), 197–212. Retrieved from http://dx.doi.org/10.1300/J377v23n01_11

Gehring, K., Van Voorhis, P., & Bell, V. R. (2010). *"What works" for female probationers? An evaluation of the moving on program.* Cincinnati, OH: University of Cincinnati. Retrieved from https://www.uc.edu/content/dam/uc/womenoffenders/docs/MOVING%20ON.pdf

Gilfus, M. E. (1992). From victims to survivors to offenders: Women's routes of entry and immersion into street crime. *Women & Criminal Justice, 4*(1), 63–89. Retrieved from http://dx.doi.org/10.1300/J012v04n01_04

Glaze, L. E., & Maruschak, L. M. (2008). *Parents in prison and their minor children.* NCJ 222984. Washington, DC: US Department of Justice, Bureau of Justice Statistics. Retrieved from https://www.bjs.gov/index.cfm?ty=pbdetail&iid=823

Global Prison Seminaries Foundation. (2017a). *Enormous progress and momentum in multiple states.* Retrieved from http://globalprisonseminaries.org/2017/07/15/enormous-progress-and-momentum-in-multiple-states/

Global Prison Seminaries Foundation. (2017b). *Women's prison seminary initiative continues in Texas.* Retrieved from http://globalprisonseminaries.org/2017/02/20 /womens-prison-seminary-initiative-continues-in-texas/

Goffman, E. (1963). *Stigma: Notes on the management of spoiled identity.* New York, NY: Simon & Schuster, Inc.

Golafshani, N. (2003). Understanding reliability and validity in qualitative research. *The Qualitative Report, 8*(4), 597–606. Retrieved from http://nsuworks.nova.edu/ tqr/vol8/iss4/6

Goldstein, E. H., Warner-Robbins, C., McClean, C., Macatula, L., & Conklin, R. (2009). A peer-driven mentoring case management community reentry model: An application for jails and prisons. *Family Community Health, 32*(4), 309–313.

Good News Jail & Prison Ministry. (2015). *What we do.* Retrieved from https://good-newsjail.org/what-we-do/

Greenfeld, L. A., & Snell, T. L. (1999). *Women offenders.* NCJ 175688. Washington, DC: U.S. Department of Justice, Bureau of Justice Statistics. Retrieved from *https://www.bjs.gov/content/pub/pdf/wo.pdf*

Greider, K. (2015). Religious location and counseling: Engaging diversity and difference in views of religion. In E. A. Maynard, & J. L. Snodgrass (Eds.), *Understanding Pastoral Counseling* (pp. 235–256). New York, NY: Springer Publishing Co.

Guba, E., & Lincoln, Y. (1989). *Fourth generation evaluation.* Thousand Oaks, CA: Sage.

Guerino, P., Harrison, P. M., & Sabol, W. J. (2012). *Prisoners in 2010.* NCJ 236096. Washington, DC: U.S. Department of Justice, Bureau of Justice Statistics. Retrieved from https://www.bjs.gov/content/pub/pdf/p10.pdf

Hall, S. T. (2004). A working theology of prison ministry. *Journal of Pastoral Care & Counseling, 58*(3), 169–178. doi: 10.1177/154230500405800302

Hallett, M., & Johnson, B. (2014). The resurgence of religion in America's prisons. *Religions, 5,* 663–683. doi: 10.3390/rel5030663

Harlow, C. W. (2003). *Education and correctional populations.* NCJ 195670. Washington, DC: U.S. Department of Justice, Bureau of Justice Statistics. Retrieved from http://www.bjs.gov/index.cfm?ty=pbdetail&iid=814

Harlow, C. W. (1999). *Prior abuse reported by inmates and probationers.* NCJ 172879. Washington, DC: U.S. Department of Justice, Bureau of Justice Statistics. Retrieved from http://www.bjs.gov/content/pub/pdf/parip.pdf

Haugk, K. C. (1984). *Christian caregiving: A way of life.* Minneapolis, MN: Augsburg Publishing House.

Healing Communities. (n.d.). *About us.* Retrieved from http://www.healingcommu-nitiesusa.com/about

Heimer, K. (2000). Changes in the gender gap in crime and women's economic marginalization. In G. LaFree (Ed.), *Criminal justice 2000: The nature of crime, continuity and change,* (Vol. 1, pp. 427–483). Washington, DC: National Institute of Justice.

Hercik, J. M. (2005). *Rediscovering compassion: An evaluation of Kairos horizon communities in prison.* Fairfax, VA: Caliber Associates.

Hoffmann, N. G., & Harrison, P. A. (1995). *SUDDS-IV: Substance use disorder diagnostic schedule-IV.* St. Paul, MN: New Standards, Inc.

Holtfreter, K., & Morash, M. (2003). The needs of women offenders: Implications for correctional programming. *Women & Criminal Justice, 14*(2/3), 137–160.

Holtfreter, K., Reisig, M. D., & Morash, M. (2004). Poverty, state capital, and recidivism among women offenders. *Criminology & Public Policy, 3*(2), 185–208.

Huebner, B. M., DeJong, C., & Cobbina, J. (2010). Women coming home: Long-term patterns of recidivism. *Justice Quarterly, 27*(2), 225–254. doi: 10.1080/07418820902870486

Hughes, T., & Wilson, D. J. (2015). *Reentry trends in the U.S.* Retrieved from http://www.bjs.gov/content/reentry/reentry.cfm

Humphreys, K. (January 24, 2017). White women are going to prison at a higher rate than ever before. *The Washington Post.* Retrieved from https://www.washingtonpost.com/news/wonk/wp/2017/01/24/white-women-are-going-to-prison-at-a-higher-rate-than-ever-before/?utm_term=.f787d6b8b262

Inciardi, J. A., Martin, S. S., & Surratt, H. L. (2001). Therapeutic communities in prisons and work release: Effective modalities for drug-involved offenders. In B. Rawlings, & R. Yates (Eds.), *Therapeutic communities for the treatment of drug users* (pp. 241–256). London: Jessica Kingsley Publishers.

James, D. J., & Glaze, L. E. (2006). *Mental health problems of prison and jail inmates.* NCJ 213600. Washington, DC: U.S. Department of Justice, Bureau of Justice Statistics. Retrieved from http://www.bjs.gov/index.cfm?ty=pbdetail&iid=789

Johnson, B. R. (2013). Addressing religion and spirituality in correctional settings: The role of faith-based prison programs. In K. I. Pargament (Ed.), *APA handbook of psychology, religion, and spirituality* (Vol. 2; pp. 543–559). Washington, DC: American Psychological Association.

Johnson, B. R. (2011). *More god, less crime.* West Conshohocken, PA: Templeton Press.

Johnson, B. R. (2004). Religious programs and recidivism among former inmates in prison fellowship programs: A long-term follow-up study. *Justice Quarterly, 21*, 329–354.

Johnson, B. R., Larson, D. B., & Pitts, T. G. (1997). Religious programs, institutional adjustment, and recidivism among former inmates in prison fellowship programs. *Justice Quarterly, 14*, 145–166.

Johnson, I. M. (2014). Economic impediments to women's success on parole: "We need someone on our side." *The Prison Journal, 94*(3), 365–387. doi: 10.1177/0032885514537760

Johnson J. E., Schonbrun, Y. C., Nargiso J. E., Kuo, C. C., Shefner, R. T., Williams, C. A., & Zlotnick, C. (2013). I know if I drink I won't feel anything: Substance use relapse among depressed women leaving prison. *International Journal of Prisoner Health, 9*(4), 1–18. doi: 10.1108/IJPH-02-2013-0009

Johnson, J. E., Schonbrun, Y. C., Peabody, M. E., Shefner, R. T., Fernandes, K. M., Rosen, R. K., & Zlotnick, C. (2015). Provider experiences with prison care and aftercare for women with co-occurring mental health and substance use disorders: Treatment, resource, and systems integration challenges. *Journal of Behavioral Health Services & Research, 42*(4), 417–436. doi: 10.1007/s11414-014-9397-8

Johnson, J. E., Williams, C., & Zlotnick, C. (2015). Development and feasibility of a cell phone-based transitional intervention for women prisoners with

210   *References*

comorbid substance use and depression. *The Prison Journal, 95*(3), 330–352. doi: 10.1177/0032885515587466

Journey with Jesus. (n.d.). *Poetry selections: Teresa of Avila (1515–1582)*. Retrieved from https://www.journeywithjesus.net/PoemsAndPrayers/Teresa_Of_Avila _Christ_Has_No_Body.shtml

Kaeble, D., & Glaze, L. (2016). *Correctional populations in the United States, 2015.* NCJ 250374. Washington, DC: U.S. Department of Justice, Bureau of Justice Statistics. Retrieved from https://www.bjs.gov/content/pub/pdf/cpus15.pdf

Kaeble, D., & Bonczar, T. P. (2016). *Probation and parole in the United States, 2015.* NCJ 250230. Washington, DC: U.S. Department of Justice, Bureau of Justice Statistics.

Kaskutas, L. A. (2009). Alcoholics anonymous effectiveness: Faith meets science. *Journal of Addictive Diseases, 28*, 145–157. doi: 10.1080/10550880902772464

Kazura, K. (2001). Family programming for incarcerated parents. *Journal of Offender Rehabilitation, 32*(4), 67–83. doi: 10.1300/J076v32n04_05

Kerley, K. R., Matthews, T. L., & Shoemaker, J. (2009). A simple plan, a simple faith: Chaplains and lay ministers in Mississippi prisons. *Review of Religious Research, 51*(1), 87–103.

Kirkpatrick, L. A., & Hood, Jr., R. W. (1990). Intrinsic-extrinsic religious orientation: The boon or bane of contemporary psychology of religion? *Journal for the Scientific Study of Religion, 29*(4), 442–462. doi: 10.2307/1387311

Koons, B. A., Burrow, J. D., Morash, M., & Bynum, T. (1997). Expert and offender perceptions of program elements linked to successful outcomes for incarcerated women. *Crime and Delinquency, 43*(4), 512–532. Retrieved from https://doi. org/10.1177/0011128797043004007

Kort-Butler, L. A., & Malone, S. E. (2015). Citizen volunteers in prison: Bringing the outside in, taking the inside out. *Journal of Crime and Justice, 38*(4), 508–521. doi: 10.1080/0735648X.2014.969293

Kristof, N. (June 11, 2016). Is it a crime to be poor? *The New York Times.* Retrieved from https://www.nytimes.com/2016/06/12/opinion/sunday/is%2Dit%2Da%2Dcri me%2Dto%2Dbe%2Dpoor.html

Kubany, E. S., Haynes, S. N., Leisen, M. B., Owens, J. A., Kaplan, A. S., Watson, S. B., & Burns, K. (2000). Development and preliminary validation of a brief broad-spectrum measure of trauma exposure: The traumatic life events questionnaire. *Psychological Assessment, 12*, 210–224. doi: 10.1037/1040-3590.12.2.210

Laub, J. H., & Sampson, R. J. (1993). Turning points in the life course: Why change matters to the study of crime. *Criminology, 31*(3), 301–325.

LaVigne, N. G., Brazzell, D., & Small, K. (2007). *Evaluation of Florida's faith- and character-based institutions.* Washington, DC: Urban Institute Justice Policy Center. Retrieved from https://www.urban.org/sites/default/files/publication/ 46791/411561-Evaluation-of-Florida-s-Faith-and-Character-Based-Institutions. PDF

LeBel, T. P. (2012). "If one doesn't get you another one will": Formerly incarcerated persons' perceptions of discrimination. *The Prison Journal, 92*(1), 63–87. doi: 10.1177/0032885511429243

Legal Action Center. (n.d.). *Securing official identification for individuals leaving prisons and jails.* Retrieved from https://lac.org/toolkits/ID/ID.htm

Leverentz, A. (2011). Good daughter and sister: Families of origin in the reentry of African American female ex-prisoners. *Feminist Criminology, 6,* doi: 10.1177/1557085111414859

Levitt, L., & Loper, A. B. (2009). The influence of religious participation on the adjustment of female inmates. *American Journal of Orthopsychiatry, 79*(1), 1–7. doi:10.1037/a0015429

Lovoy, L. (2014). *Female inmates can face a cycle of abuse.* Retrieved from https://news.wbhm.org/feature/2014/female-inmates-can-face-a-cycle-of-abuse/

Lynch, R. (December 3, 1994). 3rd strike for O.C. woman in $50 drug deal. *Los Angeles Times.* Retrieved from http://articles.latimes.com/1994-12-03/news/mn-435 6_1_june-drug-deal

Mallicoat, S. L. (2015). *Women and crime: A text/reader* (2nd ed.). Thousand Oaks, CA: Sage Publications, Inc.

Mallicoat, S. L. (2012). *Women and crime: A text/reader* (1st ed.). Thousand Oaks, CA: Sage Publications, Inc.

Mallik-Kane, K., & Visher, C. A. (2008). *Health and prisoner reentry: How physical, mental, and substance abuse conditions shape the process of reintegration.* Washington, DC: The Urban Institute. Retrieved from *https://www.urban.org/sites /default/files/.../411617-Health-and-Prisoner-Reentry.PDF*

Maruna, S., Wilson, L., & Curran, K. (2006). Why god is often found behind bars: Prison conversions and the crisis of self-narrative. *Research in Human Development, 3*(2–3), 161–184.

Maruschak, L. M., & Parks, E. (2012). *Probation and parole in the United States, 2011.* NCJ 239686. Washington, DC: Bureau of Justice Statistics.

Mauer, M. (2013). *The changing racial dynamics of women's incarceration.* Washington, DC: The Sentencing Project. Retrieved from http://www.sentencingproject .org/detail/publication.cfm?publication_id=432

Mauer, M., & King, R. S. (2007). *A 25-year quagmire: The war on drugs and its impact on American society.* Washington, DC: The Sentencing Project. Retrieved from http://www.sentencingproject.org/detail/publication.cfm?publication_id=170

Mauer, M., Potler, C., & Wolf, R. (1999). *Gender and justice: Women, drugs, and sentencing policy.* Washington, DC: The Sentencing Project. Retrieved from http://www.sentencingproject.org/publications/gender-and-justice-women-drugs-and-sentencing-policy/

McDaniel, C., Davis, D. H., & Neff, S. A. (2005). Charitable choice and prison ministries: Constitutional and institutional challenges to rehabilitating the American penal system. *Criminal Justice Policy Review, 16,* 164–189. doi: 10.1177/0887403404267386

McDaniels-Wilson, C., & Belknap, J. (2008). The extensive sexual violation and sexual abuse histories of incarcerated women. *Violence against Women, 14*(10), 1090–1127. doi: 10.1177/1077801208323160

McDargh, H. J. (October, 2010). *Called by our true names: Theological reflections on prison ministry.* Paper presented at The Boston College School of Theology and

Ministry "You Visited Me": The Urgent Challenge of Prison Ministry conference, Boston, MA.

McLeod, L. (2011). A holistic approach to the trauma of reentry. In W. W. Goode Sr., C. E. Lewis, Jr., & H. D. Trulear (Eds.), *Ministry with prisoners & families: The way forward* (pp. 129–139). Valley Forge, PA: Judson Press.

McRoberts, O. M. (2002). *Religion, reform, community: Examining the idea of church-based prisoner reentry.* Washington, DC: The Urban Institute. Retrieved from www.urban.org/sites/default/files/.../410802-Religion-Reform-Community.PDF

Meade, B. (2014). *Moral communities and jailhouse religion: Religiosity and prison misconduct.* El Paso, TX: LFB Scholarly Publishing LLC.

Mears, D. P. (2007). Faith-based reentry programs: Cause for concern or showing promise? *Corrections Today, 69*(2), 30–33.

Mears, D. P., Roman, C. G., Wolff, A., & Buck, J. (2006). Faith-based efforts to improve prisoner reentry: Assessing the logic and evidence. *Journal of Criminal Justice, 34,* 351–367. doi: 10.1016/j.jcrimjus.2006.05.002

Mercadante, L. A. (1996). *Victims and sinners: Spiritual roots of addiction and recovery.* Louisville, KY: Westminster John Knox Press.

Merton, R. (1968). *Social theory and social structure* (enlarged ed.). New York, NY: Free Press.

Messina, N., & Grella, C. (2006). Childhood trauma and women's health outcomes in a California prison population. *American Journal of Public Health, 96*(10), 1842–1848. doi: 10.2105/AJPH.2005.082016

Miller, M. K., Lindsey, S. C., & Kaufman, J. A. (2014). The religious conversion and race of a prisoner: Mock parole board members' decisions, perceptions, and emotions. *Legal and Criminological Psychology, 19,* 104–130.

Moon, D. G., Thompson, R. J., & Bennett, R. (1994). Patterns of substance use among women in prison. In B. R. Fletcher, L. D. Shaver, and D. G. Moon (Eds.), *Women prisoners: A forgotten population* (pp. 45–54). Westport, CT: Praeger.

Morash, M. (2010). *Women on probation and parole: A feminist critique of community programs and services.* Lebanon, NH: Northeastern University Press.

Moustakas, C. (1994). *Phenomenological research methods.* Thousand Oaks, CA: Sage.

Mumola, C. (2000). *Incarcerated parents and their children.* NCJ 182335. Washington, DC: U.S. Department of Justice, Bureau of Justice Statistics. Retrieved from http://www.bjs.gov/index.cfm?ty=pbdetail&iid=981

Mumola, C. J., & Karberg, J. C. (2006). *Drug use and dependence, state and federal prisoners, 2004.* NCJ 213530. Washington, DC: U.S. Department of Justice, Bureau of Justice Statistics. Retrieved from http://www.bjs.gov/index.cfm?ty=pbdetail&iid=778

National Benevolent Association. (n.d.). *Webinar: Mass incarceration and returning citizens.* Retrieved from https://www.nbacares.org/care-resources/educational-webinar-mass-incarceration-and-returning-citizens

National Institute of Justice. (2014). *Recidivism.* Retrieved from http://www.nij.gov/topics/corrections/recidivism/Pages/welcome.aspx

New York Theological Seminary. (November 29, 2012). *NYTS testimony on MPS program at Sing Sing correctional facility.* Retrieved from http://www.nyts .edu/2012/11/28/testimony-submitted-to-the-nys-assembly-standing-committee -on-correction-concerning-the-mps-degree-program-offered-at-sing-sing -correctional-facility/

Nolan, P. (2004). *When prisoners return: Why we should care and how you and your church can help.* Leesburg, VA: Prison Fellowship.

O'Brien, P., & Lee, N. (2006). Moving from needs to self-efficacy: A holistic system for women in transition from prison. In E. Leeder (Ed.), *Inside and out: Women, prison, and therapy* (pp. 261–284). Binghamton, NY: Haworth Press.

O'Connor, T. P. (2004/2005). What works, religion as a correctional intervention: Part II. *Journal of Community Corrections, 14*(2), 4–6, 20–26.

O'Connor, T. P. (2002). Religion-offenders-rehabilitation: Questioning the relationship. In T. P. O'Connor, & N. J. Pallone (Eds.), *Religion, the community, and the rehabilitation of criminal offenders* (pp. 1–9). New York, NY: The Haworth Press, Inc.

O'Connor, T., & Erickson, V. (1997). Theology and community corrections in a prison setting. *Community Corrections Report, 75,* 67–68.

O'Connor, T. P., & Duncan, J. B. (2008). Religion and prison programming: The role, impact, and future direction of faith in correctional systems. *Offender Programs Report: Social and Behavioral Rehabilitation in Prisons, Jails and the Community, 11*(6), 81–96.

Open Table, Inc. (2017a). *Open Table: Relationship transforms communities.* Retrieved from https://drive.google.com/file/d/0B7Ano_ir9SB5WFdaa 0k3R0VVYm8/view

Open Table, Inc. (2017b). *Open table white paper: Evidence base summary for government partners.* Retrieved from http://www.theopentable.org/resources/open-table-e vidence-based-practice/

Parsons, M. L., & Warner-Robbins, C. (2002). Factors that support women's successful transition to the community following jail/prison. *Health Care for Women International, 23,* 6–18.

Pelissier, B., & Jones, N. (2005). A review of gender differences among substance abusers. *Crime and Delinquency, 51,* 343–372. doi: 10.1177/0011128704270218

Penance. (n.d.). In *Merriam-Webster's online dictionary.* Retrieved from https:// www.merriam-webster.com/dictionary/penance

Percival, G. L. (2016). *Smart on crime: The struggle to build a better American penal system.* Boca Raton, FL: CRC Press.

Perez, E. (March 14, 2016). DOJ warns against jailing poor people for not paying court fines. *CNN.* Retrieved from http://www.cnn.com/2016/03/14/politics/court-fines -poor-people-doj/index.html

Perry, J. (2006). *God behind bars: The amazing story of Prison Fellowship.* Nashville, TN: W Publishing Group.

Petersilia, J. (2004). What works in prisoner reentry? Reviewing and questioning the evidence. *Federal Probation, 68*(2), 4–8. Retrieved from www.uscourts.gov/ file/23009/download

Petersilia, J. (2003). *When prisoners come home: Parole and prisoner reentry.* New York, NY: Oxford University Press.

Pew Research Center's Forum on Religion & Public Life. (2012). *Religion in prisons: A 50-state survey of prison chaplains.* Washington, DC: The Pew Research Center. Retrieved from http://www.pewforum.org/2012/03/22/prison-chaplains-exec/

Pollock, J. M. (2014). *Women's crimes, criminology, and corrections.* Long Grove, IL: Waveland Press, Inc.

Pounder, S. (2008). Prison theology: A theology of liberation, hope, and justice. *Dialog: A Journal of Theology, 47*(3), 278–291. doi: 10.1111/j.1540-6385.2008.00402.x

Prison Communication, Activism, Research, and Education (PCARE). (2007). Fighting the prison-industrial complex: A call to communication and cultural studies scholars to change the world. *Communication and Critical/Cultural Studies, 4*(4), 402–420. doi: 10.1080/14791420701632956

Prison Fellowship. (n.d.-a). *The legacy of Church Colson.* Retrieved from https://www.prisonfellowship.org/about/chuckcolson/

Prison Fellowship. (n.d.-b). *Our approach.* Retrieved from https://www.prisonfellowship.org/about/

Prison Fellowship. (n.d.-c). *Why help prisoners?* Retrieved from https://www.prisonfellowship.org/why-help-prisoners/

Proctor, S. (2012). Substance use disorder prevalence among female state prison inmates. *The American Journal of Drug and Alcohol Abuse, 38*(4), 278–285. doi: 10.3109/00952990.2012.668596

Rabuy, B., & Kopf, D. (2015). *Prisons of poverty: Uncovering the pre-incarceration incomes of the imprisoned.* Retrieved from https://www.prisonpolicy.org/reports/income.html

Richie, B. (2000). Exploring the link between violence against women and women's involvement in illegal activity. In B. Richie, K. Tsenin, & C. Widom (Eds.), *Research on women and girls in the criminal justice system* (pp. 1–13). Washington, DC: National Institute of Justice.

Richie, B. (1996). *Compelled to crime: The gender entrapment of battered black women.* New York, NY: Routledge.

Richie, B. E. (2001). Challenges incarcerated women face as they return to their communities: Findings from life history reviews. *Crime & Deliquency, 47*(3), 368–389. doi: 10.1177/0011128701047003005

Robinson-Dawkins, A. (2011). Nurturing a 'woman kind of faith': Ministry to women in incarceration and reentry. In W. W. Goode Sr., C. E. Lewis, Jr., & H. D. Trulear (Eds.), *Ministry with prisoners and families: The way forward* (pp. 82–92). Valley Forge, PA: Judson Press.

Sargent, E., Marcus-Mendoza, S., & Ho Yu, C. (1993). Abuse and the woman prisoner. In B. R. Fletcher, L. D. Shaver, & D. G. Moon (Eds.), *Women prisoners: A forgotten population* (pp. 55–64). Westport, CT: Praeger.

Saxena, P., Messina, N. P., & Grella, C. E. (2014). Who benefits from gender-responsive treatment?: Accounting for abuse history on longitudinal outcomes for women in prison. *Criminal Justice and Behavior, 41*(4), 417.432. doi: 10.1177/0093854813514405

Schaefer, L., Sams, T., & Lux, J. (2016). Saved, salvaged, or sunk: A meta-analysis of the effects of faith-based interventions on inmate adjustment. *The Prison Journal, 96*(4), 600–622. doi: 10.1177/0032885516650883

Schlosser, E. (December, 1998). The prison-industrial complex. *The Atlantic, 282*(6), 51–72.

Schneider, R. Z., & Feltey, K. M. (2009). "No matter what has been done wrong can always be redone right": Spirituality in the lives of imprisoned battered women. *Violence against Women, 15*(4), 443–459. doi: 10.1177/1077801208331244

Scroggins, J. R., & Malley, S. (2010). Reentry and the (unmet) needs of women. *Journal of Offender Rehabilitation, 49,* 146–163. doi: 10.1080/10509670903546864

Sered, S., & Norton-Hawk, M. (2011). Whose higher power?: Criminalized women confront the "Twelve Steps." *Feminist Criminology, 6*(4), 308–332. doi: 10.1177/1557085111420557

Severance, T. A. (2004). Concerns and coping strategies of women inmates concerning release: "It's going to take somebody in my corner." *Journal of Offender Rehabilitation, 384,* 73–97.

Shaw, D. R. (1995). *Chaplains to the imprisoned: Sharing life with the incarcerated.* New York, NY: The Haworth Press, Inc.

Sheridan, M. J. (1996). Comparison of the life experiences and personal functioning of men and women in prison. *Families in Society: The Journal of Contemporary Human Services, 77,* 423–434. doi: 10.1606/1044-3894.942

Sinha, P. (October, 2017). The arc of the moral universe doesn't bend itself. *Huffpost.* Retrieved from https://www.huffingtonpost.com/entry/the-arc-of-the-moral-universe-doesnt-bend-itself_us_58288529e4b0852d9ec218d2

Smith, J. A., Flowers, P., & Larkin, M. (2009). *Interpretative phenomenological analysis: Theory, method and research.* Thousand Oaks, CA: Sage.

Smith, J. A., & Osborn, M. (2008). Interpretative phenomenological analysis. In J. A. Smith (Ed.), *Qualitative psychology: A practical guide to research methods,* 2nd ed. (pp. 53–79). Thousand Oaks, CA: Sage.

Snyder, H. N., & Mulako-Wangota, J. (n.d.). *Arrests of females by age in the U.S., 2012. Generated using the Arrest data analysis tool.* Washington, DC: Bureau of Justice Statistics. Retrieved from https://www.bjs.gov/index.cfm?ty=datool&surl=/arrests/index.cfm#

Stanley, K. V. (2016). Behold, she stands at the door: Reentry, black women, and the black church. *Journal of Prison Education and Reentry, 3*(1), 56–64. doi: 10.15845/jper.v3i1.1000

Staton, M., Leukefeld, C., & Webster, J. M. (2003). Substance use, health, and mental health: Problems and service utilization among incarcerated women. *International Journal of Offender Therapy and Comparative Criminology, 47*(2), 224–239. doi: 10.1177/0306624X03251120

Steffensmeier, D. J., & Haynie, D. L. (2000). Gender, structural disadvantage, and urban crime: Do macrosocial variables also explain female offending rates? *Criminology, 38*(2), 403–438. doi: 10.111/j.1745-9125.2000.tb00895.x

Stephen Ministries. (n.d.). *What is Stephen Ministry?* Retrieved from https://www.stephenministries.org/stephenministry/default.cfm/917?mnbsm=1

Stern, K. (2014). *Voices from American prisons: Faith, education, and healing.* New York, NY: Routledge.

Stewart-Sicking, J. A. (2016). *Spiritual friendship after religion: Walking with people while rules are changing.* New York, NY: Morehouse Publishing.

Stringer, E. C. (2009). "Keeping the faith": How incarcerated African American mothers use religion and spirituality to cope with imprisonment. *Journal of African American Studies, 13*, 325–347. doi: 10.1007/s12111-009-9096-3

Substance Abuse and Mental Health Services Administration. (n.d.). *Motivational interviewing.* Retrieved from https://www.integration.samhsa.gov/clinical-practi ce/motivational-interviewing

Sullivan, W. F. (2009). *Prison religion: Faith-based reform and the Constitution.* Princeton, NJ: Princeton University Press.

Sundt, J. L., Dammer, H. R., & Cullen, F. T. (2002). The role of the prison chaplain in rehabilitation. *Journal of Offender Rehabilitation, 35*(3/4), 59–86.

Sweat, M. D., & Denison, J. A. (1995). Reducing HIV incidence in developing countries with structural and environmental interventions. *AIDS, 9,* S251–S257.

Swinton, J., & Mowat, H. (2006). *Practical theology and qualitative research.* London, England: SCM Press.

Tan, S. Y. (2013). Lay Christian counseling for general psychological problems. In E. L. Worthington, Jr., E. L. Johnson, J. N. Hook, & J. D. Aten (Eds.), *Evidence-based practices in Christian counseling and psychotherapy* (pp. 40–58). Downers Grove, IL: IVP Academic.

Taxman, F., Perdoni, M., & Harrison, L. (2007). Drug treatment services for adult offenders: The state of the state. *Journal of Substance Abuse Treatment, 32,* 239–254. doi: 10.1016/j.jsat.2006.12.019

The Council of State Governments Justice Center. (2016a). *State identification: Reentry strategies for state and local leaders.* Retrieved from https://csgjusticecenter .org/wp-content/uploads/2016/04/State-Identification.pdf

The Council of State Governments Justice Center. (2016b). *The second chance act.* Retrieved from https://csgjusticecenter.org/jc/publications/fact-sheet-the-second-chance-act/

The Council of State Governments Justice Center. (n.d.). *What works in reentry clearinghouse.* Retrieved from https://whatworks.csgjusticecenter.org/

The Sentencing Project. (2015a). *Incarcerated women and girls.* Washington, DC: The Sentencing Project. Retrieved from http://www.sentencingproject.org /publications/incarcerated-women-and-girls/

The Sentencing Project. (2015b). *Race and justice news: Why are 1.5 million black men "missing"?* Retrieved from http://www.sentencingproject.org/detail/news.cfm?n ews_id=1933&id=167

The Sentencing Project. (2012a). *Incarcerated women.* Retrieved from http://www .sentencingproject.org/template/page.cfm?id=189

The Sentencing Project. (2012b). *Parents in prison.* Retrieved from http://www .sentencingproject.org/template/page.cfm?id=189

The Sentencing Project. (2009). *Incarcerated parents and their children: Trends 1991–2007.* Washington, DC: The Sentencing Project. Retrieved from http://www.sentencingproject.org/publications/incarcerated-parents-and -their-children-trends-1991-2007/

The Sentencing Project. (2007). *Women in the criminal justice system: Briefing sheets.* Washington, DC: The Sentencing Project. Retrieved from http://www.sentencingproject.org/wp-content/uploads/2016/01/Women-in-the-Criminal-Justice-System-Briefing-Sheets.pdf

The Sentencing Project. (n.d.). *Fact sheet: Trends in U.S. corrections.* Retrieved from http://www.sentencingproject.org/template/page.cfm?id=189

The United States Department of Justice. (2017). *Statement on the institutionalized persons provision of the Religious Land Use and Institutionalized Persons Act (RLUIPA).* Retrieved from https://www.justice.gov/crt/religious-land-use-and-institutionalized-persons-act-0

Thomas, J., & Zaitzow, B. H. (2006). Conning or conversion?: The role of religion in prison coping. *The Prison Journal, 86*(2), 242–259. doi: 10.1177/0032885506287952

Travis, J., Solomon, A., & Waul, M. (2001). *From prison to home: The dimensions and consequences of prisoner reentry.* Washington, DC: The Urban Institute, Justice Policy Center. Retrieved from http://urbaninstitute.org/UploadedPDF/from_prison_to_home.pdf

Tripodi, S. J., Pettus-Davis, C. (2013). Histories of childhood victimization and subsequent mental health problems, substance use, and sexual victimization for a sample of incarcerated women in the US. *International Journal of Law and Psychiatry, 36*, 30–40. doi: 10.1016/j.ijlp.2012.11.005

Turner, R. G. (2008). *Religion in prison: An analysis of the impact of religiousness/spirituality on behavior, health, and well-being among male and female prison inmates in Tennessee* (Order No. 3307301). Available from ProQuest Dissertations & Theses Global. (304339846). Retrieved from http://proxy-ln.researchport.umd.edu/login?url=https://search.proquest.com/docview/304339846?accountid=12164

United States Commission on Civil Rights. (2008). *Enforcing religious freedom in prison.* Washington, DC: U.S. Commission on Civil Rights. Retrieved from *https://www.law.umaryland.edu/marshall/usccr/documents/cr12r274.pdf*

United States Conference of Catholic Bishops. (2012). *The two feet of love in action.* United States Conference of Catholic Bishops. Department of Justice, Peace and Human Development. Retrieved from http://www.usccb.org/beliefs-and-teachings/what-we-believe/catholic-social-teaching/two-feet-of-love-in-action.cfm

U.S. Department of Health and Human Services. Center for Behavioral Health Statistics and Quality. (2016). *Key substance use and mental health indicators in the United States: Results from the 2015 National Survey on Drug Use and Health* (HHS Publication No. SMA 16-4984, NSDUH Series H-51). Retrieved from http://www.samhsa.gov/data/

United States Department of Justice. (2016). *Roadmap to reentry: Reducing recidivism through reentry reforms at the Federal Bureau of Prisons.* Washington, DC: U.S. Department of Justice. Retrieved from https://www.justice.gov/archives/reentry/roadmap-reentry

United States Department of Justice. (n.d.). *Prisoners and prisoner re-entry.* Retrieved from https://www.justice.gov/archive/fbci/progmenu_reentry.html

Van Dieten, M. (2010). *Moving on: A program for at-risk women. Modules 1 and 6 facilitator's guide.* Center City, MN: Hazeldon.

Vigesaa, L. E., Bergseth, K. J., & Jens, K. R. (2016). Who participates in reentry programming? An examination of women offenders in a mid-western state. *Journal
of Offender Rehabilitation, 55*(5), 308–328. doi: 10.1080/10509674.2016.1181131

Vigil, J. D. (1995). Barrio gangs: Street life and identity in Southern California.
In M. W. Klein, C. L. Maxson, & J. Miller (Eds.), *The modern gang reader*
(pp. 125–131). Los Angeles, CA: Roxbury.

Viglione, J., Hannon, L., & DeFina, R. (2011). The impact of light skin on prison
time for black female offenders. *Social Science Journal, 48*(1), 250–258. Retrieved
from https://doi.org/10.1016/j.soscij.2010.08.003

Wagner, P., & Rabuy, B. (March 14, 2016). Mass incarceration: The whole pie
2016. *Prison policy initiative.* Retrieved from http://www.prisonpolicy.org/reports/
pie2016.html

Walmsley, R. (2013). *World prison population list* (10th edition). Essex: International
Centre for Prison Studies. Retrieved from http://images.derstandard.at/2013/11/21
/prison-population.pdf

Walsh, A. (2016). *States, help families stay together by correcting a consequence of
the adoption and safe families act.* Retrieved from https://www.prisonpolicy.org
/blog/2016/05/24/asfa/

Weber, L. (2010). *Understanding race, class, gender, and sexuality: A conceptual
framework* (2nd ed.). New York, NY: Oxford University Press.

Whitehead, J. W. (April 10, 2012). *Jailing Americans for profit: The rise of the prison
industrial complex [Web log post].* Retrieved from https://www.huffingtonpost
.com/john-w-whitehead/prison-privatization_b_1414467.html

Widom, C. S. (2000). Childhood victimization and the derailment of girls and women
to the criminal justice system. In B. Richie, K. Tsenin, & C. Widom (Eds.),
Research on women and girls in the criminal justice system (pp. 27–36). Washington, DC: National Institute of Justice.

Willison, J. B., Brazzell, D., & Kim, K. (2011). *Faith-based corrections and reentry
programs: Advancing a conceptual framework for research and evaluation.*
Washington, DC: The Urban Institute. Retrieved from *https://www.ncjrs.gov
/pdffiles1/nij/grants/234058.pdf*

Women in Prison Project of the Correctional Association of New York. (2006). *When
"free" means losing your mother: The collision of child welfare and the incarceration
of women in New York State.* Retrieved from http://www.correctionalassociation
.org/wp-content/uploads/2012/05/When_Free_Rpt_Feb_2006.pdf

Women's Prison Association and Home. (2003). *WPA focus on women & justice:
Barriers to reentry.* New York, NY: The Women's Prison Association and Home.
Retrieved from http://www.wpaonline.org/pdf/Focus_October2003.pdf

Women's Prison Association. (2018). *Success in the community.* Retrieved from
http://www.wpaonline.org/wpaassets/Success_in_the_Community_Matrix_2018.pdf

Wright, K. N. (1985). Developing the prison environment inventory. *Journal of
Research in Crime & Delinquency, 22,* 257–277.

Index

About the Author

Reverend **Jill L. Snodgrass**, PhD, is Associate Professor of Pastoral Counseling at Loyola University Maryland. She is a pastoral and practical theologian, a scholar-activist, and an ordained minister in the United Church of Christ. Her research interests include spiritual care and counseling with traditionally marginalized populations, with specific emphasis on individuals and families experiencing homelessness and women leaving prison. In addition to her work as a researcher and minister, Dr. Snodgrass has served as a pastoral counselor in churches, shelters, transitional housing facilities, and community centers.